AF354493

TIME
OUT

- The motorcycle ride of a lifetime

MONOCHROME EDITION

1st Edition © Robert Olesen, 2019
All rights reserved.

November 16th, 2019

To ensure the privacy and anonymity of individuals featured in this publication, names mentioned have been abbreviated and facial images has been blurred.

ISBN: 978-87-971849-2-9

Publisher:
LZB Danmark
Løget Center 71
DK-7100 Vejle

Acknowledgements

Dedicated to Ejgil Olesen, Hanne Olesen and Fr. Raymond Brennan. Thank you for providing me with the options for creating and working towards a rich and rewarding life beyond most peoples imagination.

Foreword

To quote the Danish travel agency Kilroy Travels' slogan:
"It's not the World getting smaller, it's your ass getting bigger".

Traveling gives value that can be impossible to measure on a monetary level. You may not have the chance to see the sights more than the first time you're there. Enjoy the view. Maybe the most important thing about traveling. It is not enough to just to drive by. Put your feet on the ground. Then you have "been there". When you're at the location you wish to be you should close your eyes for 30 seconds. This way, you'll "arrive twice".

You'll feel the world. It's a great feeling that is good for you and if you are careful it is not too expensive. The value of the memories can be infinite. Like many other good things travel can be highly addictive too. Traveling doesn't last forever and still costs money. So, you will have to go back to your boring everyday world. You may want to be a little cautious and plan ahead. An "open trip" like the ones I prefer should have room for changes in the initial plan. There is more to see than what your map will show.

To travel with a friend is not a bad idea. This does take a good amount of openness and understanding from your companion -and yourself. Traveling can be the ultimate relationship test. Speak your mind but show consideration. A companion gives you someone to support you and share the memories with.

There is enough to look at. A European just need to pop down to the Alps to see some fantastic landscapes. As you can tell I am very fascinated by the nature of our fantastic world.

Take time out before you are out of time.
You'll find new values in life. You'll start to appreciate what you got.

The world is bigger than you think.
Or you are smaller than you realize.

This journey was made possible after the loss of my adoptive parents. My mother died in 1997 and my father in 2003.

My father saved up for his retirement his entire life. One of his dreams was going deep sea fishing. Saving enough to do this, illness struck and had him wheelchair bound in a care home at age sixty, so having the money but lacking the health made me rethink my position on how to approach life. Turning thirty myself just a few months before my father died, I looked back at my life so far. Reviewing the dreams and ambitions. I had when I was twenty, there was a lot of things I wanted to do that just didn't went as hoped for. I wanted to own a Harley Davidson before I reached 25, become a writer, go travel around the world, cross the USA on a motorcycle. A decade on, none of this had happened.

Inspired by the 1974 book "Zen and the Art of Motorcycle Maintenance" by Robert M. Pirsig, I did start writing at 19 jotting down thoughts on life and big topics. My ideas and world views were very different then. Pirsig's book was probably also the spark which made me want to write, igniting my dream of touring the USA and ride a motorcycle coast to coast. It has been more than quarter of a century since I actually read this book. But there is no denying this has been a big inspiration for me. Even though we share the same name, I wanted to create something different, yet similar. "Zen and the Art of Motorcycle Maintenance" is a heavy read, and my writing style differ significantly. Robert M. Pirsig's work is inspirational but left me with a lot of practical questions.

So, spending time writing this I want to share the answers and solutions I found along the way. As I reread my old notes 25 years later, I definitely have changed views and standpoints in some ways and stand by the notion that you can't substitute life experience.

Being a moped kid the idea of crossing the USA never left me.
Back then, motorcycles were the coolest thing in the world.

In 1990 Honda launched the first 600 ccm sport bike that delivered 100 horsepower and after discovering Harley Davidson through *Easyriders* magazine and the now classic Arnold Schwarzenegger movie *Terminator 2: Judgement Day*, I was hooked. Hot chicks and cool bikes, what more would you want?

Then different priorities set in. Getting an education became a goal and the motorcycle dreams were put on hold. Having spent 25% of my time in school drawing, I became a graphic designer. Just like Steve Jobs got an eye opener discovering typography, this changed my view on design and the world around me. A few years after graduating I found my-self debt free, having paid off my student loan. This was a great feeling -for a fortnight. Then I went to a local motorcycle dealer to get my first motorcycle. The same model I used while taking my riders license, a used Suzuki GN250. Not my dream bike, but you really need to start small with an affordable insurance and a learner bike that you won't cry over when you drop it. The first few times this happens you'll feel awful. I broke 3 turn signals and a couple of levers in the single year I owned this bike. I initially planned to own this for two years to get the insurance premium down. But then Italian manufacturer Ducati dropped the price of the 2001 Monster 600, the last carburetor Ducati. It went down in price and caught my interest. Then the price dropped further a month later and I knew this was what I wanted. So, I got myself one of the most beautiful and cool bikes on the planet. Matt black with a black frame.
Just looking at it parked outside made me happy.

To me motorcycles are still is one of the greatest hobbies you can choose. You're right out in the open, feeling and smelling the elements, a perfect match with traveling, aka. motorcycle touring. So, deciding to spend a good chunk of my inheritance on doing this wasn't difficult. As this was what I wanted to do the most in the world, I had bought a guidebook in 1990 called "Around the USA". Nothing happened for four-teen years, so with the loss of my father I started to research how I could make my greatest wish come true. My travels are grounded on a motorcy-clists perspective but is intended for everybody who loves to travel.

The Internet was taking off and Google had already become king of the Web in 2002. Dial up modems were still a thing, but there was plenty of leads and information on how to go about traveling in the USA. I read quite a few articles, travel logs and stories. Contacting Johannes, who had published a nice travel story online, we had an e-mail conversation concerning costs of purchasing a bike in the USA and shipping it to Denmark, buying a bike and selling it before heading back home, versus renting a bike for 3 months. At the time renting would cost around $5000. Shipping a bike was around $1800. Comparing this to buying a bike and selling it after 3 months with 10-12000 miles on it, renting looked like an expensive option.

The other logical choice was to contact Harley Davidson Club of Denmark. They have a touring committee and they advised me to contact the sales manager Mogens at CAPS, the biggest Harley Davidson dealership in Denmark. With a friendly exchange and chat on the phone, the solution of buying a bike in Denmark, shipping it back and forth to and from the USA wasn't a viable solution. Therefore, I made an inquiry at the US Embassy in Denmark. Their reply wasn't complete, as they wrote back that I'd need to have my paperwork in order, i.e. valid visa and drivers license. In order to do this, you definitely want to get travelers insurance and you need to have an international motorcycle license issued. Some states, as Minnesota, requires you to have a car license before you can obtain a bike license. At the time I only held a motorcycle license. The reason for that was that when I was young, all my friends got a car license and a car. So, none of them got around to get one for a motorcycle, let alone a bike. One exception was a school buddy called Lars, who had an uncle that really was into motorcycles. He got a bike as soon as he could, and those of us in the old moped group looked to him with envy. I got a bike license eight years before getting a car license.

Having some of the best visa free travel options, Danes going to the USA are covered by the visa waiver program. This offers Danish citizens visa free entry for three months, but you need to have a passport which is valid for at least 6 months and be approved by ESTA (Electronic System for Travel Authorization) prior to entering a plane going to the USA (This also applies to transit flights). Some unfortunate people have had the same name as others unwanted in the USA or have been registered for activities or actions that prevent them from ESTA approval. Without ESTA approval, you need to apply for a visa to go to the USA. Besides that, if you got any felony court convictions you won't be allowed entry into the United States.

Not sure where I wanted to start my journey, I had contacted Fort. Lauderdale Harley Davidson in Florida concerning buying or renting a bike. They referred to motorcyclerentals.com.

I also contacted Lombardi's Harley Davidson in Staten Island, NY. Lombardi's HD wrote back that they couldn't help in the export department. Fair enough, they didn't want to make promises they couldn't keep just to sell a bike. Lombardi's HD did provide an essential piece of information for buying and riding a vehicle in the USA. You need to be able to obtain insurance and most crucial, an address where you can register the motorcycle.

I had the fortune to know Luis, one of my American business contacts, who also is a motorcycle enthusiast. Luis had seven bikes at this point, but his wife made him sell off a couple of them as she wanted a new house. His pride and joy is a 1955 Vincent Black Shadow, converted to a Black Prince that since became a family heirloom. So I got in touch with Luis in January 2004 about my plans and he offered to help. Luis would let me use one of his addresses for registering and insuring a bike. Luis is based in the Richmond area in Virginia, so this did change my search options. Luis offered to help scouting for a bike, new or used. This did limit the area where I could search for a bike and coordinating with Luis about meeting up was a little tricky as I was traveling, and Luis constantly was traveling for his employer.

With a few months before I would arrive in the USA, I decided to go for a new motorcycle, considering a Buell XB9 Lightning, Harley Davidson Sportster or FXDL Low Rider. Super cool bikes.

My American adventure was the final leg of my dream to go around the world. Plane tickets (economy) the long way around planet Earth were around USD 2,300 at the time, so these were not nearly as expensive as I had feared.

The dream started with me riding my Ducati Monster 600 to World Ducati Week 2004, which took place in May 17th to 23rd in Italy. After that I went back to Denmark by DB auto-train from Bolzano in Italy to Hamburg, Germany. This being the start of my trip of a lifetime.

I had terminated my rental agreement on my apartment and put all my earthly belongings into a storage, so instead of going home I went up to the Ducati dealership in Sorø, Denmark. From there I went to Copenhagen Airport heading to China, Japan, Singapore, Australia and New Zealand, before reaching the United States. The above-mentioned countries were on my bucket list, places I truly wanted to see besides countries I have had the fortune to visit before.

China was wild, watching the energy and buzz in Beijing in 2004 was an eye opener. At the end of the millennium some people were talking about the next hundred years being "the American century," I think they didn't see the full picture, perhaps watching the world solely from a western perspective. I believe the 21st century will be the rise of a Chinese dominated future for a big part of the globe, for better or worse.

The ability to copy pretty much any product and the rise of an entrepreneurial and innovative culture bodes for a different future for everyone. An example was when the Playstation 2 was released, it was much touted as having hacker proof copy protection, as pirated software was rampant on the original Playstation game console. A week after launch of the Playstation 2, a bootleg chip was on the market. With a one-party system, China makes a five-year plan. And, in comparison to the western democracies, they seem to implement and execute as decided.

With the concept of debt-trap colonialism, combined with no or little regard to niceties as workplace safety and Corporate Social Responsibility (CSR), China will muscle ahead. China has a population they need to keep happy. I am sure the People's Party is well aware of the countrys history, and they will do what it takes to avoid any new revolution happening. Pollution in the larger cities have had the effect that China has decided to give electric vehicles optimal conditions for proliferation. This could have the side effect with China taking the lead in this field becoming a world leader and dominant player in this product category.

I would really like to go to Japan again. Singapore was definitely not my cup of tea, clean and nice but way too controlled. Motorcycles there has to have license plates on the front too, so the speed surveillance cameras can easily track and catch you. While there, I got a surprise call from my uncle on June 12th. My sister had given birth to a baby girl, about six weeks earlier than expected. So, I was now "Uncle Bob".

The one place that truly made an impression was New Zealand. The NZ English accent sounds awful to me, but the people there are friendly, and the nature is stunning. One thing that make New Zealand stand out is the roads. Absolutely some of the best rides in the world. During my visit to Australia, I met with DOC (Ducati Owners Group) in Sydney and one of them told me that he had a friend who would ship his Harley to New Zealand every year for his summer holiday.
So, my choice for getting around was easy. Renting a BMW F650, I had a fantastic time, and that was just on the North Island. Talking to other riders I met there, they told me the south island was just as good if not better. I stayed on the North Island as New Zealand is located on the southern hemisphere. It was late May meaning it was wintertime there. I definitely recommend any motorcyclist to go ride in New Zealand if they ever get the chance.

Coming to America

Coming in on a flight from NZ I would be arriving at LAX international. Sitting next to an American, we had some interesting conversation. The housing market was going up after the dot-com bubble burst just after the turn of the millennium. He had just sold off his property with a good profit and our thoughts were well aligned, thinking the housing market worldwide couldn't sustain the rapid rise in prices. Generally, I think if you can't pay a home with two full time incomes, it is too expensive. (I needed a place to live so I did buy a condo in late 2004.) Buying a home shouldn't be used for speculation but should be seen as a place you want to live. Greed can block your ability to think rationally, and the housing market seems to work as a Ponzi scheme. When the buyers are priced out, you are basically married to your property, insolvent or having to eat a loss. I couldn't believe the dot-com bubble was allowed to happen. When things look too good to be true, it most likely is. The impact of the housing market crash and financial crisis in 2008 did happen a few years later than I expected.

Talking politics with strangers is often not a good idea, but my seat neighbor turned the conversation towards American politics. He thought that everyone in the world hates Americans and George W. Bush because of the second invasion into Iraq. I told him he shouldn't worry about that, I didn't think it was that bad. Why does so many people want to go to the USA if it was that shitty?

The excuse for invading Iraq was cooked up, but we only got to confirm that afterwards. George W. Bush might come off as a complete muppet, but if you want to find the true ghouls, you really have to look at the people standing behind the president. People fight and die to get democratic rights to vote, so how did this happen? Well, too many democratic voters didn't go to the polls. I know a few Americans that had a presidential preference but didn't get around to actually voting.
So, George W. Bush got re-elected.

The US presidential election is truly special. The result affects millions of people, or even billions around the world, people who have no say or right to vote on who becomes the next US president. This is written at a time where Donald Trump is Commander in Chief.

In 2004 some people thought things couldn't get worse.
Then a cartoon villain became president.

Arriving in Los Angeles was an experience to remember. The plane landed late at night. With a huge line I got pulled aside and my arrival was examined thoroughly. So I was the very last in line to enter "God's own country". I had made a mistake on my arrival card that I had to fill out on the plane going from New Zealand. I had not written an exact address where I would be staying. An immigration officer did accept me stating the Holiday Inn in New York as I had a plane ticket going to Newark Airport. My first impression of Americans at home was that they were crude and polite at the same time. After 9.11, no one in the TSA wanted to be the one who let the next terrorist enter the country.

The TSA has made a lot of people hate domestic flights in the USA. In 2012 I got marked out by TSA on a business trip coming in from Frankfurt, Germany. Frankfurt Airport had been hit by massive clouds, so my flight from Hamburg got delayed. I missed my connecting flight and had a layover until the next day to go to the USA. I got patted down and questioned two times at the airport in New York. At the gate I was told that I had to get patted down again. Here I got a glimpse of the boarding assistants computer screen. It was blinking bright red.

The airport staff knows people are sick and tired of the control posts, so when I told the boarding staff I already had been stopped and frisked twice they didn't bother to do this exercise again.

My plan of riding a motorcycle coast to coast started with a flight over the very same piece of land mass. I was seated at the window next to a burly guy at the very front of the plane. I got a suspicion that this would be the air marshal, as these were being deployed after the 9.11 terror attacks. It seemed as he was keeping an eye on me and scoping out everyone else on the plane too.

Being completely knackered from the overseas flight from NZ, I quickly dozed off, waking up a few hours later with a pool of my own drool on my shoulder. Long haul flights can be grueling, the problem is that your ears don't really sleep. Therefore, a lot of routined travelers use noise cancelling earphones or as a minimum earplugs when sleeping.

Looking out of the window I thought that we'd be landing soon.
With water all around we would have reached the east coast. The USA is a big place, so about ten minutes later I realized we were only just passing Lake Michigan. A great way to get a geography lesson.

Finally in the Big Apple, I got checked into a hotel late in the afternoon. New York hotels are pricey, ended up in Ramada Plaza for a spicy $150.

Sunday, July 11th 2004

Still jet-lagged as hell from yesterdays flight, I had the reception check the price for a flight to Richmond, VA form New York. A price of $400 seemed a bit much.

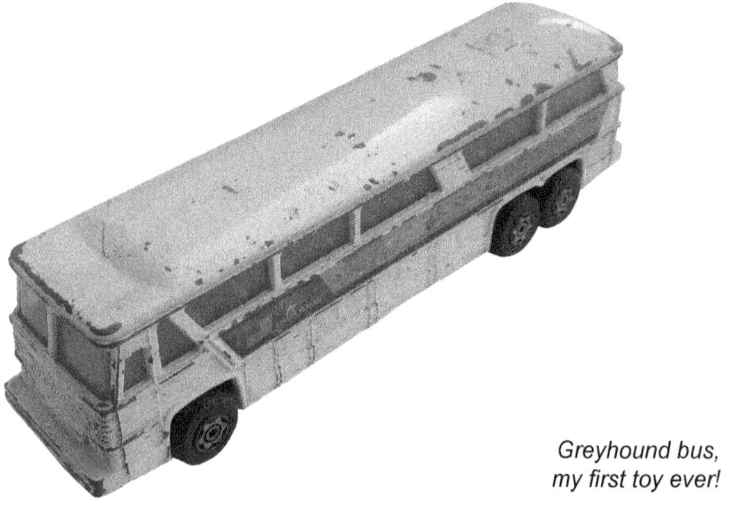

*Greyhound bus,
my first toy ever!*

The very first toy I got from my adoptive grandmother was a Greyhound bus, so I always wanted to go on a trip on one. This was a seven and a half-hour ride from the Greyhound Bus Station Broadway, including a stop about halfway. 340 miles or around 560 metric kilometers.

While not impressive, this was a fairly OK experience, the seating on economy was nothing special, but clean and tidy. With my low height of 5 foot 3 inches, leg space has never been an issue, be it plane or bus. I did notice the majority of passengers were people of color, including myself.

Taking the entire day I arrived at Richmond Bus Station on North Boulevard at sunset. I cannot recommend hanging around bus stations for extended periods of time, especially after dark. Some of the people loitering there do look like they are looking for trouble or have other problems. And yeah, being mugged isn't part of my travel plans.

I checked up on hotels and got Crowne Plaza on the line, who sent out a minivan to pick me up at the bus station. Upscale hotels do come with some extra perks. My first impression of folks in Richmond, VA was that people were friendlier and more relaxed. I didn't go out that night, I prefer to see a new area in daylight.

As I was going down to the business centre, I had received an e-mail from Luis but couldn't catch him on his home number. Luis is old school and he didn't have a cell phone. His employer did talk him into carrying one a few years later. Talking about tech, in 2004 there were no social media. The most advanced phone I had seen at the time was a Japanese guy in Australia who had an early smartphone with a camera, internet and e-mail functions that made my old Ericsson cellphone look like a brick with buttons. The concept of blogs wasn't a thing yet. So the basis of this book was an A5 sized paper notebook used as a diary. Today, my journey could easily be documented on Facebook, Instagram and other social media. I have a Facebook account and had an average amount of friends. One day in 2015 I had enough. Checking my profile so often I felt that it took up too much of my attention, one day I thought to myself: Who the hell cares about what I write online? It doesn't matter and I don't give a fuck about the crap other people post.

Online debates are often dominated by toxic individuals who render any debate they participate in a complete waste of your time.

Still having a need to be updated on technology in a professional context, I have kept my Facebook account. Instead I wrote a "farewell to Facebook" message on my feed, and then deleted everyone on my friends list. In addition to that, I deleted the app on my phone. Anyone who wants to keep in touch can send me an SMS text or give me a call. Going back to a life without Facebook relieves you of a lot of distraction, stress inducing behavior and lets you be present in a way many people seem to miss out on. Facebook provides space for an incredible amount of hate speech and threats of violence. There are numerous examples of individuals who have destroyed their careers and future employment opportunities by posting stupid remarks online. Employers like Google and many others screen people seriously before hiring. No employer wants to be the centre of a shitstorm and lose customers, revenue and reputation because of their employees' behavior online. The many hate groups on Facebook are harmful to Facebook as a business, at some point this will make people opt out of Facebook if they do not effectively address online extremism. Facebook should quarantine 6 months for all members of the hate groups that are reported and subsequently closed. Otherwise, Facebook ends up losing users and revenue. If I had a business, I would reconsider if Facebook is a good medium for me as an advertiser, especially when stories of hate speech turns up in the press. In an edited media reality, the hateful and malicious rhetoric does not have the media's attention or interest.

The worst statements on Facebook take place because there are no consequences for the people who write them. Therefore, it is important that those whose statements call for violence and other illegal activities through social media are reported. In fact, this is the only defense that exists when dialogue isn't possible.

Freedom of speech is often misused as an excuse for avoiding taking responsibility. One should not fail to recognize that the constitution provides protection from the *government* limiting your freedom of speech. You can't get arrested for speaking your mind. But the constitution protects you from the government, not societys reactions -or yourself.

6931
OUND
SEATING CAP. 55
DUCATI
DUCATI
RICHMOND
moto europa
moto europa
2.9%
2.9%
FINANCING
FINANCING

City walk in Richmond

Monday, July 12th 2004

Richmond in daylight is a nice place. But the weather in the South sure can get hot. Going on foot is a good option to check out most city centers. If distances are too long there is usually public transport. Mr. Brain has been traveling with only a solid pair of Caterpillar work boots, not recommended. I did go down to the city centre and it was quite nice. Cute little shops, I got to try out Subway sandwiches. I actually have a special connection with Subway. Reading an ad in Newsweek I applied and got approved for a Subway franchise in 1997. Unfortunately, or fortunately, I chose not to pursue this as some really wealthy folks in Denmark just launched a knockoff chain pretty much carbon copying the Subway concept. With the knowledge I have about franchising today, I'm glad I made this choice. I do like freshly made Subway sandwiches and eat a lot of them.

For years I had wanted to build and own a business on my own. As my adoptive father said, it is more fun to work for yourself than for others. It is never too late to dream, but if a good idea doesn't come to you with the right timing, you may end up disappointed. But the worst thing that can happen is that you end up in a retirement home full of regret, not having taken chances and pursuing your ideas. Therefore you need to break out, challenge yourself, and work pro-actively towards your goals while you're young or at the first chance that comes up. No pain, no gain. You will need to ask yourself what it entails, do the necessary research possible and know what you want to do after accomplishing this.

A lot of people get an education in order to make their dreams a reality later in life. This is in a way also taking a chance, thus improving your odds of success. You may pick the wrong field and after college or university. Most people end up with student debt, this is like a stuck brake pad dragging on the rotor.

Today, an education is unfortunately no guarantee for employment.

A dream that hasn't been fulfilled, is as valuable as one which is.
But is a Harley in the garage is better than no Harley in the garage?
Hell yeah. So my first business venture was started in 2005.

Getting back to the hotel, I got Luis on the phone. I needed to transfer funds so that I could pay for a motorcycle. Not informing my bank about this before going abroad was an oversight on my part, bringing a lot of hassle and trouble on myself. So I had to get in touch with my bank in Denmark and sort this out. The funds were there, just in the wrong damn bank account. Well, sometimes I'm an idiot.

My family would probably say that sometimes I am not an idiot.

Bike Search

Tuesday, July 13th 2004

Using the business center, I received an e-mail from my bank. They needed a bank account to transfer money to. Taking a city-walk of downtown Richmond I went into a Bank of America branch. I made my inquiry about money transfer and they told me I would need a bank account in advance, and I had to have legal residence to get one. My VISA card had a limit of approximately three thousand USD per month, a security measure which prevented me from just using my credit card to pay for a motorcycle. Again, the lack of forward thinking and planning was no one else's fault than my own. This being an adventure of a lifetime, I sure made it more exciting for myself.

Well, my search for a bike was on. So I went down to the business center again. Here I looked up to find out who had a Sportster in their inventory. Coleman Motorsports in Fairfax had a 2004 Sportster in yellow and Battlecycle just north of Washington D.C. in Maryland had two Harleys of interest, a 2001 priced at $8700, and a 2003 model at $10,200. Richmond Harley Davidson listed a 1200 Sportster in stock with a sticker price of $12,000.

Calling a cab ride from the hotel I asked the driver to take me to the local Harley Davidson dealership, Richmond HD. The driver fit the skinny white redneck stereotype well. Plaid shirt, mustache and a very worn-in baseball cap. Friendly guy, though. On the dash under the car radio he had a wide confederate flag sticker. I couldn't help but ask what was up with the flag. Without taking any offense to my question it was just something he thought was cool. Times have changed and I am not sure it would fly today. People can hate all they want; I don't care as long as they don't incite or commit hate crimes. It was just one of those situations where you have to note that some people's views are just different even though they aren't malicious. I do think that sticker wasn't any advantage when it came to tipping your driver. Cabs are not cheap, 17 miles cost $36. My driver did like to have my business, so we agreed that he could pick me up one hour later taking me back to the hotel.

Looking at Richmond HD's motorcycles I talked with their sales guy "Cuz". Explaining I wanted to buy a motorcycle. I didn't actually receive any sales pitches, it was more "this is what we got in stock".

Harley Davidson Motor Company celebrated their 100th anniversary the year before in 2003, so the bikes with the black and silver centennial paint scheme were all sold. While I sure liked the FXDL Low Rider available, I thought it was quite pricey and the two-tone red and silver paint didn't appeal too much to me. Buell XB9 just isn't a good bike for touring. so I ended up deciding on an XL1200 Sportster. I have fancied a Sportster since I bought my Suzuki GN 250. In 2004 the Sportster range got an all-new frame including rubber-mounted engines for reduced vibrations and improved comfort.

While registering my information "Cuz" asked for a credit card that he swiped into his system. Asking if I could do a bank transfer directly to the dealership, I was told that it was not an option and I should look into using Western Union to make a money transfer.

Annoyingly complicated.

Getting back to the hotel the bell hop asked me about my day.

Telling him about going to the Harley Davidson dealership, he told me liked the look of Harleys. He didn't know anything about bikes, to many people Harley Davidson is synonymous with motorcycles. With a market share hovering around 50% or above in the american home market, this comes as no surprise.

Later that day I got Luis on the phone. Before I could ask him, Luis offered to help with getting money transferred in an e-mail. I had to get in touch with my bank in Denmark and with Luis bank information I got a solution for paying for a motorcycle. This felt a bit like a leap of faith, transferring twenty grand is not small change. I would be meeting Luis on the weekend, Saturday, July 17th, as his schedule obviously would be packed on workdays.

I am like a woman in a shoe store when it comes to motorcycles and this resulted in me calling up "Cuz" at Richmond HD. I had decided that the Low Rider was a better choice than the Sportster for riding long distance and I wanted to ship the bike abroad after riding it. I was told that I needed to come in with a deposit of $500 so that he didn't sell it before Saturday. I agreed, but halfway through a question about lead time for saddlebags "Cuz" cut me off and told me he had another customer he had to talk to. His last words were "Rubba, rubba" and he hung up on me before I could ask my question in full. What the fuck ??? This behavior caught me off guard and I immediately dropped the thought of him getting commission on a 17,000 dollar sale. So I didn't contact Richmond Harley Davidson again.

It isn't news that a lot of Harley Davidson dealers have been a bunch of arrogant dicks for years. There are plenty of motorcyclists who can testify to this. With one of the strongest brands in the world Harley Davidsons have been selling like hotcakes. The supply increased after the Kansas plant was opened in 1996. However, the classic customer base has been getting older and many are getting too old to ride, and young people buried in student debt can't afford motorcycles, much less a Harley.

Today, the Motor Company has closed the Kansas factory. So perhaps some of the dealers will rethink the customer experience in the future. I still like Harley a lot. It is very much Americana on two wheels.

The bikes used to be pretty bad quality, but since the launch of the Twin Cam engine in 1999 and the rubber mount Sportster range in 2004, Harley Davidsons are just as good quality bikes as other brands. With the sound and vibrations Harley Davidson motorcycles have soul, and touch riders on an emotional level.

Having dropped dealing with Richmond HD, I got on the phone with the Harley dealerships Whitt's HD and Patriot HD in the Fairfax area where Luis lived, to inquire about inventory. Surprisingly, they came off just as arrogant as the sales guy at Richmond HD. So enough of that bullshit, and a one finger salute to buying a Harley Davidson. Instead, I looked up the address of MotoEuropa, the Ducati dealership in Richmond.

This being the third day in Richmond I had begun to feel stuck.
It had cost a lot just waiting to get everything going.
Itchin' to go riding.

Choosing a motorcycle

Wednesday, July 14th 2004

Getting my bank on the phone was a bit of a challenge. There is a five hour time difference between Eastern and CET (Central European Time) time zones. So I got up at 3 AM without getting through. Tried again at 4 AM and got hold of my bank advisor. At 4:50 AM funds had been transferred funds to Luis' account.

When it comes to motorcycles, manufacturers diversify themselves from their competitors by using special engine features, BMW are known for their boxer engines, Harley Davidson for the big V-twins with valve push-rods and Triumph for their triple inline cylinder configurations.

Most of the Japanese manufacturers high end performance models are inline four cylinder engines. Americans often refer to foreign motorcycles as metric bikes, as they stick to imperial units of measurement.
Some riders mockingly refer to Japanese bikes as "rice burners".

In 2002 I bought my first Ducati Monster 600 brand spanking new. The engine self-destructed on the way to a visit to the factory tour on the Italian autostrada three months later. It became a write-off in late 2003 by a cager (car driver) who got the sun in his eyes before turning left, taking out my rear wheel, totaling the bike and busting up my left knee. I did get a replacement through my insurance, in the classic Ducati red. Didn't replace my knee though.

I have a soft spot for Ducati, still lasting to this day. What makes Ducati unique is the desmodromic valve system opening and closing the engine valves by an overhead camshaft without using valve springs, most are belt driven. This creates a unique exhaust sound, different from Harley Davidsons "potato, potato, potato" idling sound, but like the American brand, it also reaches people on an emotional level. My uncle's dog could easily distinguish whether it was me or some other motorcycle arriving at my grandmother's apartment. Having experience with and preference for Ducati I do know they have a weakness, the electrical wiring system. This is prone to fail after around five years. Made in Italy, anyone who has owned an Italian car or motorcycle will be well aware of this.

As they were in walking distance just 2,8 miles away, I went to check out MotoEuropa. Half of the store was dedicated to "Ducati Richmond", the Ducati dealer in-store concept. This was a difficult choice, so I spent a couple of hours contemplating what bike to choose.
The Buell XB9 just wasn't a good bike to load up with camping gear so it was out of the picture. I couldn't easily let go of the thought of buying a Harley Davidson, I had wanted one of these for years. But having been turned off just calling the three closest retailers, I had no urge to spend any money at any of their dealerships.

MotoEuropa had a few Ducati bikes in stock that had my interest. Looking at an ST3 this probably would be the best bike for touring. But standing just 5 foot 3 tall I am a short-ass, so an ST3 would be a bit of a handful with only three years of riding experience. My passport says 5 foot 4, but that is with footwear.

Lowering a motorcycle is a bit tricky. Changing the rear suspension can affect headstock rake angle, so in order to keep the handling the front end should be lowered too. This can lead to two other problems.
The side stand being too long making the bike stand too upright when parked, you might have to shorten this. I have experienced that I couldn't even get the side stand to flip down. Besides side stand issues, the lean angle will be reduced too. At this time I am a seasoned rider going into my 19th riding season. If I can get a bike off the side stand and hold it upright with one ball of my feet, I can ride it.

Narrowing the selection down, I didn't want to go long distance touring on a sport bike. Bikes can fall or get dropped on the side, so a full fairing will get damaged and is pricey to fix. Owning a Ducati Monster already, I knew this model series quite well. The Ducati M1000ie in the store was a new model launched in 2003. Having met a (very cute girl) rider having motor issues with one of these at WDW2004, I wasn't sure if I wanted to bet on this bike as it was featuring a new engine construction and perhaps still suffering from "childhood diseases". MotoEuropa did have an offer for a new 2002 Ducati Monster S4 that they wanted to clear out, so they had it on offer at $10,999. This was the most powerful in the Monster model range basically fitted with a detuned engine from the legendary Ducati 916 super bike. The Monster S4 was a bike I would like to keep, shipping it home after riding it and selling my other Ducati Monster.

Talking to the general manager Stubbs, I wanted OEM hard side bags with mounts, an Ungo alarm system, a centre stand for easy chain maintenance, low seat option and a plus kit. The plus kit consisted of a high flow air filter, new ignition boxes and a set of sweet rumbling carbon fibre Termignoni slip-on exhausts. This was more than 3000 dollars in upgrades, configuring a super cool Ducati ready to go coast to coast.

So I made a decision and ordered the above, with an out the door price of $14,500, this included tax, title and fees.

At the time a Monster S4 was the most powerful bike I had ever owned or ridden, producing one hundred horsepower at the crankshaft.

Insurance

Thursday, July 15th 2004

Still staying at Crowne Plaza, I went down to the business centre again. I needed to get some things sorted for my trip to get things going.

In 1990 I saw a documentary on TV about the Sturgis Motorcycle Rally in South Dakota. I just had to experience this. I had done some research about the rally and knew that you needed to book camping, motel or hotel well in advance. Looking up campsites on the internet I decided to book at rushnomore.com, "Rush No More RV Resort and Campground", a ten minute ride via Interstate 90 Eastbound. At the rally there would be so much traffic going into the city that you couldn't count on this estimate to be accurate.

Needing insurance for a motorcycle, Luis had recommended contacting Progressive Insurance. So I got them on the phone. Having had an International drivers license issued based on my current license didn't pose any problem for stays under a month, but they told me that I could not be insured on a tourist stay. Progressive advised me to call a local insurance agent. Well, that didn't work as he didn't have time to for me and he asked me to try later. I didn't call him back.

Instead, I got the bright Idea to call back to Progressive and inform them that the bike would be permanently registered at the stated address at Luis' place in Fairfax, Virginia. This worked. The service operator was in doubt if I could do this with an international license or if I would need a Virginia issued license.

This would probably have been easier with a Harley Davidson as the dealerships usually have a permanent insurance agent associated or partnering with them. It turned that out my international license was sufficient.

So I got two quotes in accordance with my inquiry. Full coverage for a new 1200 Harley Davidson Sportster was $550, and a Ducati Monster S4 would be just $179 ! I had actually asked my insurance company in Denmark at an earlier point about insuring this particular model Ducati. Their price "offer" was just over an insane $1800 annually. I have no clue on how the insurance companies set their prices, but the difference was off the chart. To this day I still don't get it. The only explanation I can think of is that Danish insurance companies cannot deny you insurance, but they can set the price whatever they want, this being the same as saying no to your business.

Accepting an insurance offer for a motorcycle at less than
a tenth of the price a home wasn't a hard choice.
Life comes with more complicated choices.
Decisions with lasting influence that often come along
through life milestones.
Education, job and career. Marriage, family and children.
Making choices in this order is the most common and sensible.
Choices come with causality. One choice affects the next.
The main route is simple on a map. Then shit happens.

Choices often seem complicated,
and many factors often have to be taken into account.
And You may be forced to compromise.

To make the right decision is often hardest
when it is almost too late.

You will need to duck and come back swinging
before the world takes off the gloves.

STONEWALL JACKSON

Friday, July 16th 2004

Having a day left before meeting Luis and to get away from the hotel, I booked a seat on a guided bus tour in Richmond. Before this round trip I went on foot to the pickup point. On my way there I had my first encounter with the world-famous American portion sizes. Passing a sandwich shop near a university, I stopped and ordered a five dollar Gyros in a pita bread to go. I only realized how huge it was when the cashier handed me the bag. After munching my way through a little over half the portion, I was absolutely stuffed and had to chuck the rest. I am a small guy, so this would be a fantastic deal if two people split a serving this big. A big person would definitely not be hungry after this "man vs. food" challenge.

On the tour bus around Richmond I got to see the Old Foundry, Monument Avenue and the Federal Reserve. We just passed the Stonewall Jackson statue and Edgar Allan Poe Museum; these would require a separate visit as the main focus of the tour was on the Old Foundry which played a central role in the American Civil War. It was a bit odd to think about how geographically close the capitols of the two warring factions were during this time. Richmond has around 350,000 people living in the city and the greater metropolitan area totals a population of around 800,000 people., including around 25,000 students within the three universities. The city really takes care of the beautiful colonial architecture and Richmond brands itself as "the City of Monuments". These became an issue of conflict in 2017, including the one of Jefferson Davis, Robert E. Lee and others rooted in the American Civil War. Closely connected with slavery the monuments were became a hot topic after the 2017 white supremacist rally that killed one person in Charlottesville, Virginia. While beautiful, the city's history is dark and bloody. The sad part is that some people there seem to base their identity on this, looking backwards to the old days instead of building a better future as one nation. American history is filled with countless terrible crimes, incidents and tragedies. Healing the wounds is a process constantly hit by setbacks, such as police violence and hate crimes.

In the last decade right wingers have constantly tried to ridicule the concept of political correctness, which is understandable. It is strenuous to have to stay politically correct when you in reality oppose it. Extremist far right wingers at least says what they mean.
The right wing does not have a lower limit for their rhetoric as long as it serves the purpose and goes against minorities who often cannot fend for themselves. The hostility of the right wing is not limited to immigrants and foreigners. Political history shows that the sick, unemployed and other weak groups are targeted time after time when the right wing puts their votes to work. Using scapegoat politics works.
Blame the guy who don't speak english.

Don't be fooled, immigrants and refugees are just leverage for the next upcoming round attack on the weak. This is what I call the right wing magic trick. Cutting down on the very people who votes for them. I think it is reasonable and fair that their voters feel the consequences of their own choice. Right wing voters need to be more critical of who they vote for if they are dissatisfied.

It often turns out that many children have their opinions from their parents. If that is the world we are creating, we should ask ourselves what we want for our democracy. An important part of this issue is that the schools let a group out of the elementary schools without purpose or direction, as they must have minimum grades to get an education or a trade. This requirement as such is not unreasonable, but society cannot afford to let the weakest pupils stand without hope and prospects for the future. This creates a breeding ground for radicalization that only extremists benefit from, be it religious or political.

Since the 1960s Denmark and Europe has chosen to build up welfare societies. With the election in 2001 where the right wing won the vote based on far right parties, the Danes have chosen a new and more individualistic direction. The policy of the Danish right wing governments continues the political course set by Anders Fogh who was Danish prime minister at the same time George W. Bush was President of the USA. The right wing aims to replace the current social security with the minimal state. The consequence of this is the reduction of public services such as unemployment insurance, and services like home assistance for the elderly and sick as we see now. They do this with no revolutions taking place, instead "the salami method" is used. Slice by slice, society is changed. As said refugees and immigrants are just being used as leverage to make these changes.

In short, we get the policy that was voted for by the last election.
The real problem is when there are no jobs for the unemployed. If you can't get an apprenticeship or job because of your name, religion or skin color, this is a serious problem for all.
Feeling alienated is not the same as pulling the victim card. The last 20 years of Immigrant/foreigner/refugee/muslim debate have in my opinion, smashed the cohesion of western societies with the consistent "them and us" rhetoric. The cost of discrimination in the labor market is not elucidated by the labor market researchers. The government will rather open up to cheap foreign labor.

Discrimination is not free.
Those who are kept on the fringe of our society must live off
something, and society will receive a bill either in the form
of costs for public support or increased crime rates.
By combating the integration of minorities,
it also ensures its own political platform.

The right wing is like a consulting firm,
they do not have to solve problems,
smart people don't cut the branch they're sitting on.

Expanding on Yoda's wise words from Star Wars:

When people lose hope, they become assholes.
Fear leads to anger; anger leads to hate.
Hate leads to violence.

Meeting up with Luis

Finally, it is Saturday and Luis had time to come to my hotel. The money transfer was sorted Wednesday, so now Luis had the payment part of acquiring a motorcycle in check.

While talking with Luis about motorcycles, I could probably have saved a lot of money by buying a used Harley Davidson from a private seller. Finding one of these through Luis while traveling seemed a bit problematic as coordinating this would have been difficult. So I might have saved about 40% buying a used motorcycle. But I had decided to go for the Ducati MS4.

With plans to head up to Washington D.C., Luis gave me some of his thoughts on safety, the story of how some people had got killed there just for their shoes. I had actually heard this story; some sneakers are so sought after it is ridiculous. But Luis certainly had a point advising me to stay vigilant and not put oneself at risk, wherever you are.

Luis has some friends who are Harley riders. His opinion on Harley Davidsons is that they are heavy and slow. You can't really disagree with that. Having ridden on a 2002 FLSTC Softail Heritage, the vibrations on older Harleys are in my opinion just too much. The only Harley Davidson Luis liked was the Softail Night Train. This Harley Davidson was the precursor to the factory "Dark Custom" line of blacked out motorcycles. This was followed by the HD Sportster 1200N Nightster in 2007. Then the XL883 Iron was introduced in 2009, with all black parts and matte black "denim" paint was introduced. This no bullshit look has been super popular ever since. Harleys are classic bikes but still trendsetting. But a lot of people may not be aware of that Ducati launched the Monster 600 Dark in 1998. This was an entry level model in the Ducati Monster model range. It was the first bike to sport the murdered out (all black) look, and as earlier mentioned the first bike I bought brand new in 2001.

Luis is an old school republican who speaks his mind and don't give a shit about political correctness. Like many Americans he is direct and takes bullshit from no one. Luis is a ground infantry combat Vietnam veteran who later earned a degree in engineering. I can testify that Luis is very liked by former business partners and contacts. He was genuinely missed after retiring, and they had only nice things to say about him. Luis had seven bikes at the time, and a preference for the BMW GS all-road range of motorcycles with the boxer engines and shaft final drive instead of a belt or chain. On boxer engines the cylinders are horizontal opposite each other, with the pistons moving side to side, hence the boxer type designation.

I expected to have Luis do the payment of a bike using his credit card.
To my surprise Luis had the withdrawn the $20,000 in cash, stuffed into a thick big paper envelope. I actually never had such a big amount of cash in my hands before, or since, the second most being around $6500. This has had an influence on me, as I have had a preference for cash since.
Before that I used my credit card all the time.

Before leaving Crowne Plaza Luis made me check if I had remembered everything, stuff you leave unattended or forget has a tendency to disappear on its own. Besides clothing, I had motorcycle gear with me from my ride to Italy and onwards, including an axle wrench. I already had an HJC flip-front helmet which I bought in New Zealand when renting the BMW. F650 With everything stuffed into a big gym bag, I was ready to ride. My six days stay at Crowne Plaza Richmond tallied up to $670, not exactly cheap, not super expensive.
Signing the bill of sale with Stubbs, the store assistant Matt could start counting 145 Benjamins. While waiting for things to get sorted I did some additional shopping, I found some super handy elastic band tie downs with buckles for easy locking and removal called "ROK Straps" and to avoid theft, a Kryptonite chain with lock for $130.

Besides that I bought two copies of the book "Sport Riding Techniques" by Nick Ienatsch, giving one to Luis as thanks for his help and assistance. This is the "go to" book on motorcycle riding techniques.

Some of the extra options such as the hard bags kit I ordered on Wednesday had not arrived from Ducati North America yet, and they wouldn't be at Ducati Richmond before Monday, so we made an appointment for this to be fitted Tuesday, July 20th, along with getting the 600 mile engine run-in service done at the same time. With a print of the Progressive Insurance quote, we got the insurance in place and the bike was equipped with a temporary Virginia tag.

I wasn't keen on carrying 6000 dollars in cash so I had Luis hold onto two grand, I thought it would be good to have an emergency bundle in case I needed it later. I would still be having four grand with me, not a great or smart solution. Luis said goodbye and told me to keep in touch and to let him know how things were going.

So around 2 am I could ride out legally.

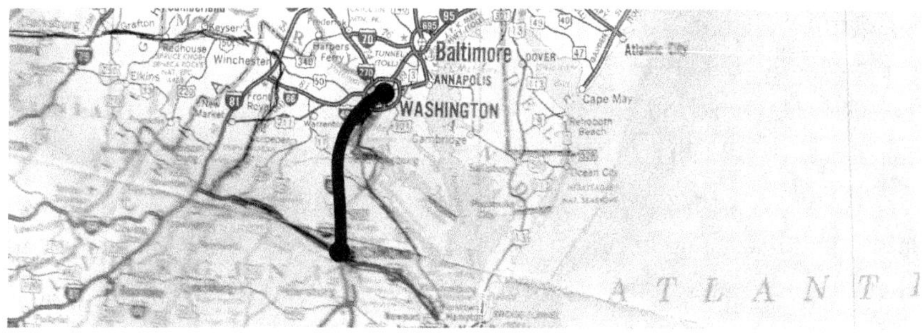

I decided to head up to Washington DC, which is a 110 mile ride away. My first impression of American driving is that they drive pretty close without enough distance from the car in front. After about half an hour on I-95 Northbound I got dizzy, and my vision got a little blurry. Without travel luggage I was riding with a backpack and had put my Gore-Tex riding trousers over my jeans, not realizing how hot July can get in the South. I had dehydrated quicker than I could imagine possible, so I got off the Interstate at the first available exit to get something to drink. This had never happened to me before, so I made an effort to avoid this happening again during my entire trip.

Arriving in Washington DC I rode around for a bit feeling tired and with a buzzing feeling in my fingers. At a traffic light on the Mall one guy yells "cool bike". Ducati motorcycles are a bit exotic, not produced on the same large scale as other brands. Looking for a place to stay I went into the downtown Holiday Inn;, the price was ok for the location and they had parking that could accommodate my brand new bike. Parking was stupid expensive, at $22 a day. Getting out of my riding gear, my jeans were soaked in sweat. At dinnertime, I decided to try the fast food chain "Popeyes, chicken and biscuit" for dinner. Nothing special in my book.

Before sunset I took a short walk in the same area as the Holiday Inn, this felt a bit upscale. My big wad of cash was locked in the hotel safety box, definitely not on my person. Waiting for a pedestrian light to change to green, a young black guy asks for spare change at a crosswalk. I think nothing of it, so I gave him the small change I received at Popeyes. With a bunch of people around, getting attacked would be unlikely, and I always keep my wallet in a zippered inner pocket. The guy was very thankful, explaining he has to scrape by to help a family member with some health problems. Upbeat and happy he wanted to shake my hand 90's style like in the Beverly Hills 90210 TV show intro. While I am a bit of a germaphobe, I have always thought that was stupid. He thanked me sincerely though and asked if I'd help him if he gets health problems himself. I told him in that I couldn't and in that case he is boned, so with a good laugh we went our separate ways on the other side of the crosswalk.
Everyone else at the traffic lights looked more worried about not having to talk to the guy. Solidarity has become less and less since the mid-nineties. There are many who have not yet discovered that the cohesion in society for many does not exist beyond their own family. But discriminating against minorities based on appearance and name is part of a bigger problem. At some point we all get all old and people who have not really experienced true discrimination before risk getting a harsh awakening later in life. Like all other discrimination, age discrimination looks very different when you are at the receiving end.

Going to bed I thought that I wouldn't roll on 600 miles on my new bike before heading back to Richmond, so the run-in service might not get done on Tuesday.

Sunday, July 18th 2004

After having arrived in Los Angeles and transferring to New York, it was time to experience the Capitol of the nation. Most government departments reside in Washington. Named after the first president, George Washington, the capitol is home for the legislative, judicial and executive powers. Washington D.C. is not a state but an independent "District". With my graphic design education I do have a soft spot for architecture. So obviously, I wanted to see as much as possible. Although far apart, everything is within walking distance. If you can't be bothered to walk there are plenty of guided bus tours available. The guided tour I took in Richmond had some limitations and just gave me some basic photo-ops. In order to experience what truly interests you in D.C, you're better off on foot and using public transport. Do make sure that you have appropriate footwear, only having my Caterpillar boots, these were heavy and hot as hell.

A good starting point is the Mall that I crossed on arrival Saturday. Quite a lot of American cities are built on a grid network where streets, boulevards and avenues have numbers instead of names. Washington DC is modeled a little differently with streets meeting in circles or roundabouts, inspired by Paris. Not too surprising since it was planned by the French architect Pierre Charles L'Enfant.

My first stop was Pennsylvania Avenue 1600. In 2004 George W. Bush resided there and the second invasion in Iraq the year before had security on their toes, with an increased safety range from the fence going around the White House. An extra barrier of concrete blocks had been set up. Not getting the right angle on my selfies, I asked a ten year old kid to take a shot of me with the White House in the background. Taking pictures was mostly done on film in 2004, so she was mesmerized by my state of the art four megapixel digital camera. One of my fellow tourists on the grass got the White House Police Force on alert, as he was ordered to step back from the fence: "Sir! Please step away from the fence!" I remember this clearly as the situation seemed like it could have escalated a few seconds later. He only moved back after the third time he was called out, and I'm sure the guard was about ready to pull his weapon. The message was delivered in a stern yet respectful tone. I was impressed, a very well handled situation.

Walking less than a mile south of the White House I went to see the World War II memorial. This had taken three years to build and was opened April 29th and had only been open to the public a few months before my visit. One of the fund-raising campaign leaders was Senator Bob Dole who ran for president against Bill Clinton in 1996. As former president George H.W. Bush, Dole was a decorated WWII veteran.

With an interest for and broad knowledge in history, this was deeply touching, especially the "Field of stars" on the Freedom Wall. With four thousand stars, each gold star represents the sacrifice of a hundred Americans. We shall never forget the 400,000 of the sixteen million US Servicemen who served in World War II to defeat the German Nazi regime and the axis powers.

The history of Europe is based on repeated examples of self-destruction due to internal power struggles. Through the First and Second World War, most Germans has learned that war and conflict do not bring any good. Since the Second World War, German politics has focused on preserving peace in Europe by cooperating in the form of the EC and the EU.

If each European country had continued to care for its own interests individually after 1945, the continent would be a much more unstable place. The EU has helped preserve peace so far, but the new situation with increased migrant flows has not been taken into account.

Denmark and Europe are a community under pressure from within.

The problems with migration have once again created a breeding ground for the forces on the extreme right that want violent conflict in Europe.

Three landmark events have been of particular importance to my perception of the weakened solidarity and a community in disintegration.

First, the Srebrenica massacre in 1995. European politicians failed and just watched idly by as eight thousand civilians were murdered within the borders of modern Europe. Only when the United States decided to use military intervention did something happen.

Second, Denmark had a general strike in 1998, locally known as "the yeast crisis". With just the treat of food shortage the Danes appeared from their hitherto most embarrassing and primitive side. The scenes that unfolded showed people arguing over yeast so they could bake bread. No one was short of anything; the issue was a result of hoarding for a just in case scenario. As my uncle says, "Civilization is a thin veneer layer on society", that can crack within days. Selfishness has become prevalent and it does not bode well. We are most likely no better than an African mud hut village if a real SHTF situation arises.

Finally there was a big discussion in 1999 if Denmark could cope and manage to receive 1460 Kosovo Albanian refugees. This figure was absolutely minimal compared to the refugee flows that we see today.

I believe the concern about an external threat to Western civilization is the wrong angle to consider the true menace. Europe self-destructed in the Second World War, so I do not believe talks of any special cohesion without the European Union. The Germans (just as an example) would not care if Greece or Italy went bankrupt if they had not committed themselves to maintaining free trade, peace and cooperation through the EU. The Germans backs the EU because of the wars they do not want ignited. The internal hassle of the rules and distribution of refugees is an image of the fragile peace that the EU has secured for years.

Europeans have spread to the rest of the planet making the Western world the richest regions, and the world's population has historically sought the best living conditions. Therefore, the migration is moving towards Europe. The same is seen in the workforce from Eastern Europe, just like Mexicans working illegally or legally in the USA.. If this development is to be halted or reversed, it is necessary to create opportunities for the world's poor in their home countries. The disparity between rich and poor is, in my opinion, the most important factor for migration. Therefore, it is actually thought-provoking that politicians also make political initiatives that greatly contribute to increasing inequality. The distance from life running smoothly to losing everything has become very short. In comparison to Americans there are many west Europeans who have not yet discovered this.

From one war to the other, I walk for five minutes to the other end of the Lincoln Memorial Reflective Pool to see the Vietnam War Memorial on Constitution Avenue. Names of the 58000 Americans who died in the Vietnam War is engraved in the black granite wall. As mentioned later, a lot of bikers has a military background and served in Vietnam.
At the site there was a laminated book with the names in alphabetical order. With a quick glance into this, I found that nine men with my family name were listed as KIA or MIA in Vietnam. Right next to the Vietnam War memorial you'll find the Lincoln Memorial. It is strange to see the sites in real life, places and buildings you only know from movies and TV. An engraving marks the place where Martin Luther King Jr. held his "I have a dream"-speech on August 2nd 1963 during the "March on Washington for jobs and freedom".

Walking east towards the Capitol I meet a young couple. Their English accent gave them away as Danes, so they did get surprised with me greeting them in Danish. Just like me, Nanna and Allan were sightseeing in Washington D.C. Getting along and with the same reason to be there we stayed together as a three man tourist group for the rest of the afternoon.

The 555 feet and 5 inch tall Washington Monument was the tallest built structure in the world when it was finished in 1884. Unfortunately, it was under renovation and maintenance thus cordoned off by a 15 foot board fence encircling it completely. But with a height of 180 meters most of it was visible. The Lincoln Memorial Reflective Pool had also been drained for maintenance, so that was a bit of a letdown and the funky smell did not help either.

While looking at the Washington monument, a group of five Amish tourists were looking at the sights too, they probably were aware of themselves being a bit of an attraction themselves sticking out with their distinctive dress style.

On the east end of the Mall is the Capitol, home of the United States legislative power, with the Senate and House of Representatives. This building is as iconic as the White House and so big one can't miss it unless you're blind. A lot of state capitol buildings has similar architecture with a dome in the middle. I think the atmosphere of corruption is pungent once inside one of these, maybe that is just me not trusting most politicians. The big Potomac River runs south of Washington D.C. Walking along this we suddenly find ourselves in front of the Watergate Hotel. Funny, this felt like we just had seen over half the set of the classic 1994 comedy *Forrest Gump*.

Ending our short time together, Nanna, Allan and myself wanted a cup of coffee and to rest our feet for a bit. Seemingly having passed one Starbucks Coffee after the other I made the claim that Union Station must have a Starbucks for sure, and if not I would buy them a cup of coffee. To my surprise it didn't. Union Station had been restored to its original look as in 1907 and is a landmark for railway buffs and trainspotters, meaning no Starbucks… While they offered to pay for their coffee themselves, I don't weasel out on a bet despite being a smart ass. So coffee on me for sure. Wishing the Nanna and Allan a nice stay in the USA, and them wishing me the same, we parted ways afterwards. This was before Facebook and smartphones, so I didn't keep in contact with them.

A grand sunny day with weather that wasn't too hot, seeing all the iconic sites and buildings. Before going to bed, I did some reading in my old guidebook to get the most out of the following day.

I HAVE A DREAM
MARTIN LUTHER KING, JR.
THE MARCH ON WASHINGTON
FOR JOBS AND FREEDOM
AUGUST 28, 1963

UNITED STATES
Internal
Revenue
Service
Building
← Visitors
Hells
Angels

Monday, July 19th 2004

It is way too risky to travel around with four grand in cash, so I went into another Bank of America branch to have my roll converted to travelers cheques, at five bucks a piece this was a pretty high tax to secure my money. But worth it.

A lot of countries are currently moving towards "cashless societies". The banks love this as they pretty much have a monopoly on transactions and fees. The argument for pushing this agenda is that criminals are the only ones who use cash as they don't want to be tracked. Not many people like the thought being under the watchful eye of "big brother", and electronics transactions make societies vulnerable beyond belief. Denmark is a small country and have privatized the electronic payment transaction system. This system has been down numerous times and caused a lot of people to become unable to get basic necessities as food and gas. Albeit, just for a couple of hours, but along with water and electricity, this would be the first target in any international conflict. So when people in Germany, Japan and the USA prefer tangible currency they are not necessarily behind the rest of the world but may actually be ahead of the curve.

Visiting the memorials yesterday, historic events does fascinate me as they have led to the world as it is today. One of them took place in Ford's Theatre, where Abraham Lincoln was assassinated on Friday, April 14th, 1865, just a few days after the Confederate General Robert E. Lee and General Ulysses S. Grant of the Union forces signed the agreement to end the American Civil War. Visiting the theatre on 10th Street I went on the guided tour as early as possible. This was the only way to see the private box in which Lincoln and his wife, Mary Todd, were watching the play with their guests. The assassin John Wilkes Booth was an actor, and this would have been a logic reason why he got the chance to get close to Abraham Lincoln and fire his Derringer flintlock gun. After having been shot in the back of the head, Lincoln was moved to the Petersen family house across the street, where he died in the morning, April 15th.

John Wilkes Booth was shot dead on April 26th, refusing to surrender after a massive manhunt for him and his co-conspirators. Ford's Theatre is one of those "must see" tourist attractions if you visit Washington D.C. In close vicinity behind the Mall is the FBI HQ. This is one of the most popular attractions in D.C. My trusty guidebook said the Federal Bureau of Investigation Museum was "newly constructed" -in 1990. For reasons unknown the Museum was closed, so I just took a few pictures of the building. When you take pictures of government buildings, I am convinced they'll take your picture too on the surveillance cameras.

On 14th and K Street I encounter a few more beggars. As it happened yesterday, they truly appreciated the little small change I gave them. Some people say you shouldn't give to panhandlers. In my opinion it depends on the situation. Once I was riding in "the tube" (London Underground), where I was approached by a woman claiming to be a refugee from the former Yugoslavia in need of money walking around the train with a sign. I didn't accept this as a fair and real need, because she would have had to pay at least a bit for a ticket to be inside the train. Sometimes greed becomes too smart for my liking.

While on foot I came across one of the most hated institutions in the USA, the Internal Revenue Service Building, the tax department.
A lot of people think taxation is theft, in Denmark it is robbery. Sales tax is 25% for everything with a few exceptions that probably can be counted on one or two hands. Hated everywhere, my experience with the tax folks in Denmark is not a happy one. They have an arrogant culture and do not care about anything besides stealing as much of your money as possible. I had a shipping container picked out for extra inspection and they had a statute forcing me to pay for the shipping company moving the container back and forth to their controlling area. Fair enough if they found anything wrong, but they didn't. Another incident was payment of sales tax for a quarter. My customers had not paid on time, so I got behind on the sales tax myself. Informing my local treasury office about this, they arrogantly told me I should consider shutting down my business if I couldn't pay. So I got absolutely no love for these people.

Back on the Mall I wanted to see the National Air and Space Museum. A great place to geek out on technological achievements.

One the biggest and most visited museums in D.C., you definitely should not miss out on this. Unusual for the United States, entry is free.
The Apollo II and Viking lander are the first things you see going in. Encapsulated and hanging off the ceiling there was the first American manned space capsule. Super cool, but the damn commies actually beat the USA for sending the first man into space in 1957.
Another national treasure hanging off the ceiling is the "Spirit of St. Luis", the airplane Charles Lindbergh flew non-stop from New York to Paris France in 1927. Looking at what looks like an amateur garage hack, this feat seems even more impressive. The planes in the old black and white films has always looked like a mix between paper airplanes and kites, and in real life they are truly fascinating. They also had a curiosity in the form of a framed movie poster from the Howard Hughes film "Hells Angels", as a motorcyclist I found this pretty cool.

At noon I went on the Metro line to Arlington Cemetery. Located on the south side of the Potomac River it is actually in Virginia.
Arlington Cemetery is 624 acres and over 400,000 people are buried here, including military servicemen and dignitaries. With over 175,000 of them, the rows of white tombstone seem endless. Arlington is a graveyard, so you want to carry yourself with the respect and dignity this place deserves. So no selfies.

John F. Kennedys grave has an eternal flame burning, whereas his brother Bobby is buried with a plain white stone cross and nameplate. While at Arlington Cemetery, a flower wreath ceremony for the unknown soldier was conducted, a very touching experience. Some of the largest losses have their own markers at Arlington Cemetery, such as the 5th Regimental Combat Team having 867 men killed in action and more than three thousand wounded.
Coming across the commemorative stones for the 7 crew of the Challenger space shuttle disaster on January 28th in 1986. I remember this vividly, watching this unfold live on TV when I was 12 years old.

The high school teacher Christa McAuliffe is the one everyone recalls as she would be the first civilian going into space. As indicated through my visit to the National Air and Space Museum, space travel is super fascinating. It is the tangible proof of how far man can go with technology and I would definitely be willing to risk my life if NASA offered me the chance to go into space.

Another special gravestone was one in memory of the armed special forces killed during a rescue attempt under the Iranian hostage crisis. I was a small child when this happened, but my father followed the news closely on TV, so I am well aware of this. Visiting Arlington can be a bit overwhelming. Ending my visit I take a look at the big statue in memory of everyone who has given their life for the USA, replicating the iconic raising of the flag in Iwo Jima.

Compared to the USA (in 2004), Denmark has a mandatory draft for men. I didn't have to do this as I am missing the sight on my right eye and stated a few allergies I could document. Growing up with the cold war, this ended before I had to go into the military. Some of my school buddies had to enroll. My opinion was that I would not try to dodge a draft. My father served in the military and so would I if my country told me to, but I wouldn't volunteer for armed service. At the time of my possible enrollment, the disintegration of and civil war in the former Yugoslavia was in full effect. I did sign up to volunteer as a civilian aid worker, but decided not to go through with it, as I felt this wasn't my war and that it simply was too dangerous. A few of my friends did get deployed as soldiers, as part of the Danish contribution to the UN peacekeeping force. Many really wanted to go and there were plenty of volunteers. As it turned out, war isn't fun and games once the bullets start flying, so a lot of the guys who went there got PTSD or traumatized, quite a few committed suicide later.

The reason the army recruits young people is that they don't think long term and look for adventure and excitement. Not thinking shit can happen to them, they are easy to sucker into serving in the armed forces. Things were of course different earlier during the cold war, back when the USA had a military draft.

I believe a draft will be harder to reinstate in the USA today, as people are more informed via media and the Internet. So it is a bit ironic that the Internet initially was created as a further development of ARPANET by the Advanced Research Projects Agency under the United States Department of Defense.

Back on the Metro I went to check out the world's largest office building, the Pentagon. As with the FBI they were closed for tours. The security guards didn't loiter around with their automatic machine pistols over the shoulder, but ready to return fire anytime necessary. At that time in 2004 the USA was engaged in Operation Enduring Freedom started 2001 in Afghanistan and the second invasion of Iraq, so everything concerning homeland and national security was on lockdown. The underground Metro station at the Pentagon is an interesting piece of architecture, it looks like a nuclear resistant bunker. Just like the day prior, a lot to take in.

Riding back to Richmond, Virginia

Tuesday, July 20th 2004

Holiday Inn is a bit upscale and like Crowne Plaza it is a part of the Intercontinental Hotels Group of brands. These are often sited at prime locations which is reflected in the price. The tab for three nights at Holiday Inn Washington DC-Central came to a total of $480 of which parking was 66 bucks. Staying in upscale hotels is a bit unusual for me, but the convenience was worth it, having everything in walking distance.

Heading back south on I-95, I turned off at Fredericksburg 50 miles south. A mandatory goal of my journey was going USA coast to coast. So whipping out my map of the USA I decided to take a 150 mile detour to Virginia Beach via Newport News. Not sure where to go I got lost in Newport News. Another bystander complimented my bike while filling up the gas tank. Worth noticing is that it at this point wasn't fitted with side bags and with my belongings strapped on top. It didn't look as sexy loaded up like a camel.

While lost I had my first experience with Taco Bell at lunchtime. Taco Bell doesn't have any restaurants in Denmark and to my knowledge just a few in Europe. Mexican food in Denmark is similar to the American interpretation of this, in the form of prefab taco shells and guacamole, etc., that we most often buy in supermarkets. Taco Bell had a meal deal for three crunchy tacos with a soft drink. I thought this was ok, but not impressive. It comes off more like a snack. My meal order was super sized even though I wasn't asked, this wasn't cool in my book.

After Morgan Spurlock's documentary "Super Size me" had premiered on May 7th, just two months prior to me coming to the USA, the attitude to "super sized" fast food deals changed. McDonald's even discontinued these after this movie was released. In 2011 Taco Bell got accused and sued for using sub-standard beef grade that couldn't be classified as meat. I hope this wasn't true and Taco Bell did some serious damage control that cost them around three or four million dollars. Taco Bell since documented that their seasoned beef was 88% beef and made sure these accusations hasn't surfaced since. I don't think Taco Bell is worse than any of their competitors. You can't have high expectations at the price point.

As I drove out of Fredericksburg I needed to see something else than the Interstate, so I went on highway 17 towards Virginia Beach. This route was very pretty and I thought that it in some areas resembled my home country, a very pleasant ride on some nice tarmac. Finally at Virginia Beach after 200 miles of riding, I had my first look at the Atlantic ocean from the American side. Well, in Virginia Beach it looks the same as from the west coast of Denmark, kinda windy too.

Before heading back to Richmond to have the ordered extras fitted, I had to do a second fuel stop. A woman asks about the bike, she hadn't seen one of those before. Ducati is an "exotic bike" and does not look like the cruiser style as is the prevalent motorcycle class in America. Buying gas is a different matter in the USA. This is one of the only goods that is sold with the price stated including sales tax as you can pay at the pump. But fuel taxes are nothing in the USA compared to Europe. I paid $5 for my first fill-up and $4 for this second. At home these would be around $20 each!

I had to be in Richmond during opening hours to hand in the bike, so no more sightseeing. Driving 110 miles from Virginia Beach on Interstate 64, I had managed to run up a little over 450 miles on the tachometer. Not voiding the factory warranty, I wanted to get the engine run-in service done early, as the Ducati dealerships in the United States are very far apart. Back at MotoEuropa around 4 pm, I checked in at Comfort Inn which was in walking distance from the Ducati dealership. At $100, this was cheaper than the other places I had stayed, but the location was just fine. Wanted to call Luis, but the dang phone in the room didn't work.

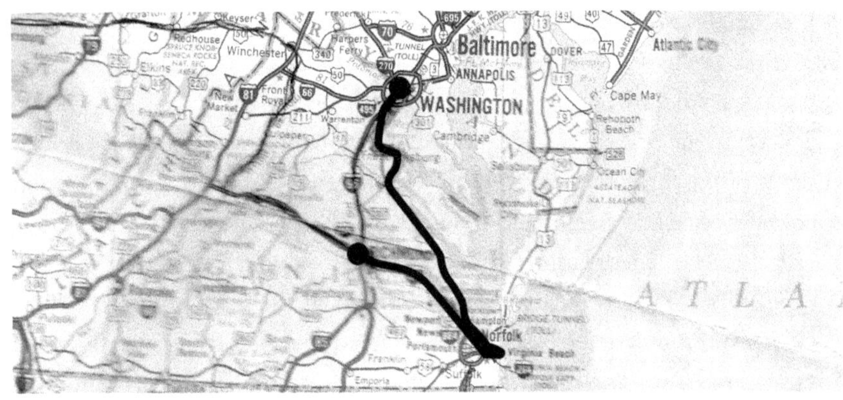

For dinner I went to Hardee's, a burger chain I'd never heard of before. Their standard burger was pretty damn good. Hardee's is also known as Carl's Jr. as the two fast food chains are have the exact same concept and menu. The name does differ as the Hardee's name is used in the southern USA and Carl's Jr. has locations spreading out from the Midwest and onwards to California. To my delight Carl's Jr. opened up their first outlet in Denmark back in 2016. I much prefer this to McDonald's and Burger King. While waiting for my order at Hardee's a couple of african american guys were joking around. In 2004 American stand-up comedian David Chapelle was at the pinnacle of his career. So one of them pulled off this fantastic one-liner: "I grew up in the ghetto, my dad couldn't afford an AK47". Guess black guy humor is dark by nature.

With more than six hours and 340 miles in the saddle,
I had no problem falling asleep.

50

Wednesday, July 21st 2004

I had to wait for the extra options to be bolted on and the run-in service to get done. With a new bike you want the initial services to be made properly and get the service book stamped in order not to void the factory warranty. Another important thing is to follow the motorcycle run-in instructions stated in the manual. Most motorcycle engines rev up to 7000 to 10000 rpm. and many sport bikes go up to 14000 rpm. and over, compared to most cars that revs up to around 5-6000 rpm. The internet is full of motorcycle "experts" who will say that this doesn't matter, but I definitely disagree. As earlier mentioned I bought my first Ducati Monster 600 from new in 2002. On the way to a visit to the Ducati factory in Bologna the engine self-destructed on the Italian autostrada, with me going 93 mph. The rear valve cam broke in two, the valve timing belt pushed out the front belt and both cut through the belt covers. I believe this could have been due to me not doing the run-in correctly. Besides the manufacturers recommended limits on engine revolutions, you also need to avoid letting the engine torque pull in the highest gear which is usually an overdrive gear. Well, make sure to bring a correctly stamped service book if your bike is still under warranty. Carrying the correctly stamped service book while traveling, this catastrophic and complete engine failure didn't cost me anything.

So there was some time to kill at Moto Europa. Having travelled for a while I had visited Ducati dealerships in Italy, Thailand, Singapore, Japan, Australia and New Zealand. Writing articles for the Ducati Club Denmark about these, I noted down some information about Moto Europa/ Ducati Richmond. Moto Europa celebrated their tenth year anniversary in 2004. Besides the general manager Stubbs, they were four employees. Sales guy Matt, wrench monkey called "T" and a hot eye candy Margo handling merchandise and accessories, such as boots, gloves, helmets and protective riding gear. Furthermore, there was an office assistant called Joyce whom I never met. Chatting with another customer whom the staff knew well as he had been spending a lot of money at Moto Europa. Trying to come up with something funny, he told me "I just bought his bike" that

moto
europa
DESMODECIMO
VIRGINIA
08 17 04
V336 084

he had been eyeballing for a while. Motorcycle shops often become like a club house with the customers hanging around drinking coffee and inhaling gas fumes without spending money. But that is part of how the business works. A motorcycle is a big purchase decision, so you want to take your time to pick the right one. I would show up just to eyeball Margo.

Two other motorcycle retailers were located right next to Moto Europa. One next door and another just across the street. Here, Big Dog Motorcycles had a showroom. The place looked nice; the bikes were custom built to order like the bikes in the popular Discovery Channel TV-show "Orange County Choppers". With the long and low chromed out style, Big Dog choppers were basically Harley Davidson clones. You can actually build a complete Harley clone from bits and parts from the aftermarket manufacturers, but if you don't know what you are doing it can easily turn out as a half baked project. There is plenty of those for sale. I got a few friends who have given up on what looked like a cool concept, but where skills and funds turned out to be inadequate.

A style of motorcycles that since became popular is the café racer.
The hipster generation loves old bikes rebuilt into this stripped down style bikes often with low positioned handlebars. A modern cousin of the cafe racer is the "streetfighter", with the common trait being minimalist styling, engines tuned for speed and responsive handling. Streetfighters were initially sport bikes that had been thrashed and instead of doing an expensive rebuild, the owners stripped these powerful machines down and put standard handlebars on them. Another motorcycle style that has become popular is the scrambler. These were standard bikes kitted out with knobby tires and higher suspension to make them useable for off road riding.

With motorcyclists getting older and young people discovering classic values and styles, the motorcycle manufacturers haven't been slow to catch on. Almost all have a factory scrambler, street fighter or cafe racer model in their model lineup. These are modern bikes but with a retro design styling.

A fun fact is that all of the above styles have roots in England.

Stripping down your bike to make it lighter and go fast from café to café, the most famous being the Ace Café in London, a must visit for any motorcycle enthusiast. The popularity of scramblers owes a lot to American actor Steve McQueen racing his modified Triumph around the Mojave Desert, with Triumph being an English manufacturer.

The motorcycle I bought for my coast to coast ride was a Ducati Monster S4. In 2005 the Monster range accounted for more than half of Ducati motorcycle sales. The Ducati Monster series are streetfighters, basically sport bikes without the full fairing. These are also called naked bikes. The Ducati Monster model range was launched in 1994 and created from surplus parts from the outgoing Ducati 851 superbike racer. Just comparing the two models side by side and there is no mistaking where the M900 trellis frame originated from. Ducati Monster can be seen as a direct response to Triumph launching their Speed Triple the very same year. The streetfighter category was created by British riders who had crashed their sport bikes and due to economy would or could not rebuild these.

All the above styles have a hint of fashion and lifestyle statement over them, but all the new factory retro models are very well handling motorcycles with great performance.

Two types of popular motorcycles which do deserve a mention as well are adventure and touring bikes. Adventure bikes are "do it all" motorcycles that go through city traffic, commuting, long distance touring and even off road riding. The adventure bike category is dominated by one manufacturers model, the BMW GS12xx range. This is the reference that all the other manufacturers tries to beat. Luis swears to this model which is often referred to as the best motorcycle in the world.

While Ducati has produced some of the most beautiful motorcycles in history, their first generation adventure bike named Multistrada is ugly beyond belief. Hence I have nicknamed this as the "Multibastard".

Touring bikes are well known by most as the big Harley Davidsons with the big classic batwing style fairings. I do think this has a big part to do with the highway motorcycle cops using them. But the competition is fierce, and the Honda Goldwing is probably the best in the motorcycle touring class, unless you are one of those who think it absolutely has to be a Harley Davidson or nothing.

At around 2 pm my bike was ready, so it was time to load up. Motorcycle touring is a crash course in minimalism. My full inventory:

6 t-shirts, including two high quality freebies from Moto Europa
1 sweatshirt
3 pairs of pants
4 pairs of socks
Riding jacket, Gore-tex
Riding Pants, Gore-tex
back protector, helmet
2 pairs of gloves, weatherproof and summer
Tools
Spray can of chain lube
Travel- and vehicle documents, including insurance papers
Sony Ericsson cell phone (emergency) with charger
Canon Exilim 4 megapixel digital camera with battery charger
Water bottle
Toiletries
Swag, sleeping bag and backpack

Moto Europa were ok with me leaving a bag with items I didn't have room for on the bike until I would be back from my round trip, this included the Riding Techniques book. I later discovered that I forgot my adjustable wrench and my t-handle spark plug wrench in the bag. The license plate would take longer to arrive, so I rode out with the temporary tag initially fitted. Valid for one month, I was insured and riding legally. With just a map of the USA I only reached the outskirts of Richmond before I had to stop at a Taco Bell and ask for directions to the Blue Ridge Parkway, one of the most scenic roads in the USA.

My first day included 82 miles on Highway 250. Thinking I had spent a bit much on hotels in Richmond and Washington D.C. I found the Misty Mountain Camp Resort. Not a lot of people there that day, most had RV's or camper trailers. My inventory list didn't include a tent starting out, but just my swag. A swag is a thick canvas sleeve with a foam mat in it. As foam insulates you from the ground and though spartan, it does the job. You just crawl into it and go to sleep in your sleeping bag. To give you a little privacy I had the bike parked in between me and the other campers. This also provides a bit of wind protection, however you really have to make sure the bike is positioned so that it in no circumstances risks falling over with you underneath it.

The main characters of the classic road movie *Easy Rider* has a swag strapped to the sissybar backrest of their bikes, just like in the old Clint Eastwood movies. And in the saddle of a bike in the Unites States, you feel like a cowboy.

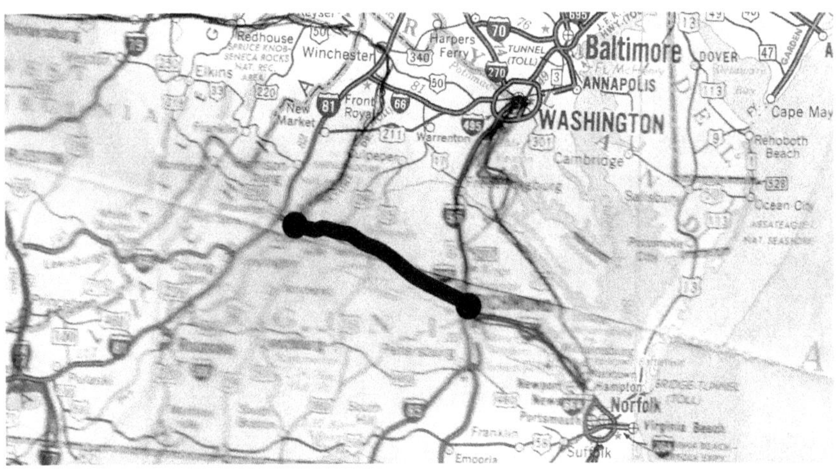

The Misty Mountain Camp Resort was $23, so a very different price point. Checking out the facilities available, they didn't have a washing machine for laundry and their dryer was out of order. Later that night I had a nature call, so I went into the campsite toilet. I found this to be very well maintained and pretty clean.

Roughing it is no problem, it is a part of the biker lifestyle.

But as you get older you do get accustomed to more comfort.

Thursday, July 22nd 2004

Waking up the next morning, and packing the bike ready to go again, I realized that I had used the ladies' facilities earlier. This time I went into the correct restroom, and the sight was typical. Dirt and feces all over the place, I never go into a mens' room without footwear. It still puzzles me why mens' toilets pretty much always literally look like crap. I avoid touching anything and fortunately I didn't have to go number two. While on this topic I also have noticed that a lot of men do not wash their hands before leaving a public toilet, this being the reason why I am a bit of a germaphobe and don't like to shake hands with other people unless the situation requires it.

Looking on the map I get a sense of how big the USA really is.
With about eight weeks of planned riding and one week in New York before going home to Denmark, I had no plan but my old guidebook had already given me a good idea of what I would like to see and experience. So back on the road again I continue up route 250. Luis had recommended the 469 mile long Blue Ridge Parkway that goes through Virginia and North Carolina, offering the most beautiful experience of the Appalachian Mountains. Turning right I went north up through Shenandoah National Park to Front Royal. The problem was that I should have turned left southbound to find the Blue Ridge Parkway.

With an idea of visiting multiple national parks such as Yellowstone NP and Yosemite NP, I bought a National Parks Pass at the entrance, valid for the rest of the year. A National Parks Pass lets a vehicle and up to four adults into each park for free, children under 16 have free entry. Where the park charges an entry fee per person rather than a per vehicle fee, the pass normally covers up to four people. Note: It doesn't include extras like tours or camping and RV use.

So on a motorcycle you can't get as much value for money as if you were in a car with the family or friends.

Making a few stops in Shenandoah NP I saw why they named the area Blue Ridge Mountains. Coming from Denmark which is flat as a pancake and no mountains or rivers, I just love visiting places with varying altitudes. I talked to a few fellow bikers about riding in the USA vs. Europe. I wanted to get an idea of how tough the cops were on exceeding the speed limit. One of them claimed that in a national park like this, they can't get you in the corners as their laser or radar guns cannot get a reading. Not sure whether or not that was true, so I didn't argue against that.

Riding through Shenandoah NP I almost collided with an eagle carrying some prey flying across the road at low height. Close calls and hairy situations happen all the time when you're on a motorcycle.

At the north end of Shenandoah NP I got on the I-66 going on to I-81. Navigating the Interstate highways is easier, but they are primarily transport pipelines that get you from A to B. With every rest stop on the Interstate highways you have the option of eating at a fast food chain, so I went to KFC. I haven't been to a lot of these in my life, so I ordered the only thing I knew beforehand, a Zinger menu. Just a few miles northbound on I-81 I realized this was going to Washington D.C., so I took the off ramp to highway 50 going west at Winchester, VA. With the bike pointing in the direction I wanted, while only passing through, I just nicked the bottom of the state of Maryland.

At my next gas stop I bought some "Reese's Peanut Buttercups", I had never tried these before and I first heard about these in an episode of the animated Simpsons TV series. In 2004 these were not sold in Denmark. At the same time I got myself a Road Atlas. They had an offer for a 2003 edition for $5, whereas the new 2004 print would be $20. Even though I got the chance to go to the USA and buy a motorcycle, I am basically a tight-ass who don't want to pay more than necessary. So no prizes for guessing which one I picked.

Money makes the world go round. Money lets you do more.
Money has only true value when you spend it.
Buy a motorcycle or a burger with fries, build a house,

The old Depeche Mode song says it best:
Everything counts in large amounts.
This makes for another point: We are not all equal.
Some stick to complaining about this claiming "The rich should share
with the rest of us". I used to think this was bullshit.
But inequality is not the same as 25 years ago, and the true problem is
the opportunity gap that has become visibly wider.

In my opinion, the self-made rich who have worked their asses off
do not have to share, but a lazy stoner who do not want to work
should be entitled to nothing.
Some wealthy people got rich from ripping off the poor and giving to
themselves. I have no sympathy for these people if they screw up and go
bust. Greed make some people turn into monsters.
By writing I am giving you my thoughts. But not for free.
And I chose to cross the USA
on a Monster.

Route 50 goes into West Virginia.
While riding in these lightly foggy and
cloudy weather conditions on this road,
reality hits me:
I AM TOURING THE USA
ON A MOTORCYCLE.

An incredible felling of joy comes over me.
I'm living the dream, baby !

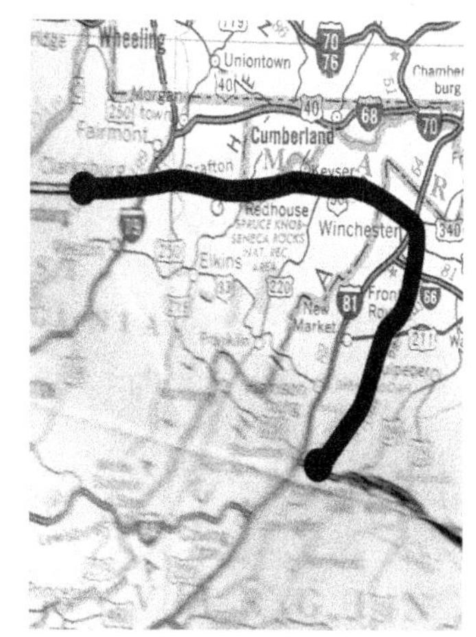

We all strive for the feeling of security or pleasure, on both a material and psychological level. Security and pleasure often come with an inner joy which is visible when it occurs.
Joy isn't a constant, maybe it is supposed to be like that.
Feelings of joy do become greater when they are attained
with a sense of pride and accomplishment.

While we are looking for independence and security, doubt causes insecurity and feelings of emptiness. So focus and concentrate on your ambitions, along with a mission and a sense of purpose. Some fill this with alcohol, others become shopaholics or develop an eating disorder. In my opinion a form of hiding, giving you a worse starting point from which to try and find happiness, independence and security.
You can hide your feelings, but you can't hide from yourself.

Continuing on highway 50 I cross over Mount Storm, riding through forests and mountainous terrain. It is a sweet route which offers a great stretch of tarmac with lots of curves. Most of these are equipped with signs stating the recommended speed. Not knowing the path of road I stick to these, as I need to get more acquainted with my new bike. I did have a close call with an oncoming car as he took a corner too fast and crossed the double yellow line. Here, I also encountered the first rain on my trip. Rain is pretty normal for the Mt. Storm area. There is not bad weather when you wear the right clothes, I almost always use protective and/or weatherproof gear. It is just a part of being on a motorcycle. After Mt. Storm I got close to hitting a deer about to cross the road on Mount Olivet, it fortunately turned around when I revved my engine. Those Termignoni exhaust pipes may not be street compliant, but they saved my ass in this situation.

Reaching Clarksburg after 300 miles of riding in 75° F (approx. 24° C) temperature, I checked into Sleep Inn motel, a fair deal at $59. Dinner was at the Golden Seagull. I noted had I developed the bad habit of buying side orders, so I decided to give "diet"- soft drinks a try. I think they're bogus, but they seem less hard on my teeth enamel.

Munching down the "Reese's Peanut Buttercups" I bought earlier, I did find these interesting, especially as I got a feeling that I might have a light degree of peanut allergy. The motel room TV had sixty channels, not sure why I ended up watching "Fit TV", a dedicated fitness channel.

Checking my new Road Atlas, I thought of sticking to US Route 50. But three high risk incidents on the bike in one day was a bit unusual, I sure hoped this wouldn't be a precursor for my trip.

Ohio reminds me of home

Friday, July 23rd 2004

While checking out of the Sleep Inn I wait for my turn to check out, some guy in the line starts telling me a story about his son and I wonder why he tells me as it is none of my concern. Blabbering babble for yak-yaks sake. This wouldn't be the last time I run into people with an urge to share their history with strangers. To meet people you do need to be open and talk to them, but getting personal matters explained within 30 seconds is a bit too forward to me.

This made me think about the things we say.
Words can be everything. Aggressive, reconciliating, liberating,
personal. Anything you say can be used to your advantage
as well as against you. Words have value.

That is why there is three thumb rules you might want to stick to.
Even though I know it is not always possible to keep your head straight,
think before you talk.
Stay alert and try to avoid letting others manipulate your thoughts.
Don't say anything you unless you mean it.
It is easy to hurt other people or yourself.
Keep your promises. It is always a good idea to stick to your word
keeping your integrity and reputation intact.
If people think you can't be trusted, you're boned.

As planned, I went back out on the highway crossing the Appalachian Mountains. The weather was hazy, but comfortable. Route 50 to Parkersburg widens and become a double lane highway. Not really aware of where I am going, I end up in Marietta, Ohio. So to find out where the hell I was, I headed north on Interstate 7.

The Interstate Highway System, the vast network of freeways across the USA, was made possible by the Federal Aid Highway Act of 1956 funding the construction. Maintenance, refurbishment and new construction is a process that has been ongoing ever since. Creating this, President Dwight D. Eisenhower was influenced by an appreciation of the autobahn network being a crucial component of the German defense system. Providing a fast track infrastructure in Germany, the concrete dividers between the opposing traffic flows can be moved to assist redirecting traffic during roadworks. What not many people are aware of is that these also were an important part of the West German cold war military infrastructure, as the concrete dividers can be moved to allow airplanes to take off and land during wartime.

The designation freeway is used for roads designed for high-speed vehicular traffic where access is controlled by interchanges, on- and off-ramps, so that no byroads are connected directly, providing an unhindered flow of traffic, without traffic signals, intersections or property access. Crossing traffic is instead carried by over- and underpasses. These are called motorways in most of Europe, Italy use "autostrada" and Germany "Autobahn". The German Autobahn deserves a special mention on its own, as half of this 8000 mile network does not have a speed limit. I have had the pleasure of getting my Triumph up to 150 mph (242 kph) there. But traffic congestion creates a natural limit on how fast you can go. The Germans has the best traffic culture in the world keeping right when possible. This is due to the rule of thumb that someone is always coming from behind, going faster than yourself.

There is constantly some German tree huggers and safety boffins who wants to implement a general speed limit, but I believe the no speed limit legislation on the Autobahn is the outlet that makes a lot of Germans accept the many other strict laws they have to live with. I must say that going 111 mph (180 kph) in the big Autobahn curves is just about my limit on how fast I dare to go. If you fail to keep the rubber side down and shiny side up and coming off your bike at this speed means you'll be boxed up and buried in case shit happens.

Interstates are not very exciting, so I soon find myself on an off ramp and on route 60 towards Zanesville. The fields in Ohio really reminds me of the part of Denmark where I grew up. This is probably also why a lot of people in Ohio are descendants of Scandinavian immigrants. Filling up my bike I see a sight I will never forget. A young woman only four foot five tall (140 cm) climbs into a full size pickup truck. This little lady could only just peek over the steering wheel. Only in America, man…

The surroundings being a bit monotonous, I headed west alternating between Hwy 40 and I-70 to cover some distance. On highway 40, I find myself stuck behind three 18-wheelers without anyone else in sight and a clear view ahead. So it is time to see what the Ducati Monster S4 is capable of. Letting the Ducati rip I overtook the three semi haulers, but decided to slow down as the needle reached 120 mph. No need to end up in handcuffs for reckless driving. In Ohio this is a flexible clause citing any "vehicle operation that disregards the safety of other drivers, passengers or pedestrians, or both public and private property". I don't think you can talk your way out of going 120 where the signs say 55.

Around Columbus, I decide to try out Dairy Queen for lunch. I had heard of them serving milkshakes, so decided to go check out their concept. Another burger munched, they kinda taste the same and I am getting tired of these. I can't blame anyone else for choosing this for sustenance. Once again without stating that I want a "regular", I get a supersized order. I really don't think this practice is ok, at least they should ask.

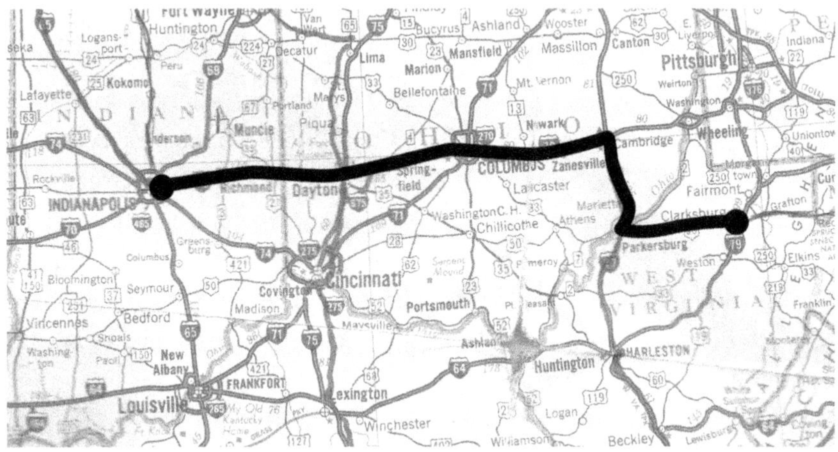

Not having spare fuses for the bike I make a stop at Advanced Autoparts. This would later prove to be a smart move. Totaling 400 miles this day I arrived in central Indianapolis at 6 pm. Here I found one of the worst motels on the entire trip. Not wanting to ride around looking for a motel in a larger metropolitan city after dark, "Motel Indiana" on one of the main roads offered a room for $45. "Motel Indiana" looked as if more than one person had been murdered there, electrical outlets hanging out of the walls and doors with unnatural foot-shaped signs of "wear". I didn't realize this until after I had checked in. I should have picked one of the big motel chains on the ring road, this was so bad I just had to take some pictures to document it.

What a shithole crapshack.

Saturday, July 24th 2004

Getting the hell out of Motel Indiana as soon as possible was a priority. So I do a little sightseeing drive around Indianapolis, the name gives it away as the state capital. The Greater Indianapolis area has a population around 900,000 people, not unlike Richmond in Virginia. Ohio and Indiana don't seem to have a mandatory motorcycle helmet law.

On a parking lot I stop and talk to a pair of motorcyclists who could explain the way to "Flat-out Inc.", listed in the dealership booklet that came with the bike. They had a moved to a completely different address, so no wonder I couldn't find them. Fortunately it was a short drive away. After talking to the shop assistant at "Flat-out Inc.", I was informed that they no longer were a Ducati dealer, but still serviced the brand. To ensure I got the right type I bought a pair of OEM Ducati spark plugs. They cost a whopping 60 dollars, and the guys at "Flat-out Inc" actually felt so bad about this price that they threw in a free t-shirt.

Business is about money and the motorcycle manufacturers in many instances treat their partners and customers like crap. This affects the goodwill of the brand through the entire supply chain. You already know my relationship with Harley Davidson, with the weak link being the dealerships acting like a bunch of miserable dicks. Harley Davidson Motor Company really need to address this, I don't think they can afford to lose any customers in the future.

> *Goodwill has a measurable influence. Everybody knows the saying:*
> *"You reap what you sow".*
> *Treat others like you want to be treated yourself.*

> *The joy of giving is not always enough. I am not afraid to give when I can myself, but those who receive from me should not be stingy when it comes to giving themselves.*

> *Put in another way: I am registered organ donor.*
> *If you don't want to give yourself, you cannot expect others to either.*

To be able to fit the spark plugs I needed a wrench, since I forgot the one I already had at Moto Europa in Richmond I went to "PepBoys", another automotive spare parts supplier, and bought one for $30.

While there I checked if I I they had the spark plugs that my Ducati used, but no luck. I guess Ducati North America knew it would be hard to get aftermarket plugs with the correct heat grade.

Without any ideas of things I would want to see in Indianapolis, besides a building with a wall which had a concrete dinosaur bursting through it, I get the Ducati pointing straight north on Route 421 West. This is a three-digit numbered highway which are generally spur routes of parent highways.

It is pretty chilly with a temperature around the low sixties (12-14° C). So I had another close call almost losing my balance at the gas station in Lafayette. Continuing north to Lacrosse, I soon found myself westbound on Route 30. In order to reach Chicago before evening I hit I-90. Here I finally started to meet other motorcycles in greater numbers. Half of them Harleys, but I would say around 25% were big Honda Gold Wing touring bikes.

Twenty-five miles outside Chicago on I-94, I made the brilliant decision that I wanted to see some of suburban Chicago, immediately getting stuck in a traffic jam at a set of intersection lights and the 30 minute Interstate drive became a sizzling hot two hour rush hour trap. With my full touring load I didn't dare to lane-split, which means going between the car lanes instead of being stuck with the other vehicles.
There was simply too much dense traffic to navigate through and I estimated this would be challenging fate in an unnecessary way. My backpack started to feel uncomfortable too, or so I thought. Mr. Brain later found out that he had been wearing his t-shirt with the back facing front the entire day.

Riding through residential neighborhoods, I got overtaken by a group of local African American sport bike riders. They greet as motorcyclists do with a nod and a wave. Wanting to be in the city centre, I ride to the downtown Holiday Inn in central Chicago. They didn't have any vacancies until the next day as it was high season. The price was also top dollar at a crazy 250 bucks per day. So I found the Esquire motel 13 miles outside the city centre at a fair price of just $59. This was run by an Indian family; I have since noticed Indians from Asia do seem to have a preference for the motel business. Having rolled 200 miles on the tach, I felt pretty hungry. Across the street I went into "El Ranchero", a Mexican restaurant that, compared to Taco Bell, felt real and authentic. The place wasn't too busy at the time and the staff was friendly. Here I had my second encounter with the American portion sizes. For just $12 I got a mixed platter so heavily loaded that I had zero chance of eating it all. Being stuffed I managed to get through 2/3 of the serving including the starter noodle soup.

The only comparable experience I have had prior to this was in Beijing, China. While in a mall I felt hungry and went past a restaurant offering a deal for around $6.75. Since I couldn't and can't read Chinese, I had pointed at the sign and made them know this was what I wanted to eat. I only realized that I had ordered a family dinner for 4-6 people after the servers just kept bringing tray after tray of food. It actually made me feel kind of bad as plenty of Chinese people could use a meal and all this uneaten food would just go in the trash.

Sunday, July 25th 2004

Leaving the Esquire Motel at 10 am, I almost slay myself riding out on North Elston Avenue. Elston Ave. is a double lane main road to and from central Chicago. Leaving the parking lot, I drive out and make a left turn. A big pickup truck was approaching from the left, with plenty of distance margin. Everything is bigger in America, so what I couldn't see was that another pickup was overtaking the closest one at the same moment. Completely hidden from view, this was one of those near miss situations where it was a matter of luck, not skill that didn't result in my trip being cut short. However, this was without discussion an error on my part. I think a collision would have been my last mistake on Earth, so the motorcycle gods must have been in a good mood. This was the fifth time I had got into a dangerous situation riding in the USA, but not the last. There are three types of idiots on the road; you, me and everyone else.

On Milwaukee Avenue to downtown, I decided to take a detour into a very mixed neighborhood. Here I make a stop at a laundromat.
After two weeks my clothes had started to get a bit funky, so I needed to get it washed. The laundromat was an interesting meeting point for the diverse population living in the city, with Latino, Polish, Italian, Mexican and Indian patrons. A latino family had their hands full while doing their laundry, also having to look after their small kids wanting to run all over the place. One little old polish woman was particular talkative and told me about her having a son outside marriage and thus being outcast by her so cial circle and family. Once again it does puzzle me how some people find it urgent to tell their life story to strangers. As I am on a motorcycle, she also warns me that Chicago has a lot of people who drink and drive. Clean clothes and life stories, I definitely got full value of the one and a half hour plus the three dollars spent there.

Meeting some average Americans in their everyday life had me thinking about how others live their lives. My thoughts of a better world in a modern society is based on a general concept of "the modern man".
This being the best starting point for a new age, a new beginning.

Esquire
MOTEL
HOOTERS
Wings

*Everything starts with yourself, nothing really new in that.
But maybe there is something new when you put everything into a
greater perspective, creating a renewed focal point when we seek to
make sense of it all. The great connect consist of harmony between
consciousness and body. With this I mean the conscious human, living
sensibly. The Ideal in perfect balance with the world. This idea enables to
seek the connections in life, as the ideal also consist of more than just one
single guideline.*

*With a view from higher up, call it holistic if you want, we are able to
see things in a different perspective, in more than one way, more than
the usual way. This leads another core value: Openness. Openness for
new impulses and ideas, making the world bigger. Here is also one of the
traps in life; Letting new impressions overwhelm you. Never forget to
stay critical, and to keep your feet on the ground. Then we see the world.*

*Going in the deep end, when we look at the world we know it is
not how it should be. Should I do something to change this
or accept things the way they are?
Some things can be changed. On a personal level.
Which moral standard does one possess?
For myself, my moral is limited to what is tangible, but I don't do any-
thing that crosses the line of what threatens my own values.
Egoistic, but natural. I am sorry to conclude that
this way of thinking will not ever make me perfect.
Perhaps it is not supposed to be this way.*

*A part of morality is respect. As we live in a world where most people are
forced to live fairly close next to each other, we should show consideration
and thereby respect. In order for this to work respect should be mutual.
I do not care to respect anyone who doesn't respect me.
It is pretty simple, know the difference between yours and mine.*

*"No touchy" means "do not touch". A first and simple rule you can apply
to almost anything. And if this isn't followed, the road to the stone age
becomes very short. Eye for an eye, here you definitely start with yourself.*

At 12:30 I arrive at the Holiday Inn Express in fine sunny weather. I am not sure if it is better to make reservations ahead, but it is one pricey option. This is located on the "Magnificent Mile", the main shopping street in downtown Chicago and near the financial and cultural district known as "the Loop". So everything is within walking distance. Having busted my left knee front ligament while writing off my first Ducati the year prior, I found that walking was good exercise for my old injury.

With around 2.8 million living in Chicago, it is the third largest city in the USA and a third of the entire US population lives within a 500 mile perimeter. No wonder I encountered some of the most dense traffic in my life the day prior. Located next to Lake Michigan it is also known as "the windy city". Chicago is also famous for being the home of legendary mob boss Al Capone. The Italian Mafia rose to power in the city during the prohibition, the federal alcohol ban from 1920 to 1933.

With countless documentaries I care more about my safety while actually in Chicago. In 2004, 448 people were murdered and 15964 were robbed or mugged. Using my guidebook, I checked up on recommendations concerning safety, about not going into the wrong area after dark and other sensible advice.

After a shower I talk to the concierge at the reception about ways to experience the city. He had plenty of options, but I had no problem deciding as he asked if I was interested in architecture. Chicago is famous for the skyline and riding into the city I took pictures of Willis Tower with its distinct two antennas; this is actually more commonly known by the old name "Sears Tower". I decided to take a city cruise by boat to experience as much as I could in the shortest time possible. Staying at Holiday Inn Express cost an arm and a leg, but again, the location was worth it. In 2004 internet access wasn't mobile like today, so online searching and booking ahead would only take place on computers. Bringing a laptop on this trip would be problematic, given the size of these back then.

I can recommend taking a boat ride in the cities which offers such. Chicago is particularly great as the Chicago River lets you to see the architecture from a little further away, most often without anything obstructing the view. The Chicago River is special as the water flow has been reversed so that the polluted water from the city doesn't seep out into Lake Michigan. Instead it is routed into the Mississippi River. Whether or not this was a smart move by the city planners, thinking ahead wasn't a big thing. When you have a river nearby you can make your problems flow, or float, out of sight to end up being someone else's problem.

Coming into the city I had crossed some of the steel bridges the tour boat sailed under. The driving surface is steel mesh, so you definitely want to be careful on a motorcycle. With the guide providing names and other information on the buildings this was a great value for the price of just $26. The weather was sunny and the skies clear, so I had the best conditions for taking a lot of great pictures.

On the Magnificent Mile, all the stores were open on Sundays in the high season. The temperature was around a comfy 65º F (18º C). In 2004 people were still buying CDs and DVDs, so I visited Virgin Megastore. Excellent porn section too. Obviously there is an Apple Store on the Magnificent Mile. They were a new concept at the time, but today I find them boring, visit one and you have pretty much seen them all.

Harley Davidson also had a merchandise store on Michigan Avenue. They had three very beautiful vintage Harleys on display. Unfortunately, it wasn't possible to get close up to see these in detail. Harley Davidson has for sure mastered the art of branding. They offered all sorts of HD crap as HD pool balls, HD mouse mats, HD knives, HD drinks coolers, HD dart arrows and not least, HD T-shirts. Some people buy anything as long as it has Harley Davidson written on it. The joke being that HD is an abbreviation for "hundred dollars", the usual amount you end up spending after visiting a Harley Davidson merchandise store or dealership. And the biggest motorcycle club in the world is the "Harley Davidson T-shirt Club"…

The World famous Route 66 starts on Adams Street (Westbound). Here you can find the "Start Historic Illinois U.S. Route 66" marker sign at Michigan Avenue. Going on Route 66 is a dream for many but checking the actual route it is no longer the best for getting to Los Angeles fast, and there is not that many big "must see" attractions on the way. You may be able to see and meet a lot of Americans living their everyday lives taking this route. I later went down to the promenade facing Lake Michigan. While there I got inspired by looking at the shoreline, so I decided that instead of taking the short route up to Milwaukee, I would go the long way around the great lake, counterclockwise.

Walking around downtown I came across Original Hooters on North Wells Street, the first Chicago location of this legendary of restaurant and sports bar chain. With the slogan "Delightfully tacky, yet unrefined" they are world famous for the waitresses outfits consisting on tight tank tops with a canyon view and orange shorts. And Buffalo Wings.
So I just had to visit one of these. Since dinnertime was coming around, the timing couldn't be better. I got seated by one of the lovely ladies and ordered some Buffalo Wings, a Samuel Adams beer and some curly fries. Samuel Adams is a big Americans brewery and I must say that I have grown fond of their Boston Lager. A mainstream beer that I highly recommend. Some American cuisine has funny names so for those not familiar with Buffalo Wings, that is chicken that usually has been deep-fried then coated or dipped in a sauce consisting of a vinegar-based cayenne pepper hot sauce and melted butter prior to serving. The Buffalo wing was

invented in 1964 at Anchor Bar in Buffalo, New York, hence the name. I noticed that I have started to eat more during my trip. For dessert I ordered cheesecake and coffee, totaling $21. Americans are world champions at two things, entertaining and branding. So I bought a $5 calendar too.

Women's groups have been up in arms for years accusing Hooters of being male chauvinists exploiting women. During my visit to Hooters on North Wells Street I saw families with kids too. Being offended has become the norm and times have changed, so Hooters has re-designed the uniform options for their employees. Hooters is harmless fun.
Everyone likes hot women. And hot food.

The concept of "breastaurants" is not limited to Hooters. In 2005 rival chain Twin Peaks was founded in Texas. One of the founders were formerly executive at Hooters Inc. "Breastaurant" chains have been growing at a rate of 30-40% per year, while the general restaurant industry as a whole has only grown about 3–5% annually.

This type of restaurant appeals to bikers, including myself. A few Hooters franchises have had the foresight to locate near Harley Davidson dealerships. So the big boys can go to the toy store and go eat some comfort food and see some fine ladies while getting their bikes fixed.

Twin Peaks in Texas had one famous biker fight on May 17, 2015.
A shootout erupted at a Twin Peaks restaurant in Waco where Bandidos MC and Cossacks MC tried to solve an argument about political rights for Texas as an exclusive territory. With 200 bikers present, nine bikers were killed, and eighteen others wounded or injured.

Back at Holiday Inn, I went down to the business centre and e-mailed the family at home, still no pictures of my niece. I did send an e-mail to Luis to let him know how things are going. He had been a bit worried that I was traveling alone, so he was happy to hear my trip was going well. Besides the e-mail from Luis another e-mail had landed in my inbox.

Internet dating was taking off in 2004. At the time there were more than 800 lifestyle and dating sites, a 38% increase since the start of the year. I had signed on to a site called Asiansinglesconnection as they had offered a lifetime membership for $35 to get people to sign up. As I was born in Thailand, this was an option I decided to go for, I had tried other dating sites earlier without much success. Asiansinglesconnection changed their name to or merged with Chistianmingle as the original dating portal couldn't maintain their traffic rate and became an online ghost site. I got in contact with Nancy, aka. "Smiling4U" in Minneapolis, and we had been communicating for a while. Telling her about my travel plans Nancy had e-mailed her phone number in her last message.

To get the most of my stay in Chicago I asked the hotel concierge about options to see Wrigley Stadium. Tours were only on Saturdays, the 9.11 terrorist attacks in 2001 had an impact here too. I have never understood baseball fully and watching an MLB game at a later opportunity, I learned why stadium beer sales are high during the baseball season. Homer Simpson said it best in season 7 where he is at baseball game while abstaining from beer for a month: "I never realized how boring this game is".

Monday, July 26th 2004

My architecture experience continued with a visit to the John Hancock Center, only a 11 minute walk from the hotel. At 1128 feet (around 370 meters) and 100 stories tall, this is one of the most famous buildings of the structural expressionist style. The distinctive X-braced exterior shows the structure's skin as an integral part of a "tubular system", one of the engineering techniques which the designers used to achieve the record height. The name was changed to 875 North Michigan Avenue in 2018. But just as Willis Tower is known as Sears Tower, I am sure this skyscraper will continue to be referred to as the John Hancock Center. On a curious note, the John Hancock Center was featured in the movie *Poltergeist III*. The observatory is located on the 94th floor and has a 360° view of the city, up to four states, and a distance of over 80 miles (130 km). This is the highest building I have enjoyed the view from, and the entrance fee of $11 was well worth it. As this is the fourth tallest building in Chicago, I didn't feel a need to go into Willis Tower.

Back on street level I bought a couple of postcards and $8 worth of stamps. Postcards were still a thing in 2004 and do possess a certain charm and personal touch that social media can't replicate. Time to brag to the family and let them know that everything is good. Besides that, Facebook, Instagram and Twitter only became prevalent after the launch of the iPhone and other smartphones in 2007, three years later.

Walking around I come across a Bang & Olufsen concept store on Oak St. This is the super stupid expensive high-end entertainment brand from my home country. Looking around, they had a 50" Beovision 4 plasma TV that I wasn't sure was available in Europe. At "just" $13,000 it was cheaper that the 50" model sold in the Danish home market. No prizes for guessing why Bang & Olufsen is struggling to become profitable.

At Grant Park I took a stroll through Millennium Park not mentioned in my guidebook. It had just opened July 16th, 10 days prior.
No wonder it looked absolutely spotless.

A graphic designer by trade, I would like to look at some art.

My graphic design course included art history, so I went into the Art Institute of Chicago. Located next to Grant Park on the Magnificent Mile, this is one of the oldest and the second largest art museum in the United States. Recognized for its curatorial efforts, popularity and 300,000 works of art, the museum hosts approximately 1.5 million visitors each year. I was lucky enough to go in at a time where there wasn't a lot of people there. For the $12 entrance fee plus a $1 for wardrobe service, they offer Indian, American Indian, Japanese, Chinese, Japanese art and artifacts. The Art Institute of Chicago does have some of the most famous art in the world and if you care about art, you definitely don't want to miss this.

Among the must see artworks are: Van Gogh self-portrait, Georges Seurat's most famous work, "A Sunday Afternoon on the Island of La Grande Jatte", made with a pointillist technique, Edward Hopper's "Nighthawks", the oil painting of an American diner and Grant Wood's iconic "American Gothic", the one with the couple where the man is holding a pitchfork. Iconic masterpieces indeed. Taking a few pictures, one of the wardens make sure and ask to assure that I don't use a flash on my camera in order to avoid damage to the artworks. Her job must be a lot harder today with everybody tooling around with their camera phones.

Art is a strange topic. At times it can be very difficult to understand why something is art and other things are not, and how a selected few for some unknown reason has the privilege to determine this.

Back in the 90s artistic and creative people were dressed in an unofficial uniform, wearing all black. Popular culture does offer some answers to the question of "why something is art," as some artists and artworks has had the fortune to get exposure in mainstream media. English artists Banksy and Damien Hirst are two examples of this. Banksy is famous for his street art and Damien Hirst has gained high fame and status through "The Physical Impossibilities of Death in the Mind of Someone Living" in 1991. This artwork features a large tiger shark suspended in formaldehyde. The latter is a good example what art is all about.

The street art of Banksy has a bastard cousin called graffiti. When I was a kid in the mid-eighties, it was the new big cool art thing from New York. Today I think tagging walls is basically vandalism. It is done by idiots and on a more serious level, it often relates to territorial gang activity.

A Chilean artist, Marco Evaristti, gained notoriety for an installation he called "Helena" in the year 2000 that featured ten functional blenders containing live goldfish. The display invited guests to turn on the blenders, which caused a huge uproar and debate. Besides the back story of the installation concerning life and death, the installation didn't require any craftsmanship or skills. Any asshole can put ten goldfish in blenders. Using animals and killing them for the sake of art or to make art is not really revolutionizing anymore, so this isn't really in vogue today.
But what Marco Evaristti did was provoke emotions. This is my definition of art. Whether it is paintings, installations, statues like the ones in Richmond, music, movies, written words, performing arts or anything else, true art is a catalyst that ignites thought, reflection and emotion.

Music as art is special as you often associate this with social interaction or certain periods in your life. I do think music has to be experienced at a higher audio volume level for you to experience the full range that a song or instrumental number offers. Listening to Prince's classic hit "Purple Rain" is just one great example for you to try.

After a couple of exhausting hours I leave overwhelmed with impressions, again full value for money. It has started to rain so I went into a Dunkin' Donuts to rest my feet, I still only had my caterpillar boots to wear. As with many American franchise chains I had never been to one of these before. The donuts were a bit dry, and the coffee scolding hot, so I took some time to write some greetings on the postcards I bought earlier. Walking with my coffee, now having a drinkable temperature, a guy sells "Streetwise", a magazine that the homeless sell to be able to support themselves with some income. This idea has iterations all over the world. So I bought a copy. On earlier occasions I have been short-changed by sellers of these. I don't like to be suckered while trying to help, so I actually don't buy these magazines very often.

Needing to get a couple of things sorted. I get the pictures on my memory card burned onto a CD in a photo store. They erased the memory card afterwards which I didn't want them to, as a disc could break getting squeezed in with my other belongings on the bike. Outside I decided to give a pan-handler with no legs all my small change, albeit less than a few dollars. With the close calls I had on the bike I wanted to improve my karma. Small change is actually annoying when you travel on a bike, you don't want that to rattle around in your pockets.

On my way back to the hotel I walk along some of the streets where the Metro rails runs above, the first thing on my mind is the Gene Hackman movie "the French Connection". Popular culture sure has had a huge impact on the world.

I decided to go find some dinner. Inspired by the Edward Hopper painting I chose to go into Cambridge House on Ohio St., a classic American diner. Ordering an unimpressive cheeseburger which has a single thick pickle , a single tomato slice and a side order of thick cut fries. The ice cubes in my drink had a hint of chlorine taste. But still better than McDonald's. The tab is $8.05, so out of small change, I pay $10. The tipping culture in the USA is usually adding at least 15% to the bill as appreciation for the good service. This sometimes feel like an extra tax. The upside is that you can leave nothing if you think the service was crap. Servers often get paid a pittance per hour and rely on tips to uphold a decent income. I think this does motivate employees to give customers a good service, but at the same time it is demotivating for employees to use their time in a low-paying job if they could make more money elsewhere.

It was getting dark so I chose to head back to my hotel. In a convenience store I bought three classic American treats, beef jerky, Lays Chips and Oreos. I had heard of beef jerky and Oreos but had actually never tried it. After emailing the folks at home from the business centre, I send "Rush No More RV and Camp Resort" a follow-up e-mail too, as they haven't sent me any booking confirmation.

Munching on the Lays chips I bought I watched some TV, Al Gore and Bill Clinton sure were in top shape at the 2004 Democratic Convention. What a day.

BANG & OLUFSEN
CHICAGO HARLEY-DAVIDSON
HARLEY-DAVIDSON

Tuesday, July 27th 2004

At 10 AM the bike is loaded up. Studying my Road Atlas, my journey around Lake Michigan was on, so I fired up the Monster and rode down to Highway 41 going south onto I-94E. I wanted to take a ride along the shore where I could see Lake Michigan. Well, with four lanes and the need to have full attention on the other vehicles, I didn't see any of the shore going through the city traffic. I had yet another close call on the merging ramp onto I-94, another error that no-one else could be blamed for. Repeating myself, sometimes luck counts just as much as skill.

The gas tank needed a refill, and I turned in at the first gas station on my journey which requires payment in advance. "Drive-offs", people who fill their vehicle and run from paying the bill, is a widespread problem. Especially in the larger cities, and during economic downturns, the last being after 9.11 2001 at the time. Without any particular or direct connection, there is a cop sitting in car outside. I wonder if they get discounts on donuts and coffee.

After 60 miles I reached Michigan City around noon. So I turned off the Interstate to White Castle. Another fast food chain I had heard of, but never tried. White Castles claim to fame is that they are regarded as the first fast food chain starting in 1921, and their signature product is their small 2 inch wide sandwiches with steam cooked square meat patties, also known as sliders. I order a "Variety Sack" with some sort of paté, battered fish patty, burger and cheeseburger slider. Not really impressed, this was my only visit to White Castle during this trip. What I didn't know was that the now legendary stoner movie *"Harold and Kumar go to White Castle"* would be released on the 30th of June, just three days later. This was a piece of collaborative marketing genius which since made White Castle famous worldwide.

The best about White Castle was actually the kid admiring the Ducati in the parking lot, telling me that "I like your bike". Oddly, this was the third time someone used those exact words about the Monster S4.

Ducati hit a bullseye designing the Monster range. I do find the design changes after 2014 less sexy than the earlier iterations, acknowledging that the later models probably have much improved handling performance.

Without a GPS I wasn't sure how long it would take me to go around Lake Michigan, so I decided to at least get some distance away from Chicago. Getting off the I-94 thirty miles northeast, I ride into Stevensville. Here a cop rolled down his window and asked: "How big is that engine?" I don't think a Harley Davidson would generate the same type of interest as my "Italian Stallion", probably more in the way of checking for gang affiliations. No longer on the Interstate I try to stay on Route 32. During this day, I managed to take more than one wrong turn resulting in a detour. When lost I had to pull out my Road Atlas, and when it got too confusing I went onto the freeway.

Following I-196 the weather was fairly cold, but it stayed dry without rain. In Muskegon I turned off I-196 after another 100 miles and onto Route 31. After 60 miles of riding I pass north through Ludington and then further 36 miles along the east coast of Lake Michigan to Manistee. With my knees being stiff from the chilly temperatures, I had covered 360 miles in 7.5 hours, so the day was mostly a point A to point B ride.

Checking into Comfort Inn, this sounded just like what I needed. But I found $79 + tax a bit steep, so I ask at Super 8 Motel. So at $63, the latter it was. It is my experience Motel 6 and Super 8 usually offers the best value for money.

Needing a few camping items I went to K-mart. Here I bought a Leatherman Multitool for ($70), a microfibre sleeping bag ($14) and a pen size Mag-Lite ($7). The cashier clerk is a 21 year old flirting chick with braces and a positive and happy attitude. Pretty cute even though she is missing a tooth in the right side. She had to have me sign a waiver concerning the Leatherman tool as it has a knife blade in it. So I can't sue if I clip my digits or somehow managed to cut myself up.

Manistee looks like an ideal little place. It has everything a cozy American smallville town needs and I am sure quality of life there is pretty sweet with McDonald's, K-mart, Taco Bell, Subway, motels, well-groomed neighborhoods, a beach (Michigan is a freshwater lake) and little white picket fenced houses that looks like dollhouses. Taking a short ride on the bike I go down to the lakeshore and watch the sun set in the West. Looking at sunsets around the world, it always dawns on me that no matter where you are, it is the same sun anywhere.

When everything looks perfect, shit happens. So my camera fell out of my jacket while maneuvering the bike, breaking the sensor chip. Fuck.

It would be a boring world if there were no option or room
for interpretation. Putting things into a different perspective,
it is easy to end up with the wrong answers when you don't
ask the right questions. You'll need to find these yourself.

Stay open towards new and different input and impulses.
If you just see things in one single way, you won't be able
to see the world as it should be seen.
With a critical stance.
Criticism isn't always negative and can be constructive,
but negative criticism is often made in capitals

overshadowing many positive angles.
It is not always oneself that shut out new impulses.
You're not always as independent as you think or would like to be.
The opinions of your peers affect your opinion in a big way.
The difference between right and wrong is a product
of common sense and your social environment.

Everything depends of the eyes that see.
Each and every one of us are individuals with different views,
so stay critical to more than one world view.

Questions often opens debates where things are pretty much set,
maybe for the better, maybe for the worse.

Maybe we can grow wiser if we look more than once.
With a wider perspective the world becomes stronger – and closer.

There is more than meets the eye,
those who believe or claim that they have all the answers
are wrong.

Because new questions will always arise.

At Super 8, annoyed about breaking my camera, I had 80 TV channels to surf through. Still not having opened the packs of beef jerky and Oreos I bought in Chicago, my first impression of beef jerky was mixed. Good but it can get too much.

So I tear open up the roll of Oreos. Dry as cardboard I wonder how the hell these ever managed to become popular. This is still a mystery to me today.

Guess it is like White Castle,
I should take another look and give them a second try.

(I did, Oreos are still awful.)

Wednesday, July 28th 2004

Peter Fonda's "Captain America" character starts off in "Easy Rider" with chucking his watch on the ground before he and Billy begin their ride to Mardi Gras in New Orleans, throwing away the shackles of having to get everything done and be somewhere by a certain time.
I didn't bring a watch either, the bike has a clock in the lcd dashboard. Leaving Manistee at 10:20, I realize the bike is on Chicago time. I wanted to get on the road at 9:20. This wasn't the last time not having a watch messed with my travel plans. Besides the time issue I didn't have a GPS, these were pretty expensive in 2004, and as mentioned smartphones were only introduced in 2007. The United States is a big place and it is a pain in the ass having to pull out the Road Atlas every few hours, each time you get lost.

Coming into Manistee on Hwy 31 I ride out on this route too.
Turning left to M 22 at Bear Lake, I ride up close along the east shore of Lake Michigan to Frankfurt continuing to Empire and on to Lake Leelanau. On these 70 miles a lot of cars lugging jets skis and fishing dinghies on trailers. This is a very nice part of Michigan State, I get the feeling this is an expensive area of the USA. I pretty much only met caucasians and no cops. Making a few stops to take pictures, I tried the adjustment options to fix my busted camera. The sensor had an iffy connection and some picture came off like looking at 3D images seen without 3D goggles. No land speed records were broken on this little coastal motorcycle cruise. After 21 miles with the bike pointing towards Mexico on highway 645 through Cedar and Traverse City, I got stuck in a traffic jam. Route 31 goes through Traverse City and I stayed on this highway for another two hours after reaching Mackinaw City and Interstate 75 north.

North of the city I cross Mackinaw Bridge. It was undergoing repairs and is constructed so the driving surface is a steel mesh like some the bridges in Chicago. You can't make any emergency braking on a motorcycle on this type of driving surface. The Strait of Mackinaw marks where Lake Michigan and Lake Huron connects. I decided to let a pair of Harleys have a sampler of the Termignoni exhaust rumble when I quickly passed them. Of course one of them couldn't handle being overtaken, so he whipped it up to 70 mph and overtakes me. I decided to tag along behind him. As the lead rider in front usually rides the fastest, that is the guy whose day the police will want to ruin.

On Mackinaw Bridge I contemplate if I should do a quick excursion into Canada. But with no idea on eventual visa requirements, my insurance coverage, what I wanted to see in Canada and a temporary license tag, I decided to give this a miss. Thinking about this for a bit too long I miss the interchange exit to US Highway 2 as well.

After a quick consultation with Mr. Road Atlas, I ride behind a Harley Davidson going about 75 mph (120 kph). A bit later he slows down to stop and refuel at a Manistique gas station, so I passed and discovered that it wasn't a Harley, but a Victory or Yamaha. Harley Davidsons have a classic look that their competitors try to copy, replicate or knockoff, sometimes you just can't tell the difference. Harley-Davidson even filed a sound trademark application for its distinctive V-twin engine sound in 1994, but dropped this in 2001. Nine of the Motor Company's competitors filed comments opposing the application, as cruiser-style motorcycles of various brands use a single-crankpin V-twin engine which produces a similar sound. These objections were followed by litigation.

On Highway 2 I notice there is quite a lot of roadkill and bit of exploded tire fragments. After 132 miles my fuel warning light came on, making me a bit nervous. I was unsure how big a reserve my gas tank held and when the next gas station came up. Sixteen miles later I reached Rapid River and Highway 41 where there is a gas station. I found out that the S4's gas tank has almost a gallon of reserve capacity. Like the watch thing this issue would become relevant later.

For dinner it was "Yo Quiero Taco Bell" again. For those who don't know this slogan, it was a part of a Taco Bell campaign featuring a talking dog (chihuahua) saying "I want some Taco Bell" in Spanish. Those crunchy tacos were just what I craved. A kid and his dad were super interested in the Ducati and had all sorts of questions, guess there isn't a lot of those in this corner of the US.

Having ridden enough for the day, I camp at Pioneer Trail Park in Escabana, 12 miles further south. A paltry $12, especially compared to the Holiday Inn Express in Chicago charging $250 a day. So traveling in the USA can be done for a very reasonable cost, but would require more planning. Compared to 2004 this is much easier to do in advance with the proliferation of smartphones with Internet access and GPS. However, some areas have poor cellular coverage or none at all, so a problem free solution doesn't exist yet.

Camping in Escabana, I am still in the eastern time zone.

So the clock on the bike was just 59 miles from being correct.

Milwaukee, home of Harley Davidson

Camping doesn't encourage sleeping in, so I find myself heading out of Escabana at 9 am (eastern time). The sun hasn't risen fully so it is chilly, riding in a t-shirt, protective riding jacket and pants down road 35 following the west coast of Lake Michigan. This part of the trip has been around a 1,000 extra miles that I had not planned to do in advance, but decided to do watching the shoreline in Chicago. An impulsive decision. Today was different as I wanted to reach Milwaukee, which is 230 mile south.

In Menominee 59 miles down the shore I see a guy jumping up and down wearing a gorilla costume to attract attention to a Family Dollar discount store. Pretty funny, but I prefer mascots who can perform some great dance moves. Overtaking two Harley Davidsons, one being a girl on a trike (3-wheeled motorcycle), passing Harleys had become a habit. I think there is something to what Luis said, Harleys are heavy and slow. When I had just bought my first Ducati in Denmark, a member of the Hells Angels MC rolled up next to me. Let's just say the Hells Angels do not want to be last from the traffic lights. And I didn't want to ruin a brand new engine by drag racing it.

Crossing the Menominee River, I almost get slain by a white Chrysler Grand Voyager in Marinette. The driver is an old duffer failing to yield as he was supposed to, and then blocks two lanes. Fortunately, I managed to swerve and avoid an accident. I doubt this would have been possible on an H-D Low Rider with slower handling.

From Marinette it is a one hour ride 55 miles down Route 41 to Green Bay. Here I got one of those "chill down your spine" moment most motorcycle riders sometimes experience as I almost skid out on some fresh tar. And along the way I get bit by a ton of insects. This is not my day riding; maybe Wisconsin drivers are worse than average too?

The only thing I know about Green Bay is their football team playing in the Super Bowl. Driving through, I come by a custom motorcycle shop and "McCoy's Harley Davidson", the local dealership. Checking out the inventory, McCoy's had a used 2002 Low Rider on the floor in a two-tone pastel green and cast wheels priced at $18,000. A new one had a list price of $19,000 !

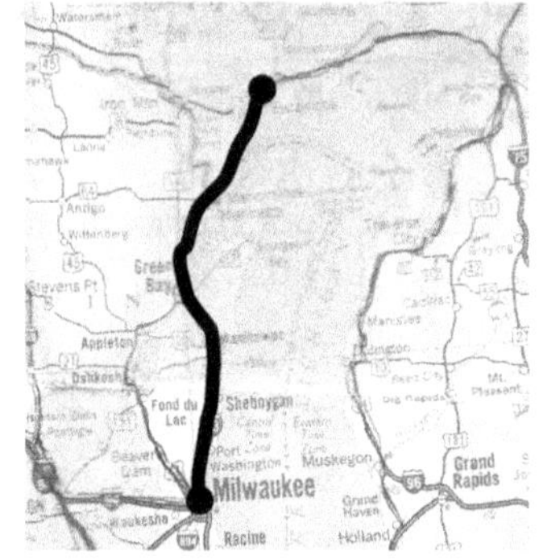

In a period from 1990 to around 2005, people were putting deposits on bikes and being charged up to 50% above msrp by the dealerships was widespread. Well, the sales manager probably knew the ugly ass color on that bike would make it hard to get rid of, as he was ready to do a trade-in on my Ducati right away. I thought I had seen it all at the Harley Davidson merchandise store in Chicago. An HD bar stool? Guess you can buy HD furniture too. I bought a "shit happens" sticker instead. Yeah, I dared to challenge karma. So this sticker was put on the bike the next day. When shit happened.

Trying to find a way through Green Bay I managed to take a wrong turn on Route 41 and ended up south on Route 32/57 as the highway split into two I missed the off ramp. Along the way I made a stop to check out a La-Z-Boy dealership, as I had been looking into buying a reclining chair. The building was using the old franchise building design and logo. Having to update this, they told me that it would be a 3-500,000 dollar store remodeling job. Ouch. But as with Subway, franchising is business where you really have to research the implications and know what you're getting yourself into.

Finally arriving in Milwaukee I stop and check out a Vespa dealership, they had tons of cool stuff. Piaggio, the brand owner and manufacturer of the Vespa scooters, has definitely learned something about merchandising from the Americans. What I really wanted to find was 3700 West Juneau Avenue, the home of Harley Davidson HQ.

Driving around for an hour lost again and again, as more than one section of Juneau Avenue had been blocked off because of roadworks. It was with a bit of awe I parked the bike in the parking lot. The receptionists are used to motorcyclists coming through their doors and they handed me route instructions to the production facility on W. Capitol Drive which manufactured engines. Not reading the map properly I ended up taking exit 42 instead of exit 44. My reward for being a numbskull was another two hours wasted, stuck in commuter traffic and an extra forty miles ridden. Eventually I found the plant, but it was too late in the day for a tour. Just before the underpass leading to the factory, a guy on a Buell had an accident and was receiving treatment by emergency services with his bike on the side, all dinged up. Having found the W. Capitol Drive Harley Davidson plant, I decided I would return the next day, I definitely didn't want to miss out on a chance to go on the factory tour.

Finding a place to stay overnight I ended up in Motel Baymont on Silver Spring Drive and Highway 100 west just three miles away from the W. Capitol Drive plant, minimizing my risk of riding around in circles for half a day. For $70 I got a non-smoking room -with an ashtray. In the motel lobby I talked with two guys on a BMW LT1200 and an HD Road Glide. They suggested a different factory five miles north of the motel! They must have been referring to the Menomonee Falls Harley Davidson plant. I thought to myself that I would stick to the initial plan for the following day, getting lost again would just make me mad now.

When asking Americans for directions, they often refer to driving distances in the time they estimate it'll take you to get there. Makes sense if they know the area and amount of traffic. And having them give you a metric reply doesn't happen, so you often need to do a little math. In retrospect, I would have loved to have a GPS on this trip. At the end of this day I had ridden 300 miles because I had got myself lost so many times it was beyond stupid. North-to-south highways are odd-numbered, the lowest numbers in the East, and highest in the West. East-to-west highways are typically even-numbered, with the lowest numbers in the North, and highest in the South. Major North–South routes like the Pacific Coast Highway have numbers ending in "1" while major east–west routes as I-90 have numbers ending in "0". If a GPS is for pussies, you can call me "Hello Kitty".

At this point, the total mileage on the Ducati just ticked over 2500 miles.

Suspected of industrial espionage at Harley Davidson

Breakfast at Motel Baymont was waffles. I have never had this for breakfast before, I consider waffles and pancakes to be desserts. Food customs really differ all over the world. Americans do things their own way, while inventing all sorts of bastard concoctions. This trend has spread all over the world. Some of the worst beer I've had was "chili beer". Yech.

Arriving at W. Capitol Drive at 11 AM, I park the bike along the many other motorcyclists there. Most were Harleys, but a Yamaha YZF R1 and a few Honda Gold Wings was also parked out front. Harley Davidson is super cautious about industrial espionage, so before going in on the factory tour I had to hand in my phone and camera equipment and go through a security check. Well, I found this a bit cumbersome, so I put my phone and camera into one of my lockable panniers.

On the factory tour I wrote the following notes in my travel diary:
The W. Capitol Drive Harley Davidson plant primarily manufactures Sportster and Buell engines, 450-500 employees machining and assembling 350 units per day, totaling 80,000 units per year. HD's total production being 300,000 motorcycles per year.

Harley-Davidson has a second Powertrain Operations facility located on Pilgrim Road by Exit 51. With a production of 350 units and total of 900 employees doing three shifts, they produce 1000 big twin engines per day. Simple math would see them produce around 220,000 engines annually.

An employee at a stop on the factory tour shows off a gearbox assembly that the visitors may try to hold in their hands. Mr. Brain then holds it at an angle, so the gears come apart. Oops. This was fortunately not a problem as the gearbox demo guy put the pieces correctly back together in just a few seconds.

Employees perks include a 20% discount on Harley Davidson motorcycles. The final vehicle assembly plant is located in York, PA.

While jotting down the above, a six foot five black security guy asks me to come with him and I was led into a side room that looks like a classic interrogation room the cops use. Two staffers kept me under tight observation, while we wait for some engineers to come and have a look at my diary. As there is no proof of me doing anything wrong, they made sure to stay courteous and neutral. I think they didn't want to risk getting sued and lose their jobs. Small talking with the big security guy, I asked and find out he is called Richard and his female colleague moans about that the lunch is burgers again. The engineer arrived and I translated some of my diary. Finding no issue, they let me continue my factory tour. If Richard didn't stop me he wouldn't be doing his job, so all fair and good with me. Security can be tricky, a thing that I found out later in Minneapolis. At this point the rest of the tour group had moved on. With no guide I just waited to tag onto the next tour group that came by a minute later. I decided not to make any further notes during the tour.

Back outside on the factory parking lot, the Harley Davidson Demo Truck was parked so visitors had the chance to get a test ride on pretty much any model Harley Davidson produced at the time. I have always grabbed any opportunity to try a new bike, often bikes which are out of my price range or totally different from what I have tried before. To this day I still go for it if I get the chance to test ride a motorcycle or two. This time was a little different, I decided I wanted to test ride the two bikes I didn't buy in Richmond. So I signed up to try a Low Rider first. This is one step up from a Super Glide, the entry-level big engine Harley and has a nice analog rev counter in the dash whereas the former only had a digital rev counter. The Super Glide was since discontinued and is now replaced with the Street Bob in the model line-up. Reading the waiver was kinda fun, and I kept this to get it framed later. While waiting for the bike to return from another test ride, I talked with one of the other riders present and she helped me out by taking a picture of me on the Low Rider. As mentioned earlier the 100th anniversary colors were black and silver. The signature color scheme used on the 2004 model range was two-tone gold and black. Looking at the shot later, that bike looks pretty sweet with me sitting on it. The test ride route was marked by small orange flags and included city, highway and a short stint on Interstate 41.

I had only ridden on a Harley once before and this was my first ride on one in the USA. Getting the bike up to speed, I got one of those "wow" feelings of achievement again. "Ride on a Harley Davidson in the USA " was another one off on my bucket list. Whoo-hoo!

Returning from the ride, the test ride staffer asked if I liked the bike and I burst out "My next bike is going to be a Harley!". With an inseam of 29 inches, the handling on the Harleys with the Dyna frame were definitely more manageable for me than the older Softail framed models. Big twin Harleys with the Dyna frame has since been replaced by a new generation Softail frame, when the Motor Company decided to streamline their production. I must say this frame design will be missed as they maintain the looks of the Harley motorcycles from the 1960s and 70's. The new Softail frame is better handling, but I think the Dyna Harley will gain cult status just like the old FXR Evolution frame. The 1980s FXR range was actually not very popular upon launch but has since been hailed by many as the best handling frame Harley Davidson has produced before the 2018 Softails. It later turned out my next bike wouldn't be a Harley, but a Triumph.

Time flies when you're having fun. So at 2:10 pm it is time for me to try a Buell XB9S Lightning. These are no longer produced but sported some pretty unique features such as having the gas tank integrated inside the frame, and a radial front brake rotor mounted on the front wheel rim. The staff told me to be very careful with the front brake, my Ducati has double 320 mil front rotors so I said they shouldn't worry about that. I soon found out what they were talking about. That was the most extreme brake I had ever tried to this day it still is ! The seating position was sport-bike style, as with the torque delivery at 5600 rpm. Not useful for long distance touring, I was glad that I didn't go for one of these for the trip. Could I do it all over again I would have bought a Low Rider instead of the Ducati, but I might not have survived the previous day.

The W. Capitol Drive site is no longer producing engines. The site now houses some of Harley Davidson Motor Company's R&D. The Motor Company's Powertrain Operations facility is now on Pilgrim Road in Menomonee Falls, Wisconsin. This where the big twin Milwaukee-Eight 8 valve and Sportster engines are made today.

At the time I visited, the bigger powertrains were the Twin Cam type, the previous generation big twin engine. Harley Davidson has assembly plants in more parts of the world now, giving the Motor Company better options for offering their products in the BRICS nations. There are now assembly plants in Brazil, India and Thailand. The latter covering the ASEAN nations. As foreign vehicles are met with high import tariffs in many countries, having the parts imported and assembled locally bypasses these. Harley Davidsons domestic customer base is dwindling, so expansion abroad is the way for the company to create growth, basically becoming a multinational company.

Harley Davidson in Milwaukee is Mecca for many motorcyclists, who has to visit at least once in a lifetime. The Motor Company's Powertrain Operations facility in Menomonee Falls therefore have visitor tours like the old plant. In 2008, the Harley-Davidson Museum opened on 400 W Canal Street in Milwaukee, giving visitors more to see and experience. I'll go there for sure if the opportunity arises.

I-41 northbound runs right next to W. Capitol Drive and I was immediately met by the sign for Milwaukee Harley Davidson at Exit 46. Still excited from my test ride, I decided to visit the dealership. They had the XL1200 Sportster priced $1400 lower than Richmond Harley Davidson! I would be annoyed if I had bought that same model Sportster in Virginia. This might have been due to the factory worker discount. Every local would know about this, and thus not be willing to pay more than them. Well, without any Low Riders available I avoid being tempted to trade in the Ducati. Still happy with the "Bologna Rocket", I went onto Highway 16 to Wisconsin Dells, 85 miles west. This seem to be very touristy. Time to try the International House of Pancakes, aka. *Ihop*, a sit-down restaurant chain. Feeling hungry, dinner included a T-bone steak, fries, salad and a roll. For dessert, obviously a couple of pancakes.
Let's just note most of the salad and roll did survive this $16 munch-fest.

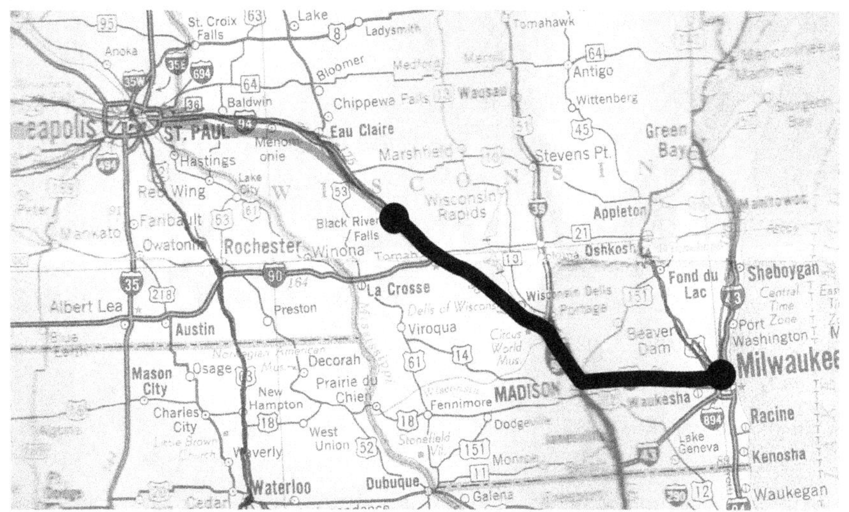

With some extra weight to compress the suspension on the bike, it is back on I-94W. Stopping at a Super 8 Motel I got an "offer" charging $110 for a room. Nein Danke, I had a similar experience once riding through Germany. In 2002 the old Deutschmark had just been replaced by the Euro. The motel owner smugly demanded €70 for a room which I am sure had cost the same in Deutschmarks, i.e. just half the new price a few months prior. Motels know that if you're tired and don't feel like driving further, they often get away with charging a higher price. Super 8 usually deliver a fair quality, but not $110 value. For a little more you can stay at the Holiday Inn.

Standing next to the Ducati on the parking lot outside Super 8, the bikes kickstand sunk into the hot asphalt. While checking my Road Atlas I did not notice this until it was too late. So the bike tipped over to the left, with me underneath it !

Scratches on the left pannier and a broken clutch lever is not the way you'll want to customize or personalize your motorcycle. Putting on the crash bungs sure looked like a smart choice this moment, saving me for serious damage to the tank and engine.

To get some distance done I rode another 85 miles on I-94 westbound. I noticed that most drivers increase their speed after sunset. Ending up at "Motel 95" in Hixton and for the handsome sum of $46, I had begun to get an idea of what I should and was willing to pay for a motel room. There was a "for sale" sign on the front for people with more than 46 dollars to spend. Going over to the adjacent restaurant "Club 95", this was full of middle-aged white folks small talking about life, garage sales and how children are impossible to deal with… Talking to a young guy that looks like a total redneck, he recommended the buffet. All the good food must have been eaten earlier as there wasn't much on the trays around 8:30 pm. I think they might have renamed "Hicks Town" as Hixton. His girlfriend looked kinda cute, I did notice she had some junk in the trunk.

Drinking a couple of beers and getting a little information about the area, the bigger city of Osseo has a population of 50,000 people and is located 20 miles up I-94. Hixton has consists of a few thousand souls, not unlike the suburb I grew up in myself. And the tachometer said Hixton is 215 miles from Milwaukee when you don't have to take any detours whilst being lost.

This sure was an event filled day. At my last gas stop I had bought some Krispy Kreme donuts, another thing I had never tried before.

What do they put in these? One bite and I am addicted. Maybe it was because I was comparing them to the crappy ones I was handed at Dunkin' Donuts in Chicago. Circle shaped diabetes to go.

Last order of the day was preparing for the next one. I should reach Minneapolis Saturday, so I call up Nancy! This is the first time I hear her voice and she sound pretty friendly. And it was very exciting to finally talk to the woman I had been e-mailing back and forth for six months. Having seen just two pictures and facing the possibility of having been catfished, I am a bit nervous. Nancy could meet on Sunday in Brooklyn Center where she lived, so I would call back when I had arrived in Minneapolis.

Getting some travel info, Minneapolis is about 146 miles away, so I should get there without having to sit on the bike for a full day.

Having the best breakfast ever, fighting drug use and riding to the Twin Cities

Saturday, July 31st 2004

In Osseo I decide to go to McDonald's for breakfast and buy a McGriddles value meal. This was a complete eye opener. With bacon, egg and cheese with two syrup-infused mini-pancake griddle buns, this sandwich is super fatty and greasy, but is the absolutely best thing on the entire McDonald's menu. I don't know why McGriddles isn't offered all over the world. I am sure it would be a massive hit for Mickey Deez. The value deal included a deep fried oval potato patty the Americans has refer to as a "hash brown" and a cup of really hot coffee. The coffee cup had the hot beverage warning embossed on the lid; this was implemented in 1994 after a now legendary product liability lawsuit. A New Mexico civil jury awarded $2.86 million to plaintiff Stella Liebeck, a 79-year-old woman who suffered third-degree burns in her pelvic region when she accidentally spilled hot coffee in her lap after purchasing it from a McDonald's restaurant. Liebeck was hospitalized for eight days while she underwent skin grafting, followed by two years of medical treatment. This lawsuit ultimately ended with Liebeck being awarded just $640,000 and the creation of a false urban legend about the woman who sued McDonald's and became a millionaire.

On the topic of great tasting junk food, the best item McDonald's big competitor Burger King serve, is their "BBQ Bacon Double Cheese" burger. I have only seen this in the UK, and also don't understand why it isn't sold everywhere. If bacon and cheese cause cancer, I'm doomed.

With just 146 miles to Minneapolis, I was in no rush. From Osseo it was ten miles west on Route 10 where a log hut says "Velkommen til Strum" in big letters on the porch. Directly translated from Danish it means "Welcome to Strum", so I just had to make a stop in this town. Asking the first person that looked like a local I am informed that this is actually Norwegian. From 1537 to 1814, Norway was largely subject to Danish rule.

The history of Norwegian immigration to America started about a decade later in 1825, the colonial period where the Norwegians joined the Dutch seeking profit, religious freedom and trade opportunities. Later in the 1800s disasters such as crop failures, blights and poor harvests leading

to poverty led to new waves of Norwegians uprooting and seeking a new and better life in America, not unlike the many coming in from South America today. The climate and seasonal weather changes in Minnesota are similar to northern Europe, and it is one of the states with the deepest ties to Scandinavia and especially Norway. Some trivia facts for you: Norway has a population around 5.3 million today, while 4.5 million Americans claimed Norwegian ancestry in 2011. A-Ha. (Get it?)
In comparison, my home country Denmark has 5.8 million living there and about 1.5 million Americans are of Danish origin or descent.

While in Strum I discovered that a local car club held an exhibition with vintage, classic and muscle cars. Being a motorcycle guy, cars are for me a question of getting from point A to B in the most comfortable way possible. As cars goes there is only one engine which counts in my book, the almighty V8. The sound just makes me happy. And the participating exhibitors at the Strum car show seemed to agree, as most of the cars displayed were equipped with this engine type. There were quite a few hot rods on display in the style used in the 80's ZZ Top music videos. And yeah, ZZ Top rules too.

Besides showing off some fine automobiles, the event was held to raise funding for the local D.A.R.E and the entrance fee was just $1, with higher donations of course being appreciated.
D.A.R.E is an abbreviation for "Drug Abuse Resistance Education" and is a police officer-led series of classroom lessons that teaches children from kindergarten through 12th grade how to resist peer pressure and live productive drug and violence-free lives. D.A.R.E. was founded in 1983 in Los Angeles and has proven so successful that it is now being implemented in 75 percent of school districts in the USA and in more than 52 countries around the world.

During my travel around the World I have noticed that young people love cool cars - and their mobile phones. So combining the fight against proliferation of drugs with a car show is a damn good idea, an example of the fact you don't need drugs to have a good time.

VELKOMMEN TIL STRUM
MUSTANG
SHIT HAPPENS

Drugs are the one thing I almost always have been serious about. I have only made experiments with cannabis and a single dab into methamphetamine. More than enough. It just doesn't fly. It is a lifestyle I just don't find acceptable in any way. I am uncompromising in this matter and like Yoda I think "Do or do not, there is no try". I prefer my mind clean and sharp. Besides, you should only ride a motorcycle in a sober and clear state.

Most users think they "control" their cannabis usage. A little bit won't harm. A little bit here and there harms. Most people make their first acquaintance with weed through friends, a social connection. Like the D.A.R.E program knows: The hook is in the social pressure. Is legalization the answer? Curbing some crime is a plus, and the cops could then concentrate on harder drugs. But weed will be a problem, legal or not. I have yet to hear about hard drug addict who didn't start with weed. If I ever meet one that'll be a unicorn farting rainbows.
"Mind expanding", or rather mind numbing hard drugs usually destroys lives within a very short amount of time. Just look at some "before and after" picture comparisons. Strong, healthy people with a nice house, job and the complete family package that transforms into homeless cast members of *The Walking Dead* in less than a year.

> *Living a rock'n roll lifestyle can be cool for a while but won't last.*
> *Leaving you in a helpless state of indifference,*
> *You're better off finding genuine and lasting values.*

Back on the Ducati, I actually haven't met a lot of motorcycles this day, so it was nice to meet a group of 4 sport bike riders in the opposite lane. They were going in a very leisurely speed. Meeting their two buddies a few seconds later, this was understandable. A State Trooper had decided to ruin their Saturday ride by tailgating the group in his patrol car.

What a dick move.

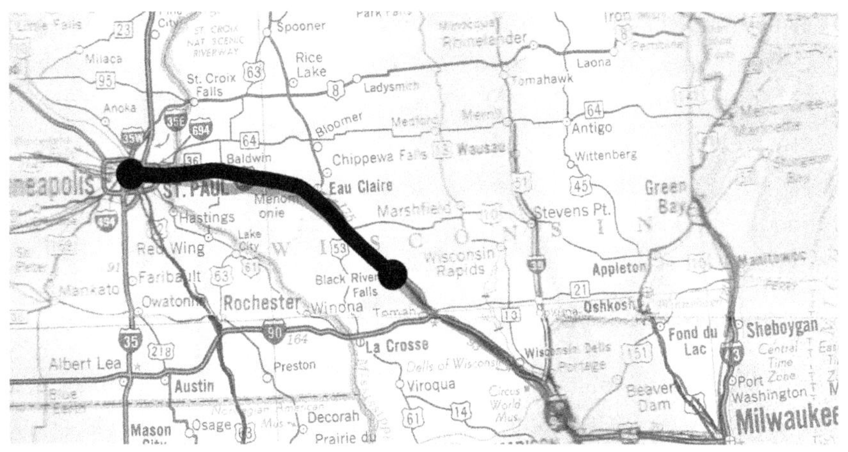

Minneapolis is located on the west side of the Mississippi. On the east side you'll find St. Paul, which is the capitol of Minnesota. A few famous people have roots in St. Paul such as F. Scott Fitzgerald, Robert Zimmermann (Bob Dylan) and my favorite, Rogers Nelson aka. Prince.

Together, Minneapolis and St. Paul has a population of 3.3 million and are also known as the Twin Cities. This is the 16th largest metropolitan area in the USA. Coming in through St. Paul, I met a group of African American riders of a wide variety of bikes, HD, Yamaha Star, Kawasaki and Honda -without helmets. These are hung off the side of the passenger pillion pads. Riders who don't wear protective gear and helmets are usually referred to as "squids". Coming off your bike hard without proper protection can see you thrown onto the asphalt as a mollusks. I guess wearing a helmet and gear you'd be a crustacean in a similar situation…

And minimize your risk of increased and unnecessary injury.

Some motorcyclists wave to each other upon meeting other riders, we do the same in Denmark. But two out of three Harley Davidson riders I met in the USA tend not to wave to riders on other motorcycle brands. I am actually not really a fan of waving to other motorcyclists. If you're rolling onto an intersection you'll need to have both hands on the grips. In such instance this becomes a safety issue. When I started out on my first 250 cc Suzuki I had all the time in the world to wave and greet everybody, as my bike was slow and underpowered as fuck. But later on I must say I do find it a bit annoying.

Waving to other riders is a part of motorcycle culture but waving to someone I don't know is pretty pointless. However, I will stop and help when I see another motorcyclists on the roadside who looks like they may need assistance.

Of course I had to take a wrong turn on this day too, as I missed the rest stop by the river where I wanted to take some pictures. It didn't matter as it started to rain as I crossed the Mississippi for the first time.

The Ducati was no longer a new motorcycle. The tires were still road legal, but after 2994 miles (4818 km), the tire thread was getting close to being worn down to a road safe limit. The engine coolant was at the minimum marker and the clutch fluid was no longer clear. I had a broken clutch lever and a scratched pannier side bag from the bike keeling over the day before. So I located the local Ducati dealership "Trackstar Motorsports". Again, the dealership list booklet turned out to be outdated. My bike was a 2002 model, so in two years a lot of the dealerships had moved, changed name or terminated their partnership with Ducati North America. Trackstar Motorsports had changed their name to MotoPrimo. On Saturdays they closed at 4 pm, so I had to come back later.

Fixing the scratched left side bag meant applying the sticker I bought at McCoy's Harley Davidson in Green bay. Motorcycles are made to be used, and a little scrub or ding now and then comes with the territory.

Checking in at Comfort Inn for $100, my choice of accommodation was not the most economical. The weather forecast had warned of tornadoes and thunderstorms in the evening. So I didn't feel like city riding in rainy weather conditions whilst scouting for a cheaper option.

Meeting Nancy

Calling up Nancy before noon as agreed in Wisconsin, she gives me driving directions to her apartment in Brooklyn Center. Only missing one exit, I arrived in front of her apartment block just in time. Online dating has been stigmatized and some of my friends would never meet anyone they only met via the internet. Times have changed and online dating is viewed as just another way of meeting people. The negative labels people associated with online dating has sure dropped over the years. The basic safety rules does still apply, any first meeting should be in a public place and you might not want to meet what is basically strangers on your own. Some people pose online as someone they're not, lie about themselves and don't use pictures of themselves having created a fake identity on a social network account, usually targeting a specific victim. This phenomenon of deceptive activity has been labelled as "Catfishing" and there is actually a TV show exploring, investigating and exposing people who does this to others. Catfishing is often employed as romance scams for financial gain on dating websites.

Nancy let me have her home address and I thought that was pretty unusual. Having described myself and my red motorcycle I am easy to recognize. Waiting a few minutes Nancy arrived in a car with an Asian guy called Aloun. Aloun is a pretty buff guy, and Nancy is fortunately not a six foot mugger. This is the first time I met what since would become two really good friends.

Bringing a friend when meeting someone provides a sensible safety precaution, especially for women. Greeting each other and having some friendly introductions on the parking lot, we went to a Super 8 motel nearby that has a more economic room rate of $50. Parking my bike at the motel I drop my belongings in the room, we got in Nancy's minivan and she took me to The Mall of America in Bloomington. Asians are often accused of being poor drivers. I am one of them, my sister and brother in law don't want to drive with me behind the wheel if they can avoid it. On the way to Mall of America, I can't ignore that the front airbags had been deployed.

The explanation was that Nancy had an accident a few weeks prior, a collision with another car. Still waiting for the insurance claim to come through, the airbags had not been replaced yet. Being very attentive, I also check out Nancy's legs. Nice.

Opened in 1992, The Mall of America is, with a floor area of 4.87 million square Ft (452,000 m2), the largest shopping mall in the United States and the twelfth largest in the world. I wouldn't have visited this place on my own, but with an indoor theme park in the center of the mall, it is an attraction in itself. The theme park features roller coasters and other rides and amusements. This is actually the USA's largest indoor theme park. Well, when you're traveling on a motorcycle shopping becomes an issue, as you have to lug anything you buy within a very limited amount of carrying capacity. Nancy wanted to give me a present, so she bought a "Mall of America" T-shirt. I got no explanation why; but I've noticed American t-shirts often are of a quite good quality and fit. Nancy told me that Minnesota doesn't have sales tax on clothing, so someone must have been lobbying hard to help the retail industry. We buy a couple of music CD's at HMV. Music taste is actually interesting as it is a way to find out more about others. Checking out Nancys choices, I am sure she also took note of mine.

At dinnertime we went to "Quang's" a Vietnamese restaurant where the appetizer was fried shrimp with yams and a main course of Vietnamese meatballs and noodles. Learning a little about Nancy, I knew she is two years older than me and she had a 9 year old daughter. As I am getting older, I think it is to be expected that women over 30 have kids. I have never had problems getting along with any dates' offspring, as none of them have been annoying brats. One kid did stand out by telling me her real dad's name was Johnny, I couldn't help but ask if she was sure about that…
Having to explain a bit about myself, I obviously was into motorcycles, traveling and have an ever expanding movie collection. I have also enjoyed video games ever since I was a kid. The evolution of video games has been amazing compared to the 1980s, these can almost match movies within the foreseeable future. Video games can tell stories that moves and engages just like books and films, and the on- and offline competitive play against

others can be a very social and fun pastime. I think there is another upside to video games that will show itself in the coming years. The generations who have grown up with video games will have something to keep them occupied when they get older and their health won't allow them to stay as active than earlier.

Asian mothers hate video games like the plague, and it was evident that Nancy is one of them. Video games are entertainment and can be great. The problem with these is like in earlier times where mothers weren't fond of comic books. Video games can easily lead to procrastination of other educational and more productive activities. This is a legitimate issue that should not be ignored. So video games can for some end up along with smoking weed, shit that prevent you from moving forward.
Generation X, born from the early 1960s to late 1970s, was among the first to embrace computers and I was one of them. My parents were baby boomers who didn't really understand the attraction of computer and video games. So both Commodore computers I had as a kid I bought myself. I fondly recall managing to save up $800 to buy an Amiga 500, after having saved every penny I could for one and a half years. (Adjusted for inflation this would be over $1700 in 2020.) Being authoritarian, my father did warn me that if it affected my effort at school, he would take it away even though I had paid for it myself.

I didn't say anything to Nancy about my preference for graphic novels (comic books) instead of reading novels. I firmly believe that comics will improve a child's reading skills just like books, and that barring or banning your kids from reading comics is a mistake. Of course I got a favorite comic, *Judge Dredd*. This is centered around a sci-fi cop who rides a big motorcycle and beat up citizens. Two concepts do stand out, as the ideas of airbags and dinosaur wildlife parks were featured in Judge Dredd more than a decade before this became a thing in the automotive industry and Hollywood. (When it comes to books, I prefer educational/tuitional books that provide me with new knowledge and insight.)
I was nice to meet Nancy, and I decided to stay in Minneapolis a bit longer to get to know her better. It wasn't love at first sight, but also not without potential. Besides not liking video games, I learned that Nancy doesn't

drink coffee. Not a dealbreaker as long as she didn't forbid me to drink it. I did offer to pay; I think the guy fronting the bill is the only way to go on first dates. But Nancy insisted on paying her half. So maybe it wasn't a date. Or a date on equal terms with an independent woman.

Finding love ain't easy. Most people are aware of the basic needs.
Sleep, food and warmth. The latter is more complex than just rest and
nutrition. When I say warmth I mean love from another person.
A physical and psychological attraction and attachment.
The physical aspect can be filled with more or less indifferent relations.
This can be cool enough if you ignore the risk of an incurable STD
that can kill you. I can tell you that waiting for the results
of an STD test sure isn't fun at all.
Casual relations isn't a sustainable solution in the long run.
Also, the idea of one love is a part of the socialization process.
Even Hugh Hefner decided to get married a couple of times.

The concept of finding the love of your life doesn't seem to be going away.
It is also a search for a kind of security.
Many times this is not for the better.
With the risk of sounding stupid I think that this comes down to instinct.
An unconscious road to self-destruction.

Searching anyway, we follow emotions we do not control.
Taking chances, only this way we live and learn:
Falling in love is an addictive intoxicating drug.
We lose control. We need more. Again and again.

You give yourself away. You are bound to get knocks, cuts and bruises on
your journey. It is hard to find a positive angle on bad love, learning
from your mistakes.

Love makes blind. I am actually born with vision on my left eye only,
which probably also contributes to my lackluster driving skills.

Monday, August 2nd 2004

The temporary tag was valid for one month, so a bit of due diligence was needed. Moto Europa had run into a snag with the license plate, as the DMV wouldn't deliver the license plate to them without a social security number. So I had to call Moto Europa back on Tuesday to see if they had managed to find a solution. Luis would most likely be at work on a business trip, so getting him to pick up the license tag wasn't a possibility that could be relied on for sure. Again, I could and should have planned more ahead before arriving to the USA.

With the small things that needed attention on the Ducati, I found my way back to Moto Primo on East 32nd and Hiawatha Avenue without any problems. The clutch lever was not in stock and it costs $96 ! So screw that, I just left the snapped lever as is. I can ride without the round end tip, although it probably isn't legal. Chain cleaning spray is also out of stock. Having checked the brake system for leaks, I found none. So this was a cheap visit as I only bought a bottle of engine coolant to top up and to have some in reserve. You don't want to destroy your engine by ignoring too low coolant or oil levels.

MotoPrimo had a 2002 Monster S4 just like mine on sale for $9300. I paid $10,999 for the bike alone, so a difference of $1699. If you're scouting for a bike in the USA, it might be a good idea to look in the Midwest. Mentioned earlier, Milwaukee Harley Davison had a XL1200 Sportster priced $1400 lower than Richmond Harley Davidson. There might be more riders and thus demand for motorcycles in the sunnier states that don't get buried in snow a big part of year.

My riding jacket was a cheap piece of junk and the velcro had started to come undone, annoying the hell out me. Scoping through the gear selection, they didn't have any that would fit a short guy. Finding clothes and shoes that fit has often been an issue for me. While living in Germany I couldn't locate any cargo shorts in my size, so with a little luck I found some nice ones in the teen kids section. The upside is that I only had to pay kid prices. Saving 30% on shoes as well is all right with me.

While MotoPrimo was easy to find, the opposite was the case when meeting Nancy and Aloun for lunch at a riverside restaurant near South Main St. in Saint Paul. After 30 minutes of riding around in circles, I finally found the cafe in a very nice and clean area. Eating lunch I had started to leave food uneaten on the plate.

Nancy is originally from Thailand and of ethnic Hmong origin. She came to the United States as UN refugee. Aloun is an art teacher, a friend, not family related to Nancy. Aloun left Thailand in the late seventies when he immigrated to the USA with his parents and siblings. Hailing from the Isaan region in north-east Thailand, Aloun is culturally more Lao than Thai due to the regions geography. I later learned that they have been dating for a bit but decided to just be friends.

Laos is the most heavily bombed country in the world. Intended to target Pathet Lao and North Vietnamese forces, the United States dropped two million tons of bombs on a country the size of Michigan, during a period lasting from 1963 to 1974. More than the amount dropped on Germany and Japan combined during World War II, this was a "secret war" and the CIA's largest paramilitary operation. When the bombing was expanded into Cambodia, the story of this bombing campaign was leaked.

Nancy had booked seats on a boat cruise on Lake Minnetonka in the evening. With 15 lakes Minneapolis is also called the City of Lakes and the state of Minnesota uses the slogan the "Land of 10000 Lakes".
Picking me up at Super 8 Motel after work, we drove 15 miles southwest of Minneapolis. There was an unimpressive pizza buffet, a food selection that couldn't offend anyone. I noticed we kinda stuck out as the rest of the cruise guests were caucasian older folks. Sailing past some very expensive lake view mansions, Prince was still alive at the time and he had owned property at Lake Minnetonka.

We talked about life and love. About meeting people online. Explaining a bit about my ride so far going around Lake Michigan, Nancy told me she had crossed Lake Michigan by car ferry, an option I wasn't aware of. On June 1st, the first high speed auto passenger ferry in the United States re-established the historic Lake Michigan ferry route between Milwaukee,

WI and Muskegon, MI. Crossing Lake Michigan in just 2-1/2 hours, The Lake Express ferry is much faster than the traditional car ferry that takes four hours to cover the 60 miles between Manitowoc, WI and Ludington, MI. This could have cut the distance riding around the Big Lake in half. I am not super keen on cruise ships and ferries. My uncle's uncle used to be captain on the ferry going from my hometown in Denmark to the UK. Having used this route three times, being on a cruise ship feels like a floating prison, even though it was a trip that just took around 22 hours.

Being independent was obviously important to Nancy. Pursuing a license for working in real estate, Nancy wasn't chasing a Mr. Right. Material things wasn't a problem, Nancy had tons of clothes and I think two or three automobiles. She actually wanted to get rid of most of these. Minimalism and simple living has since become quite popular and I have tried to get into this way of living myself. But as many other hobbies, motorcycling quickly becomes a money pit where you need new gear as gloves, helmets, etc. So it is easier said than done. But cutting down on things you don't need, having less crap and clutter is liberating for your mind too.

Talking about interests and occupation, Nancy used to own a restaurant with her ex-husband. The way it was explained, he seemed like a douchebag to me. Coming from a well off family, going to Las Vegas to blow thousands of dollars living the high life while seeming not to care about his family. Nancy no longer has anything to do with her ex-husband. Being adopted myself, I find it important for kids to have relations with both their parents if possible. But I found it understandable that Nancy had decided to cut all ties and move on.

As our talk went along we both realized that there wasn't any romantic spark and just being friends was how far this would go. Fine with me as any uncertainty and high-flying expectations about our relation could cause unwanted tension. As this wouldn't be an issue, we could relax and be ourselves.

Personality is one of the first traits I observe when making new
acquaintances. I find it important, as I more or less consciously look for
something reflecting myself in others. If I can find traits in others that
reminds me of myself, I am likely to be more open than usual.

With an opinionated personality, I manage to do some deep
and fine thinking while riding on my motorcycle.
We shouldn't be too quick to judge each other.
Others have told me that I am a unique and unlike anyone else
they've ever met. As an older me, very friendly.
My own perception of myself differ from how others perceive me.
I think I am becoming an old, cranky duffer.

Everybody needs personal space. Privacy matters and a lot of
people can't be immediately "read".
Hiding their true colors but trying to "read" others themselves,
can actually make a person's true personality shine through.
This form of hiding can ruin the options for leaving
an honest first impression, even leaving others with a wrong perception.
So when your true self appears, or is discovered, you risk coming off
as a dishonest individual that can't be trusted.

A good personality is found within a mature person.
Not perfect but recognizing and owning ones mistakes.
Everything others see has importance. So be 100% yourself.

Keep it real.

Tuesday, August 3rd 2004

On the news this morning, the Statue of Liberty in New York re-opened, albeit with limited access. This was the last monument to reopen after the 9/11 attacks. Homeland security reports of a "terrorist threat against the Republican Party Convention in New York 2nd-5th of September 2004". Back on the phone with Joyce at Moto Europa in Richmond, she unfortunately confirmed that the DMV can't or won't send the license plate without a Social Security ID number or ID card. With the bike registered in Fairfax, I would try to get in touch with Luis about this. A solution to this problem was that Moto Europa could send me a new temporary tag valid for another month. They were legally allowed to do this once, as the registration process couldn't finalized within the first month.

I decide to take a ride around downtown Minneapolis. Before starting up the bike, the alarm system beeps twice, an indicator that the alarm has been activated at some point while parked in front of Super 8. The chain lock wasn't the smallest one Moto Europa offered, and my experience is that people will fuck around with your vehicle if they can get away with it. And your bike is obviously the most at risk when you're away from home.

I am generally hard on my toys, so the Monster hadn't been washed since I bought it. So I tried to find a place where I can get this done. Asking at a car wash the staff won't touch the bike, only cars. This is probably due to company liability guidelines.

At lunchtime I took the easy solution and visited another McDonald's. An african american kid who looked to be about seven years old was totally smitten with my motorcycle in the parking lot. His mother smiles and trying to say something intelligent, I told him if he does well in school and stay away from drugs, he could own one before he knows it.

Well, sometimes I say some stupid shit that the recipient for obvious reasons is unlikely to understand. I think that it might have been a bit far fetched for a seven year old kid to comprehend.

Nancy is late because of work and she has to pick up and drop off her daughter Mindy in St. Paul. Mindy was 9 years old at the time. I didn't see her on this trip but met her on later visits. Great kid. With a fairly strict mother she was an honor student in school and since gone on to earn a college degree in marketing.

The "correct" upbringing does not exist. We're all individuals.
But some basic values should be passed on.
With this I mean to be a good role model. Economic security is impor-
tant, but if there is bread on the table the butter isn't.
It is easier for children to grow up on a solid foundation.
Build on your own opinions but observe how your kids will watch and
mimic your behavior. That is why they most likely will end up with some
of the same personality traits as yourself. So you have to be perfect.
That's difficult as hell and you will drop the ball time after time.
But your kids will see that even in failure you won't give up.
You are still an idol who have to lead by example.

A parent will also have to give warmth and sense of safety.
Here I feel at ease. My adoptive parents have given me all of the above.
I can never repay or thank them enough.
And I am not supposed to.
The hard work and all they have sacrificed for the family has shown me
how I should go about treating my own family when it is time for that.
I do criticize my role models too.
My own values are obviously not exact the same as Olesen Sr.
I am aware that I have much in common with my parents.
Sr.'s work ethic. Mom's wild ideas she just chose to go for.
These are values that cannot be measured.
If you don't have a good family, material things won't matter.

On the topic of kids. They can be a roadblock or an invaluable part of
your life that can't be measured in money. It all depends on the circum-
stances. Once the shackle is on, a lot of dreams are scrapped. Of course
there are young people who really wants to procreate as soon as possible.
On the other hand, many only dream of having kids, with the

difference that they economically are well funded and able to give their
offspring a good and stable upbringing, where mom and dad aren't on
separate sides of an abyss, having thought things through and ready for
starting a family.

When talking about having kids you can't ignore abortion.
Some people really get riled up and are up in arms about this matter
of conscience. By its nature it will likely affect the mother the most.
So in my opinion the mother should have the 100% freedom
and right to make the choice concerning abortion.
I do not think abortion is right, but accept it as a necessary evil.
Abortion should be avoided in any way if possible, you kill life.
Man and animals has always killed, but your offspring?

Earlier I would have chosen the motorcycle if the choice was
"Children or bike?". Today, my view of this has changed.
Kids are an extension of yourself,
a motorcycle is just a substitute that rusts.

Kids are also a confirmation of love, even though I think romance is
highly overrated. Perhaps this form of escape from reality is better than
weed and alcohol. Perhaps a value that overshadows anything else?
You'll feel best when you know your kids aren't missing anything,
both materially and mentally. That you can provide security for them.

You can have both motorcycle and kids if you really want.
Just make sure to have the motorcycle paid in full first.

Once again, Nancy picked me up at Super 8 Motel, she needed to buy some groceries, so I got to see the inside of a Costco. Having my camera hit the asphalt in Michigan, I pay Best Buy a visit to see if they got any replacement worth the investment. Not finding a camera that isn't too expensive, I stuck with the one I had. It did work off and on, that is, not all the time.

Maybe Nancy wanted to see my reaction as she took us down to Mall of America again. On the fourth floor she took me to my favorite breastaurant. Yep, she brought me to Hooters. No complaints here, those chicken strips were pretty good. And I like that Nancy has a sense of humor and don't get easily offended. Talking about life and experiences I told her about me being approached by a pimp in China, Nancy found it funny and asked why I didn't go for it. I actually never have visited a hooker. What other people choose to do is their problem, but my thoughts on prostitution is that I wouldn't want my mother or daughter selling their bodies, so I don't go buy sex myself.

I think Nancy wanted to see my reaction to Hooters. Well, Denmark was the first country in the world to legalize porn, so I am hard to impress.

The plan was to go see a movie, saw a poster for Blade: Trinity, but that didn't premier until December. From experience I know that you let the lady company choose which movie to see when at the cinema. M. Night Shyamalan's "The village" was on but I am not sure why, but we ended up watching The Manchurian Candidate with Denzel Washington. I managed to see the first 20 minutes before I fell asleep. Waking up once during the movie and when the rolling titles started, Prince Charming has no recollection of the plot of this movie. I think Nancy was being nice as she didn't say anything, but I am sure she noticed me dozing off. It was 1:30 am when I got back to my motel, so I think Nancy had a tough day at work on Wednesday.

I do love watching movies like The Matrix, Godfather, Terminator 2, The Dark Knight or Pulp Fiction. True classics. My favorite movie ever was released in 1987 and is about a police officer who has a very bad day at work, so he wakes up discovering that he has become a cyborg.
Paul Verhoeven's *Robocop* is a timeless masterpiece and everybody who disagrees with me knows nothing about true movie art. Like the most of my movie collection, so I have bought Robocop three times, on VHS, DVD and Blu-ray.

With my interest in motorcycles there is a few movies I consider must see for any biker, even though most are not that good. *The Wild One* from 1953 with Marlon Brando is a classic biker movie loosely based on an incident that took place in Hollister, California. A motorcycle rally organized by the American Motorcyclist Association (AMA) in 1947 saw a lot more motorcyclists than expected showing up and a few of the bikers got too rowdy. This is known as the Hollister riot and this was sensationalized by the press with reports of bikers "taking over" and "pandemonium". The strongest dramatization of the event was a staged photo published in Life magazine with a drunken man sitting on a motorcycle surrounded by beer bottles. The Hollister riot helped to give rise to the outlaw biker image and the 1% designation. This Brando movie would be total crap if it wasn't for Lee Marvin's appearance as Chino.

The quintessential biker road movie is *Easy Rider*, with Billy and Captain America's ride to Mardi Gras. Everyone knows this, so instead I can recommend *Harley Davidson and the Marlboro Man* from 1991. Starring Mickey Rourke on a uber cool custom FXR Harley and Don Johnson, the plot is paper thin. The first five minutes is pure motorcycle porn, the rest is hot garbage. It may have come from the same roll of film as *Stone Cold*, which was launched the same year. This action movie features former Seattle Seahawks football linebacker Brian Bosworth as an undercover cop who infiltrates a motorcycle gang called "the Brotherhood". This is so far out I consider it a comedy. But if you love motorcycles, this is just too fun to miss. An honorable mention should go out to *Wild Hogs*, a Disney comedy of four riding buddies taking a road trip from Cincinnati to the California coast. Two of them are going through a midlife crisis and one having social phobia, the fourth guy is a perfect match with this book, as he is a pussywhipped short guy called Bobby. He had taken a year off to write a book, and as he hadn't finished this after 12 months, his wife sent him back to work as a plumber.

Being an 80's kid I am not very high brow when it comes to movies, all they need is sex or violent action sequences.
Or even better, a bit of both.

Wednesday, August 4th 2004

Finding the US Postal office in Brooklyn Center was easy, just six minutes from my motel. The Department of Motor Vehicles was on the same road as where Nancy used to live. So I sent some postcards to the folks at home and went in to talk to the folks at the DMV. Lampooned for shitty service in a lot of TV comedies and cartoons, there wasn't much of a queue and they could easily answer my questions. They didn't see any problem in getting a license plate on the bike, I just had to pick it up in person. In Richmond. In Virginia. With limited time on my tourist visa that would be a problem. So I thought I should try to get the bike registered with Luis as an owner or co-owner.

I finally got to see Nancy's apartment, it looked like a standard public estate rental, nice and clean. While waiting for Nancy to get ready to go, I got to use her computer so I could check my e-mail. "Rush No More RV Resort and Campground" had sent me a confirmation of my booking, so for once I felt ahead of the curve.

Nancy had arranged for us to go see a theatre play with Aloun and a couple of other friends joining too. The play was a comedy called "Triple Espresso". I have never been a big fan of theatre, this play was an ok experience, but I prefer shows with vertical chrome poles. After the play we went to "Malina's", which is an Asian bar. Aloun had worked there as a bouncer earlier. Here he had plenty to do as Asians generally can't drink too much before becoming wasted, and during our stop, there was plenty of drunk people to check out.

Having a fun night out, Aloun offered me to stay at his house saving me the cost of the motel. I think Nancy had vouched for me being a friendly and trustworthy guy, this was a truly nice offer.

Friends is a fleeting term.
The people you meet daily are often colleagues, classmates and equal
minded peers. Colleagues, classmates and buddies are telling of your
relationship. You know each other by name and actions.
But not necessarily of mind.

A friendship does not consist of a common interest only.
The most important is trust.
Trust has to be built and therefore takes time.

A real friend will do pretty much anything for you.
This does require that this is mutual.

Therefore, a lot of friendships are like a house of cards. They can collapse
anytime, especially if you built it too fast, not being stable enough, noth-
ing to support it.

It isn't easy to know whether or not trust lasts.
You're basically taking a chance.
But put short, it is great to have friends.
They will be there to help when you need it, almost like family.
Having friends and family comes with responsibility on your end.

In the motorcycling world this is often taken a step further, with
people referring to each other as brothers and sisters.

My own network is a mixed bag. They are all fairly good people,
but you just have to wait a bit before their true personalities shows.
I only have a few friends.
The number doesn't matter as I know they are true friends.

It's hard to find real friends, but a good enemy is for life.

Paint, pizza and party

Still trying to get a proper license plate instead of the laminated cardboard temporary tag, I got Stubbs from Moto Europa on the phone. Joyce, whom I talked to on Tuesday, had disappeared without notice on the same day. So no solution today either.

After checking out of my four day stay at Super 8 Motel I rode towards St. Paul. For gawd knows which time I miss the correct exit, this time by seven miles. The driving directions Nancy had jotted down for me were illegible. I don't point fingers at anyone for this, as my handwriting is just awful too. Me being left-handed makes this even worse.
On I-94 going through Minneapolis and St. Paul, I spotted a big sign for the local HD dealership. In the mood for inhaling some Harley odor I decided to pay them a visit. St. Paul Harley Davidson is the biggest HD store I had visited. HD car mats, HD foosball table, a big clothing and apparel section and a real big selection of bikes, they sure got a serious setup. I later found out that they even have a merchandise store in MSP, Minneapolis- St. Paul International Airport.

After some fumbling around with the Road Atlas I found Alouns house. With pizza boxes, plates piled up and leftovers, my first impression is that it was part construction site, part bachelor pad. Aloun had asked me if could give him a hand and help paint the kitchen. With plenty of time until Nancy finished her workday, I grabbed a paint roller and I guess as long I didn't get paid I wouldn't be working illegally. I am not sure if the orange and pinkish peach color Aloun had picked was a good choice, but hey, it wasn't me who had to look at it on a daily basis. Choosing the right wall colors can have a big impact, I once rented an apartment with a baby blue bedroom interior. Waking up to this just made me absolutely cranky in the morning, so I had to change this within three days of moving in. When I bought my first condo the walls were all a light cream color, and with my new sofa set in a similar hue, it felt like living inside a doughnut. Had to change this too in order not to go crazy.

Aloun has three brothers. The youngest one was living at Alouns house too. Charlie is a couple of years younger than me, a bit of a stoner smoking too much weed and what you could call a "perpetual student".
Having finished painting the kitchen on my own, Charlie asked if we should split a pizza and so he ordered one from Papa Johns. I don't know why this franchise chain has become as big as it is. That was not a place I would order from again.

Waiting for Aloun and Nancy to come home from work, we watched the Dave Chapelle Show on DVD. This is just too funny and some of the most classic skits were new in 2004. The Charlie Murphy skits where he plays basketball with Prince and beating up Rick James are still insanely funny today, as is the Clayton Bixby story.

One of the most important things in my life is humor.
It is like the butter that makes todays stale bread go down.
It adds spice to life and a lust for more. One of the indispensable layers
of life which actually can be priceless. Humor is broad concept, but one
common thing is having fun.
It is easy to take things too far. Especially jokes about jews, muslims,
gays, disabled people and other minorities. There is a thin line between
humor and being an antagonizing dick. This category of joke is often
relatively crude. I don't find these very funny,
why I don't care about trying to remember them.

Crossing the magic bridge we will find ourselves in a
fantastic new world. The path of irony and caricature.
A cultivated and refined way to a good laugh.
Good caricature often builds on extremes. If the setup is too grotesque,
a lot of people may fail to get the pointy bit and you lose the audience.
I my opinion less conscious and open-minded people fail to see humor.
Delivery is key, otherwise only a few catches the point.

Dave Chapelle was king in 2004, and he is still great.

Back from work, Aloun found a parking spot so I can get the bike off the street, so no-one got tempted to screw with it. I did notice some of the neighbors yelling at each other, Aloun told me some of them seem to have "issues" and general attitude problems. Aloun fired up the barbecue and Nancy came around with some spicy papaya salad. This was pretty powerful, in fact so much she had some problems eating it herself. It could make anyone sweat for sure. Talking to Aloun's family and friends, they found it funny that I had helped paint the kitchen and did find it typical for Aloun to talking people into helping him. We have this skill in common.

With the University of Minnesota alone having 50,000 students, there are plenty of clubs open on a Thursday. So we went to "The Quest" in Minneapolis. Thursday is "Asian nite" with an entrance fee of $10. There were quite a few gang bangers looking to start fights in the crowd, so the security staff was a bit jumpy, and when we were going in they asked me repeatedly where I was hiding my gun. Not sure if I looked suspicious, I did change my clotting style back when I was 19, after some teenagers came up to me and asked if I had some weed for sale.

On the dance floor the Quest held a rump shaking contest. Biased decision maybe, I'm not sure. I was thinking the world doesn't really need blondes, Asians look better. Talking to a few girls at the Quest, they are not impressed with me crossing the USA on a motorcycle. Or the fact that we were among the oldest people in the club. Last time I got stopped for ID at the entrance as my party primarily consisted of twenty-somethings. The bouncer was surprised to discover that I was 40. Today I am too old to go to clubbing. Besides that, I have always thought you have to be on drugs to endure techno music.

Nancy can't drink, just three or four drinks and she was completely wasted. After leaving the Quest we dropped Nancy off at home, and Aloun decided to go up with her to make sure she got into her apartment safely. Getting older myself, I can't really drink more than 3-4 drinks today before I have had enough. My all-time record was at age 18 where I drank 36 beers within 24 hours without getting sick or puking. Today, I actually hate waking up with a hangover and wasting a day where I could be out riding my motorcycle or do some other fun activity.

Friday, August 6th 2004

After a hard night out I woke up around 11 am. Having checked my e-mail and writing to Luis and Moto Europa, I went to meet Aloun and Nancy for a farewell lunch. Riding out of Minneapolis at 2:30 am, it was a bit sad to say goodbye to my new friends.

Well, I kept in contact so Aloun and I met four years later in South Korea. Aloun had a job teaching art for five semesters at a high school in Jeon-ju and I was on a business trip visiting a business contact in Seoul. Aloun had gotten married and had a son. Traveling down south from the Korean capital, I met Julie and AJ. Julie is like my sister; she came out of a jumbo jet's vagina. Yup, both were adoptees from Korea. Aloun had a couple of cheap small bikes there, so we went on a short ride in Jeon-ju. I actually didn't know that Aloun was into motorcycles.

While I got really close in 2005, I am not married and never have been.
Therefore it is debatable if I am qualified to talk about this.
Despite the divorce statistics, plenty of people get married today.
Built on a dream or an ideal of forever love, the dry numbers
do not look good. In any marriage you need trust and patience.
Put short, marriage isn't always rosy on Monday morning.

Looking for the love of our lives, the one that feels "right",
he or she will provide a security and warmth,
even if the rest of the world was hit by a new ice age next week.
As I was younger, I didn't want to get married before I had made some
decent attempts to reach my other dreams and goals.
Back then, marriage was the ball and chain moniker. So I didn't.

I was not sure I would find "the one" quickly.
I would be making a bet, and the risk looked too big
when looking at the daughters turning into the
potential mothers-in-law I had met.

But at 45 I have changed my view on this.
If the right lady comes along I would be willing to get married.
I have met women that whose personalities were so great
that I'd take my chances with them any day.
The woman of my dreams is intelligent, independent, responsible
and shouldn't have bigger hands and feet than me.
Looks doesn't matter too much anymore either.

Everybody get chubby and get wrinkles, never forget that the beauty
queen is only at the pinnacle on borrowed time.

Going west on I decided to pass on "the World's biggest rolled bar of yarn" even though it was announced numerous time before Darwin located south of Litchfield on Route 12. I don't knit and have no plans to. Ever. Following Route 23 to highway 14, I met a lot of Harley riders who did not want to greet or talk to me. One of them drops something from his bike. You don't have to be friends with everyone, but if you don't want to talk to me I don't care about you either. Following a BMW going 75 mph, the girlfriend on the pillion wears a spaghetti strapped top, a bit chubby her rolls of side fat flaps in the wind. 'Murica baby!

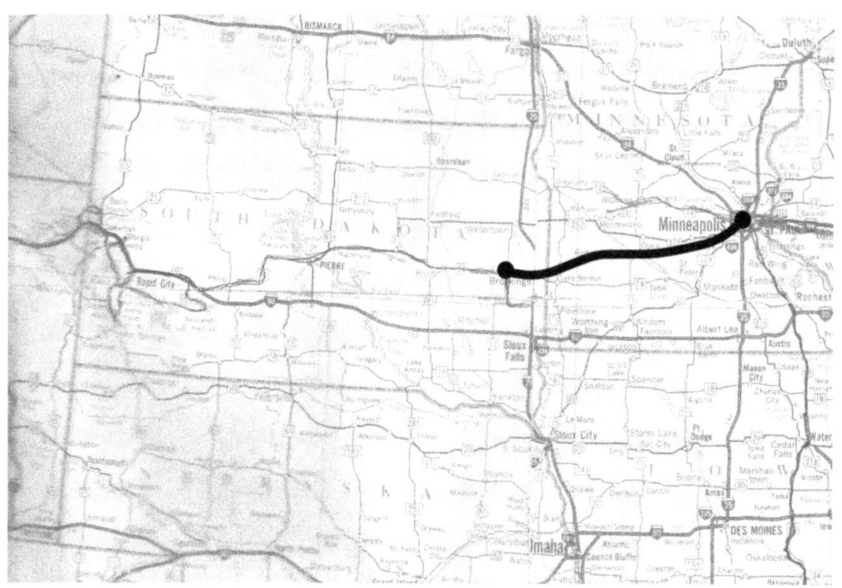

A bit later I eet four bikers. Three guys on big twin HD Road Kings and an outlier on a Kawasaki Vulcan 800 cruiser. The Harley Davidson Road King models sure looked sweet. I still think it is the coolest Harley Davidson in the touring range, like a civilian version of the cop bikes without the batwing style front fairing. Just like me they're heading to Sturgis and none of them had been there before. Tagging along with Wayne, Al, Ron and Joe on the Kawasaki, we end up in Brookings in South Dakota. Motel Brookings cost $71.

Staying at hotels and motels while touring the USA is half price per person when you travel two up or more, sharing a motel room can cut the accommodation costs to a third or even less compared to traveling alone. My riding buddies shared a single room with twin queen size beds, cutting their cost to a quarter. Eating out is a different matter as the price would not be different from dining alone.

Wayne, Al, Ron and Joe are really cool and pours me a whiskey cola at the motel. The group actually remind me of the cast of *Wild Hogs*, four middle class guys from Cincinnati out on a road trip. The odd guy out rides a Sportster in the movie, where this group have a guy on a Kawasaki.
And they're from Chicago.

My new riding buddies decided to go out and have a few drinks, having ridden 240 miles I chose to stay in the motel. At 2 am the guys return, couldn't help but notice this as the alarm on my bike goes off and someone yells "hey!". The guys had tried to put some potted plants in basins around it and block my bike in.

Kinda lame.

Into the great wide open

Starting up the bikes at 8 am, I realize the motel was next to I-29. Where there is a truck stop you will often find motels, fast food chains and strip clubs nearby. The latter was just on the other side of the I-29, so I got an idea about where the gang went the night before. Some people would say it isn't cool to go to strip clubs if you are married. I think it is ok to look at the menu, even if you're on a diet.

After just twenty minutes on the road, Joe had a puncture on his rear tire. Having a can of tire foam we managed to get rolling again quickly, with a couple of guys tilting the Kawasaki thus lifting the wheel and another filling the tire with foam. Using tire foam is an emergency measure that you can't ride fast or far on. So we end up at Interlakes Sport Center, a motorcycle shop in Madison nearby. This is actually not a detour, as we got near I-90 that leads straight to Rapid City located south of Sturgis. Joe's Kawasaki had spoked wheels and this means his tires has tubes inside them. My Ducati Monster has tubeless type tires as most other modern motorcycles. If you use tire foam in this type of tire, you need to tell your mechanic about this. It can create an unholy mess if he is not warned about it first. Joe might have gotten the concept of fixing a flat tire wrong. Normally you would replace the tire tube, but Joe replaced the entire motorcycle. Before the shop had the bike ready, Joe decided to trade in his Kawasaki Vulcan 800 for another cruiser, a Vulcan 1600, twice the engine size. So Joe got in touch with his bank to sort the financing and had to get the paperwork sorted too. Americans have a funny attitude with money. Fortunately, Joe didn't have his wife around to discuss this choice. Probably a smart move.

Buying a motorcycle, I personally think $20,000 is the limit I feel comfortable paying for any bike. That is just my opinion. I do know people who have a dream motorcycle, but don't want to buy a bike until they have all the money saved up for it. My father told me a life lesson about money that I have kept in mind ever since.

Money borrowed has to be paid back -with interest.

Driving off the lot on a brand new motorcycle is a great feeling, warranty and all. I have done this with four out of the seven bikes I have owned. Riding on a bike that is paid in full is a great feeling as well and it shouldn't be underestimated. But it is my opinion that life is too short to postpone buying a bike just because you haven't the saved up the full purchase amount. You can of course educate yourself on Annual Percentage Rate (APR), etc. But doing the numbers on financing a bike isn't rocket science. You need to have the down payment and have calculated that you can afford the payment installments, insurance and other costs in your budget.

Take the monthly installment and multiply this with the number of installments, then add the down payment sum. From this result you subtract the out the door price on the vehicle. Then you have your total costs for the financing. Dividing this number with the number of installments will let you see what the monthly financing costs actually are.

A quick imagined example on a Harley Davidson 883 Sportster
with an OTR/OTD price of $9200

Monthly installment $124 x 84 months
+ 10% down payment ($ 920)   = $11,336
Subtract OTR price   - $ 9,200
Total financing costs   = $ 2,136
Monthly average financing costs ($2136 / 84)   = $ 25.43

The example above excludes debt repayment as this is a way more complicated calculation. But it is super useful as a simple tool to compare different financing offers. If you are doing a partial trade-in with your old vehicle, you just add the equity of this to the down payment in the above calculation. You can also use it to compare the cost of financing different motorcycles, if you are spilt in deciding which motorcycle you want to own.

Finally, a way to answer what you can afford, is to look at the monthly amount you can manage to put aside each month. If you can save up $300 monthly for the down payment, you should most likely be able to afford an installment of the same amount per month.

Waiting for Joe, there was plenty of time to check out Interlakes Sport Center. Talking bikes with Ron, his son wanted a Buell. Ron was amazed how light my bike was. With my bags and gear off the Ducati, this becomes a nimble bike with a dry weight of just 426 pounds (193 kg). In comparison, a Harley Davidson Ultra Glide weighs 820 pounds (372 kg)!

Riding a Ducati or Kawasaki along with Harley Davidsons "you're not really part of the group, it's just the way it is" as Ron put it. I had intended to buy a Sportster, and he told me that he had been on a trip with a guy who rode a Sportster. The smaller gas tank made some extra fuel stops necessary, which slowed the group down so they would cover a significantly shorter distance in a day.

When it comes to tribes, you are either an outsider or a part of it.
A group has great strength due to its size.
If you choose to follow or join the group you have to adapt.
By adapting you sacrifice individuality.
How much depends of the group.

Each group has written and unwritten rules.
Break these and you never come out on top and get punished right away.
You even find that your group can get penalized.
An example is the immigrant population. Some make crime.
This wakes resentment and makes many people judge the entire
demographic group. The same happens to motorcycle clubs.

While you try to adapt you need to look critically at the group you
try to fit into. Does it give me what I want and need?
Is there a group that is better for me?
Consider what you are willing to accept.

If you on the other hand choose to be an independent lone wolf,
you isolate yourself in many ways. But you will soon find where you
stand. To survive you have to adapt to lesser extent. It has always been
like that and there is no way around it. But to put on the positive
goggles it'll give you something to relate to.

The guys were having a laugh sitting on a new Honda 250 cc "Rebel" cruiser. Like my first motorcycle this would be fine to start a motorcycling career on, but you will for sure want to upgrade after a very short time.

In Europe there is a three tier motorcycle license system where you have to pass a theory and a practical test for each tier. Too many young people got themselves hurt on motorcycles so the European tier one allows you to ride a 125 cc, basically an oversize moped. The second tier or "A2" license can be acquired if you are 19 or 20 years old depending on the country and you may ride a bike with a maximum of 47 hp.
The full tier 3 license allows you to ride any size motorcycle, sidecar included, you have to be 24 years old to obtain this. Each license can be had by passing a theory and practical test. In the USA, a kid with a freshly minted motorcycle license can legally ride the biggest bike in the world if he can afford it. It used to be the same in Europe, but too many young people got themselves killed.

Interlakes Sport Center had a bike in their showroom that I had never seen before, a Honda Rune. This model is based on the F6C Valkyrie and was a "Limited Edition" model. As with the Honda Valkyrie it is based on the big touring Honda Gold Wing with 1,832 cc engine, but has solid lifters instead of hydraulic, more aggressive camshafts, a free flowing exhaust, and a different ignition timing for increased performance. The styling is unique, and I found myself studying this for a very long time while in the shop. This motorcycle is so rare that it is highly likely to become a collector item in the future. At 2 pm we were finally ready to ride out. The lead bike decided to go north on Route 14. With 366 miles to Rapid City, we had a long ride ahead. Out of Madison, we rode through the prairie, which looks just like in Clint Eastwood masterpiece *The Unforgiven*.

On a motorcycle, everything has to be strapped tight, you risk losing anything fluttering. So I noticed Joe's bandana came flying off his bike. When we stopped for fuel and lunch at Burger King, I told him about this. Joe had been thinking too. He thought I was stupid wearing a helmet riding in 95 degree weather (35° C). Ten minutes later a monstrous rainfall started and continued for twenty minutes. This is in the top three of the worst downpours I have experienced while on a motorcycle.

Stopping at a roadside restaurant, the others turned around as a party member had been lost from the group. Riding in rain can be painful and feel like needles hitting your face. And without a helmet it quickly becomes unbearable. Wayne, Al, Ron and Joe caught up and overtook me shortly after the rain stopped.

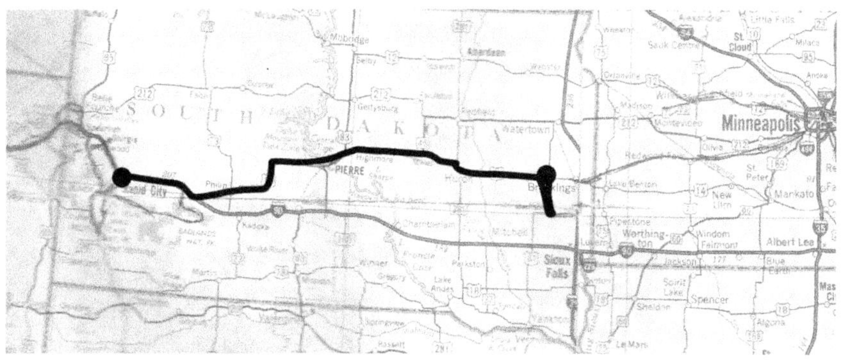

A little later the lead bike pointed his foot at the ground, there was fresh oil on the road. I can never remember the hand signs used when riding in a pack (biker term for riding in a group), these are actually pretty intuitive but the only one I remember is tapping the top of your head or helmet which means police ahead. When you ride in a group you often rile each other up to go a bit faster. I prefer to ride alone so I can choose the speed myself. The downside of this is that you don't have immediate assistance if you come off your bike.

Getting closer to Sturgis, more bikes started to crowd the highways, even though the Sturgis Rally officially didn't start until Monday. The Harley riders go fast, and the cops are out in force. Entering Rapid City close to sunset, there were now so many bikes that I got lost from the group. The Sturgis Rally is so big that I never found them again.

Because of the motorcycle rally, prices are jacked up and the Rapid City Ramada Inn charged $225 for a room! Foothills Inn asked for a more reasonable $116. I could have tried to find Rush No More RV and Camping Resort in the dark, but after riding 400 miles, I just couldn't be bothered.

Getting ready for the rally at Shotgun Willie's

To prepare myself better for my time in Sturgis, my swag would be too spartan, so in Rapid City I had my first visit to a Walmart. With a population of 65,000, Rapid City is the closest larger city. Parking spaces sure have different dimensions than in Europe. I recall Allan, with whom I was sightseeing Washington, noting and laughing at a parking spot designated "Compacts only" having an Audi A4 on it. In Europe an Audi A4 is considered a mid-size car.

My shopping included some items for the motorcycle and some camping gear. So I bought a three person dome tent, batteries, a copper brush and Tyre Pilot spray foam for punctures. Having an only partially functioning camera, I checked out their digital camera selection as well. They had a Vivitar 3765 ViviCam 3 megapixel model for $120, so I decided to go for that. While at Walmart, I also got some pictures transferred from memory card to CD-ROM.

On I-90 I turn in at Black Hills Harley Davidson. In connection with the rally this has been turned into an equipment orgy marketplace offering HD clothes, HD coasters, HD baby onesies and an HD spare wheel cover for your 4x4. Outside on the parking lot there were a lot of trucks with stalls. Thought I had seen it all, but HD merchandise is an endless line of items of which 50% is absolute junk.

One tip though. If you got a van or you don't want to put any Harley stickers on it as you increase the risk of people breaking into it or, as you may have a valuable motorcycle they'll want, following you to your house. Some criminals see a Harley logo as an indicator for something inside worth stealing.

Luis has another notion about Harley Davidson riders. They all want to be "unique". So they customize their bikes to make them personal. But with a lot of them assembled in one place they all look the same. Bikers are the same story on repeat, wearing jeans or black leather, black t-shirt with the Harley logo. Actual pretty comical when you see it in real life. I managed to spot a single Ducati 999R sport bike here, besides my own Monster.

Buying a t-shirt and cap at Black Hills Harley Davidson, I wanted to ship this right away, but as it was Sunday, the post office was closed. Talking to a guy here, he told me that two people were killed in traffic on Thursday, three days before the official rally opening. Well, no surprise, as wearing a helmet isn't a big thing in Sturgis. South Dakota obviously do not have a mandatory helmet law. Back home, "real bikers" could legally avoid wearing a helmet with a medical certificate from their doctor stating that they "had implications" such as dizziness or headaches if they wore a helmet while riding. The politicians have since tightened the laws, so that if you can't wear a lid, you can't ride a motorcycle.

With my Walmart loot it was time for some maintenance on the Monster. Black Hills Harley Davidson also offered the biker favorite, a bikini bike wash for $20. I did pass on that. Checking oil is easy, as my Ducati has an inspection window on the engine case, and I tighten up the chain. After checking the spark plugs and brushing them off with the copper brush and filling the gas tank, I was good to go. The rear tire is super square at this point as the trip mostly consisted of long daily stretches on highways and Interstates.

Foothills Inn had some rally information and rally newspapers. In one of these I saw an ad for "Shotgun Willie's" on W. Main St. I decided to pay them a visit. Their bouncer was a huge guy and no photography were allowed, so I deposited my camera at the entrance. Being on my own and wanting full value for the $4 entrance fee, I took a vacant seat up front. Watching five girls drop their bras and dropping 1-3 dollars for each, the dancers were very different from each other. Some dancers looked like their minds were completely elsewhere. One idiot patron stopped a dance by trying to strike up a conversation with the dancer, basically making the stage empty and leaving the crowd bored. A few of the dancers were paying attention to who dropped some paper, and apparently I managed to make myself noticed. One of them yanks me so hard forward that my beer tips over. A bit later another dancer tries to say something to me, but the loud music made it hard to hear. Finally figuring out what she said, she pulled me forward for some great motorboat action. Her boobs were pretty small and greased up in lotion and stripper sweat, so no wonder she wanted me to take off my glasses. Small knockers are just fine, although most women I have known has had big ones. Or maybe it just seems so as my hands aren't that large.

Drinking a Coke, a Miller Draft and a tipping over a Miller Lite I sure had a fun hour at Shotgun Willie's. I like watching hot dancers and any woman who wants to keep her man happy should master pole dancing and/or stripping. I think it isn't that hard, it is all in the hips. I definitely love to find a wife who can wiggle it, not having me go elsewhere spending money to watch titillating moves.

The girls at Shotgun Wille's kept their g-strings on and I actually prefer to leave a bit to the imagination.

It doesn't take much to keep an idiot happy.

The biggest motorcycle rally in the world

Monday, August 9th 2004

I had my last proper shower at the Foothills Inn before the 64th Sturgis Motorcycle Rally and Races. Waking up to the sound of Harley Davidson motorcycles was already getting to me, the sound of a revving Ducati is better in my ears. Harley Davidsons do have the upside with the "potato, potato, potato" sound at engine idle. Going to the post office, I mailed my broken camera home.

"Rush No More RV Resort and Campground" is just seven miles south of Main Street in Sturgis. Their driveway was a bit crap, so you had to be careful riding in and out. They do have a loading ramp for pickup trucks. Pretty smart as it makes it a lot safer to get an 800 pound motorcycle unloaded. Adding to this, there is a lot of entraining videos on the internet with people dropping their bikes trying to get them on and off their trucks. Scoping out a spot to set up my tent I managed to lay the Monster down on the side trying to do a u-turn on a sloping piece of grass. Pretty stupid, as I did the same shit two years earlier on an Italian mountain road with my first Ducati at World Ducati Week 2002. So a bit of riding advice is to do a three point turn if you need to make a 180° direction change to go the opposite way on a steeply sloping road.

Two other campers were quick to give me a hand getting the bike upright again as it still had all my crap strapped on top. Fortunately, this was on grass, so the only damage was the gear pedal being bent a little.

Another riding tip is not touching the front brake when riding on wet or moist grass. This will easily lock up the front wheel. If the front wheel lose grip on a motorcycle, you go down. Especially on grass. I have seen this happen so many times it is ridiculous.

Finding a nice spot, I raised my brand new dome tent and threw in my belongings. Taking a walk around the Rush No More Campground, a Harley Davidson V-Rod VRSC (V-Twin Racing Street Custom), modified to take a huge 320 width rear tire really is an attention-grabber.

Launched in 2001, this was just the second water-cooled double overhead cam (DOHC) model produced by Harley (The VR1000 race bike from 1994 was the first). The V-rod engine is called the Revolution and was developed in collaboration with German car maker Porsche. You do see a lot of these in Germany, but I believe lacking sales figures worldwide made Harley Davidson stop the production of the V-Rod range in 2017. I had a test ride on a VRSCA V-Rod Muscle in 2010. While they are pretty cool, it wouldn't be my first choice of motorcycle. Motorcycle manufacturers always come up with new models, and Harley Davidson has announced some new offerings featuring water-cooled engines in the future.

Time to set course to the Mecca of American motorcyclists, Sturgis.
The town normally has around 6,600 residents and is named after the Civil War Union General Samuel D. Sturgis. Sturgis Motorcycle Rally and Races is competing with Daytona Bike Week about being the biggest motorcycle rally in the world. Held in Florida, Daytona Bike Week has an attendance of around half a million visitors. The Sturgis Motorcycle Rally and Races in South Dakota has about the same number of visitors, but in 2015 the official registered attendance count was no less than 739,000 and the South Dakota Department of Transportation made a traffic tally of a full million actually making the 2015 Rally a mega-event like the Olympics! Held every year in the first week of August, with a few exceptions during World War II, the Sturgis Motorcycle Rally and Races celebrate its 80th anniversary in 2020. Among Harley riders all over the world, Sturgis is a legendary destination that you just have to experience at least once in your lifetime. Learning about the Sturgis Rally through Easyriders magazine and a TV documentary in 1990, I had always wanted to experience this Started in 1936, this is big business and the City of Sturgis has calcula-tions documenting the Rally brings over $800 million to South Dakota annually. The rally's founder is Clarence "Pappy" Hoel, the former owner of the Indian motorcycle dealership in Sturgis. Hoel died the year before I first heard about the rally, he was inducted into the American Motorcycle Association (AMA) Hall of Fame in 1998.

Getting into Sturgis from the campsite wasn't any problem. Northbound on Interstate 90 and taking Exit 32, it took me 20 minutes to reach Main Street. Motorcycles take up less space and Main Street is cordoned off and reserved for bikes. My guess is that 95% of the motorcycles are Harley Davidsons and the riders 95% caucasian. The Harley riders look like a walking free range exhibition from the HD clothing and accessories catalogue.

One thing I definitely wanted to see was the "Wall of Death"-riders. Riding in what is basically a big barrel shaped construction, they race with no hands on the bars on a vertical wall, relying on centrifugal force and their bikes not stalling, hence the name. Those guys sure got some big nuts. No insurance company will touch them, so they have to rely on spectators tips and donations.

The city center is a marketplace with bars and stalls selling all things a real biker would need, from t-shirts to knives. And alcohol. There are so many vendors that it quickly becomes samey to me and it looks as many vendors are selling the exact same merchandise. Prices are jacked up too, a serving of fish and chips cost $10, so I ended up at Mickey D's.
I did buy a raffle ticket at the Black Hills Harley Davidson stall, the grand prize being a new 2004 HD Heritage Softail. The opportunity to get a new tattoo is also all over Sturgis. I used to think tattoos were super cool, but as a teenager I didn't have money to get any. Today I am happy that I don't have Guns'n Roses tattoos or any of the of the other crap that I thought was cool at the time. Tattoos on women are a big turnoff for me, I just don't like it. Tattoos are for boys; earrings are for girls.

The town centre is a big traffic jam, so the cops are making their presence clear on every corner on Sturgis Main St. to make sure no one breaks the rules. Being too rowdy and drunk driving is met with a zero tolerance by Sturgis Police. At least in front of them.

Over the years Sturgis has been the scene of some violent biker conflicts. Just having parked my bike on Main St. at noon, I walk behind a Sons of Silence MC member. This MC (motorcycle club) was founded in Colorado in 1966 and is regarded as an "outlaw" club as they are not sanctioned by the American Motorcyclist Association (AMA) and don't adhere to the AMA's rules. Instead the clubs have their own set of bylaws reflecting the outlaw biker culture.

The US Department of Justice uses the designation "outlaw motorcycle gangs" (OMG). The most famous or infamous groups are the Hells Angels, Bandidos, Pagans and Outlaws. These are also called the "Big Four". The most recent violence involving motorcycle clubs during the Sturgis rally, prior to 2004, was in 1990 when a Sons of Silence member shot an Outlaw MC member during a bar brawl in Gunner's Lounge and Casino. Two other Sons members were stabbed here too.

Rooted in the aftermath's of World War II, the first outlaw motorcycle groups were founded by war veterans having problems returning and conforming to civilian life. Later wars have spawned new groups such as the Bandidos MC and Sons of Silence MC founded during the conflict in Vietnam. The typical internal organization of a motorcycle club consists of a president, vice president, treasurer, secretary, road captain, and sergeant-at-arms threading back to military ranks and order. Each club house or location is usually referred to as chapters or charters.

Easily identified by the patches on the back of the vests, the patches are also called colors and the vests are referred to as "cuts". The most common is to have the club logo is in center with an MC patch stating that the wearer is a motorcycle club member. The two arches are referred to as the top- and bottom rocker. The top rocker has the club name and the bottom rocker the territory, state or country.

A lot of american outlaw motorcycle clubs has spread out establishing chapters all over the world. Among the first to expand beyond the USA was the Hells Angels MC. Digits and colors are also an identifier for many clubs as colors are regarded as gang insignia and thus banned in some countries. Hells Angels MC use the colors red and white, Bandidos MC use red and gold. Where banned, Hells Angels often use "Big Red Machine", "Red and White Support" and "81", representing the eighth and the first letter of the alphabet, thus spelling "HA". Neo Nazis actually use the same alternative branding method, with the number 88 standing for "HH", representing "Heil Hitler".

The expansion by other motorcycle clubs has led to many conflicts, as the Hells Angels MC has always sought to maintain a dominant position within the outlaw subculture. The worst example actually took place in my home country Denmark, during what is known as "the big Scandinavian rocker war" in the 1990s. This culminated with a member of Bandidos MC firing an anti-tank rocket into in the Hells Angels club house in Copenhagen while it was filled with people attending a party. Two were killed, it could just as well have been fifty.

Some of the club members wear a "1%" patch. This is a fixture used by many outlaw motorcycle clubs labelling themselves as "one-percenters". This stems from the 1947 Gypsy Tour motorcycle rally sanctioned by the American Motorcyclist Association (AMA). This since became known as the Hollister riot in California as earlier described. The AMA didn't want to be associated with this, so they released a statement saying that they had no involvement with the Hollister riot, and, "the trouble was caused by the one per cent deviant that tarnishes the public image of both motorcycles and motorcyclists" and that the other ninety-nine per cent of motorcyclists are good, decent, law-abiding citizens. This has since been denied being an official statement by the AMA, so it has become both legend and lore within the biker subculture.

Being a member of a one percent club comes with the perk of respect. This is a bit ambiguous as respect for a club patch is used by many wearers as a tool for intimidation and creating fear. Well, in my book is fear not respect, but just an asshole exploiting being part of a gang.

Membership of an outlaw MC is not open to anyone. Starting out as a friend of the club or "hang-around", some manage to become potential member, a "prospect" or "probationary". One thing is certain, you cannot have applied to become, be or have been a police officer prior to becoming a probationary in an 1%'er club. After prospecting, members are accepted by a unanimous vote by a chapters full-patch members.

Outlaw club membership is not possible for women. Earlier many clubs didn't allow members of color either, and the Bandidos MC and Mongols MC were in part founded by people who were denied access into Hells Angels. So the Hells Angels earlier policies might have spawned new competing clubs. This has since changed and in Germany there is now an immigrant fraction with Turkish roots within the Hells Angels in Germany, leading to internal power struggles. And people dying of unnatural causes.

Non-outlaw motorcycle clubs, such as party, family, women's and christian motorcycle clubs, have adopted similar insignia, colors, organizational structure and trappings, such as leather outfits typical of outlaw clubs. This does make it difficult for outsiders and law enforcement to tell the difference between the two. These other groups are attracted by the mystique of the outlaw image while objecting to the suggestion that they are outlaws. As such most motorcycle clubs are basically party and riding clubs.

As a kid, around 11 years old, I remember my father hoping I wouldn't get involved in the outlaw motorcycle culture. At the time the Hells Angels had only had a single chapter in Copenhagen for a few years. They were at war with another group, but the outcome was pretty simple. The members of the rival club were killed off one by one until they disbanded. Some of these later became members of Bandidos MC when the club expanded into Denmark.

In my late teens I became infatuated with motorcycles and the outlaw culture did spark my interest. When I realized this wasn't an option as a non-caucasian, the idea was shelved. Outlaw biker culture does attract young people looking for an identity and offers a sense of community. But being a bit of a loner, club life wasn't for me.

While only for a short period, I did join a riding club later. Just like the motorcycle industry is fighting to "recruit" new riders, the riding clubs' membership numbers are also dropping.

Having experienced that I was the only one showing up for Sunday rides a few times, and the other members being pre-occupied with other things such as grandkids, golf, etc., I started to question my membership. When some members started to post political stances on the clubs social media pages I made the choice to leave.

Compared to riding clubs, outlaw culture and clubs has had a renewed interest with the TV show *Sons of Anarchy*. This tends to glamorize outlaw bikers, as I know that plenty of them aren't beyond petty theft and opportunist burglary. While entertaining, it is also pretty outlandish.
The main character kills 46 people during the show's seven seasons.

I am definitely not an outlaw biker, but I have had plenty of encounters with the police. Knowing that most laws are made to slap others with, it isn't pleasant to have the complete works land on your head. The same applies when it is just a few pages. Society's defence against anarchy is exercised firmly by our beloved and at the same time despised corps of black clad lawmen. Hated by many, they have plenty of problems and cops are some of the only people who will never run out of things to do.

Starting with yourself, it always helps to be courteous and concise.
No need to escalate any situation involving the cops, being aware that they pretty much can screw you in any situation. The right to remain silent in order not to incriminate yourself is important to know and use, my experience is that cops will try to make you admit breaking the law, especially if they don't have any proof.

In Denmark, you are obligated to identify yourself with name and birthday. This is fair enough; you could be another person than the owner of the vehicle you're driving. I remember a guy a couple of years older than me refusing to supply his name to a police patrol, so he got his ass arrested. It took him two days before he realized he could be held indefinitely, until he identified himself. People still laugh about this dumbass today.

There will always be criminals and therefore a need for police.

The unfortunate situations where the law is being upheld too harshly for no sensible reason, has caused the police to lose the trust of many people, especially as errors and unlawful actions has gone unpenalized. When I started writing this book Rodney King just had the shit kicked out of him by the LAPD. Today everybody can video document everything on their smartphones, hopefully this puts a damper on excessive police force.

I break the law like almost anyone else but won't try to run if I am caught. This usually just makes matters worse. Cops are too burdened to take it easy if you cause them to chase your ass.

I am fairly ok with most laws, but I find some laws I find wrong or too restrictive so I do violate these on occasion. Like most people. I jump a red light, go speeding and on rare instances ride without a helmet. It looks cool and the feeling with the wind in your hair is admittedly great.

Speeding is not a crime unless you get caught.
Or is stupid enough to admit it.

And if you haven't guessed it, I don't like cops.

Tuesday, August 10th 2004

It had been a pretty cold night with a bit of rain. So buying a tent was a good choice. With no cell phone coverage and a queue at the campsite's payphone, my pre-paid phone card wasn't activated, the operator told me I needed to drive to Minnesota to do this. The phone company wouldn't allow me to recharge this with a foreign Visa card either. Buying a new phone card, I again talk to Stubbs at Moto Europa about a solution concerning my license plate. We agreed on him overnighting a temp tag through FedEx. So, I emailed Moto Europa the address to Rush No More RV Resort and Campground. Things sure are easier today as all of this can be done one handheld device.

The Sturgis Rally is located in the South Dakota Black Hills. These offer an exciting variety of attractions the traveling motorcyclist should not pass on, even if you miss coming in the first week of August. So besides the Rally and races the area has some great rides. Talking to a guy called Monty on a Yamaha Star 1600, I get some tips on where to go.

My trusty guide book had set my first goal 52 miles out of Sturgis, Mount Rushmore National Memorial. In 1927 work began on carving out the four Presidents heads. Fourteen years and 450,000 tonnes of removed granite later, George Washington (1st potus), Thomas Jefferson (3rd potus), Theodore Roosevelt (26th potus) and Abraham Lincoln (16th potus) was ready for the public to view from the auditorium at the visitors centre. Mount Rushmore is a must-see if you're in South Dakota. Entry is free but parking at the visitors center was $8 and valid for the rest of the year. The faces are around 65 feet (20 meters) in height. This is a bit more impressive than the version I had seen in Legoland as a kid, but with the difference in scale and viewing distance the size perception actually is not that far off.

The memorial can also be seen from highway 244 and a lot of bikers had stopped there to take pictures. Here I talked with a girl there about her bike. Being a little shorter than me, she was riding an HD Fat Boy like Arnold Schwarzenegger in *Terminator 2*. Arnie was 6ft 1 tall (187 cm) in that movie, and this chick was 5ft 2. So I just had to know what she

thought of it. I later had a test ride on a Fat Boy Special, the floorboards
was an eye opener as they are super comfortable. No problem when rolling, but that is one heavy bike for slow maneuvering. Most Harleys can be
customized with OEM "Reach-"seats and handlebars. The suspension can
also be lowered for shorter riders. A sight for sore eyes, she looked like a 12
year old on that big twin. Small people on big bikes can look pretty hilarious. I see one every time I pass a window reflection.

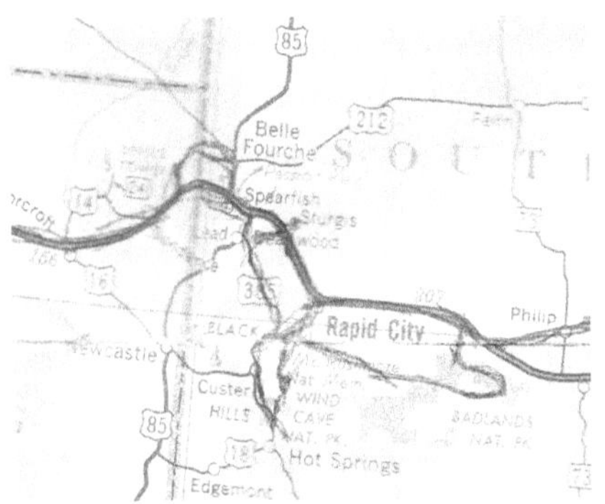

Up the Peter Norbeck Scenic
Byway from Mount Rushmore,
this 70-mile loop will take you
through the winding roads and
granite tunnels of Iron Mountain
Road, into Custer State Park, past
the Needle's Eye and Cathedral
Spires of the Needle's Highway
and Harney Peak.

Going south on Highway 16A, onto Iron Mountain Road, there was a lot
of motorcycles, so the average speed is low. A fun route where you don't go
racing but take time to enjoy the sights. There is one particular point where
you can take a photograph through a tunnel and capture Mt. Rushmore.
Super cool if you can get the shutter and camera focus to work.
Custer State Park is located 58 miles from Sturgis and had an entry fee of
$5. Encompassing 71,000 acres of the Black Hills, it is protected land home
to abundant wildlife. Driving through I made a stop to get some pictures
of some of the free roaming bison. Watching with a ton of other bikers,
I think if the Bison could talk they'd say "oh, it is Sturgis Rally time
again". They didn't look fazed at all. The many state parks offers a lot
more than what you can see driving through, so if your interest is hiking you really want to research the many options before arriving. With
my Caterpillar boots, I had no intention to do more than city walks.
Custer State Park looked very clean and well maintained.

Continuing on the loop on Highway 16/385 I arrived at Crazy Horse
Memorial. Defeating general Custer at Little Big Horn and never sign-

ing any treaties, the Native Americans wanted to create a tribute to the legendary Lakota chief who was killed at Fort Robinson in 1877. In 1947 Chief Henry Standing Bear, a descendant cousin of Crazy Horse, shared a message of hope and reconciliation, inviting Korczak Ziolkowski to carve a Memorial to honor the Oglala Lakota tribe.

The project began in 1948 and it yet to be finished. The memorial is being carved out of Thunderhead Mountain, on land considered sacred by some Oglala Lakota. Well, once again I must say that everything is bigger in the USA. With a planned height of 558 feet (170 m) and a length of 624 feet (190 m), this memorial is on a scale that matches the Egyptian pyramids. The eyes themselves are 17 feet (5 m) wide. The $4 entry fee goes to fun-ding this massive project. I talked to a few other visitors and they told me that the project is based solely on private donations as the Crazy Horse Memorial Foundation has rejected government offers for funding. They didn't expect it to be finished in their lifetime, but the symbolism makes sense that the Monument is being built by people who wants to create cross-cultural understanding and to mend relations between Natives and non-Natives.

Back on my bike I continued northbound on Highway 87 onto Needles Highway, a 14 mile scenic byway constructed in 1922, thirty miles south of Rapid City. The name stems from the pointy rock formations found on the route. With its sharp turns and narrow tunnels the construction of this road is truly impressive, you want to take your time and make some stops to take in the views. At the west end of the Needles Highway, I decided to ride to Deadwood 53 miles north on Route 385. Founded in 1876 after gold was discovered in the Black Hills. The gold rush was to no surprise a big reason to why the Native population got screwed. Deadwood is most known for the legendary scout, lawman, gunfighter, gambler and showman, James Butler Hickok aka. "Wild Bill" Hickok being killed during a five-card stud poker game at Nuttal & Mann's Saloon. This is also known as the "No. 10 Saloon". The hand of cards which he supposedly held at the time of his death has become known as the "dead man's hand": two pairs of aces and eights. Wild Bill Hickok has reportedly killed six or seven men in gunfights himself. The current No. 10 Saloon is not at the same location as the original.

SALOON
BROKEN SPOKE
ORIGINAL LOCATION SALOON 10
Wild West Winners
"The Journey"
SPOKE

Today Deadwood is home to around 1,270 people and is a nice clean place with stone covered sidewalks. The town has benefitted from the state of South Dakota legalizing gambling in Deadwood in 1989. Hollywood actor Kevin Costner even owned a stake in the Midnight Star casino and restaurant. This opened in 1991 after Costner fell in love with Deadwood when filming the Oscar winning movie *Dances with Wolves*.

The Midnight Star shut down in 2017. With more states legalizing gambling, the competition has grown and Deadwood's revenue from gambling has gone down in recent years. With all the motorcycles attending Sturgis, the parking spots on Deadwood's Main St. were crammed with motorcycles too. Going slow over a pedestrian crossing, the lights turned red halfway across and some stupid pedestrian just walks out in front of me, so he yells "Stop, god damn you!". Fortunately no collision.

Well, motorcycles are dangerous. On the previous day, Monday, four people were killed in traffic connected with the Sturgis Rally. One died at 2:25 am in Spearfish Canyon, two died at 4:30 in Boulder Canyon and one trying to avoid a deer on Interstate 90. His friend behind him actually hit the deer but survived without any injuries. A lot of American riders prefer to ride without a helmet, and some of those who do just use what is commonly known as "bucket"-helmets. These are basically an open face shell without any proper padding, useless in case of a spill. In Richmond, Virginia, I saw a guy on a Suzuki Hayabusa wearing one. Note: A Hayabusa has a top speed of 186 mph (300 kph)…

Returning to Main St. Sturgis, I basically people watch for a while. Bikers have always loved to pose, to see and be seen. Before social media and selfies, Paisano, the publisher of Easyriders magazine even had a publication called "In the Wind" dedicated to this. I think some of the older women at Sturgis Rally dresses like teens. Or how their own teen daughters would dress if they tried to look like sluts. Some shit you just can't un-see. Topping this off, I got to witness the cops arrest two card game con artists operating on Main St.

Walking into the "Broken Spoke Saloon" I just couldn't believe one of my all-time favorite rock bands were performing on the stage, ZZ Top!

Doing some research later I found out that ZZ Top indeed were in Sturgis and had played a concert 10:30 pm at the Buffalo Chip Campground on Monday, August 9th 2004. Since it wasn't announced, there actually weren't a lot of people present at the impromptu performance at the Broken Spoke. Singer Billy Gibbons is a car and motorcycle enthusiast, and he had a twin pair of custom motorcycles built in 1991, named "Hogzzilla". These were featured in the January 1992 issue of Easyriders Magazine and complements "Cadzzilla", one of the most fantastic custom cars in the world. Not a car guy I think Cadzzilla is one of the most beautiful cars ever created. The Cadzzilla is a custom hot rod car based on a 1948 Cadillac Series 62 Sedanette and built by legendary car customizer Boyd Coddington for an amount of no less than $900,000. Adjusted for inflation this would be around $1.7 million in 2020. The name is a combination of three words: Cadillac, ZZ Top and Godzilla. Logically, Hogzilla is also combination of three words: Hog, ZZ Top and Godzilla. Both bikes and the car is just insanely cool.

To fully understand the story above, the word "hog" means a pig but the term is also a nickname used for Harley Davidson motorcycles.
In the 1920s, The Wrecking Crew was a successful Harley Davidson team at board and dirt track races. During this time race team member Ray Weishaar acquired a pet piglet, which was quickly adopted as the team's mascot. A tradition soon began of riding a victory lap after each win with Johnny the pig sitting on the gas tank. Following this, journalists named the racers "the Harley Hogs" as well as noting that Harley was "hogging" all the victories from Indian and Excelsior. As the years passed, the Motor Company embraced the moniker and now "HOG" is used as an acronym for the Harley Owners Group as well as the Harley-Davidson Motor Company's listing on the New York Stock Exchange in 1986. Oh yeah, a one year membership of "HOG" usually comes free with the purchase of a new Harley Davidson.

Back at the Rush No More campground I talked to a couple of female Harley riders, Kathy and Sarah, who seemed ro be in their late-thirties. They were riding on a Heritage Softail and a Low Rider. Having sold an old Ironhead Sportster, a Twin Cam Low Rider sure was a sweet upgrade.

My Ducati was in their opinion like a Japanese sport bike, or "crotchrock-et" as Harley riders call them. They preferred the "in the bike" feel you get on a cruiser compared to sitting on top of other bikes. Some cruisers kind of "lock" you in the seat if they are cushioned too much towards comfort. The Low Rider was in a ghastly yellow and purple factory color scheme, a bit gay if you ask me. I did have a really hard time telling whether or not they were a lesbian couple or not. My knowledge of lesbians is limited to those appearing in er, "instructional yoga" movies.

I used to have a very negative view on homosexual men.
Like everyone else, they have the right to a life without having to put up
with being harassed or attacked.
Still I feel something is off. I am not sure I can say what it is.
I used to feel disgust when I saw two gay men walking down the street
holding hands. But I was a different person when I was 19.
I found homosexual men were deviant from the norm, unable to adapt
and conform to society, unable to be men.
Since then I realized that this doesn't matter, bother or concern me if
a guy want to play for the home team. I have had a gay colleague, gay
business contacts and sub-let an apartment from a gay dude who had a
side gig as a drag queen.
Gays are also minority among motorcyclists or bikers.
Here their presence is not welcomed by unwritten macho laws that
condemn without mercy. Against my preconceived opinion when I was
young, it was probably myself that was a roadblock.
Not being part of the solution I was a part of the problem.

I was basically an ignorant idiot. Acknowledging this dark side is the
first step towards a greater understanding and thus a better world for
all. My old opinions were influenced by my environment and some logic
I haven't been able to explain. Not then, not now.
But I do still think that gay men are just dudes
who has given up on women too early.

Lesbians are cool though,
as long as they don't look like truck drivers.

Wednesday, August 11th 2004

Starting the day with a mail call from the campground office, my new temp tag had arrived, I must say that the efficiency of domestic courier services impressed me. It had taken less than 21 hours to get the envelope delivered 1700 miles from Richmond. Relieved that my trip could continue uninterrupted, I rode to Sturgis Man St. where I dipped into the tourist office and bought an official 64th Rally t-shirt and rally patch. Many vendors offers a lot of different designs, but the official patch is in my book the best and right one to get. Having sent my busted digital camera home I bought a couple of single use film cameras. Which I also managed to drop on the ground.

The plan for the day was taking a ride to see Badlands National Park south-east of Rapid City. Taking SD Highway 44, the scenic access to the park, this intersects Highway 377 two miles from the Interior Entrance. With all the other bikes, a nice leisurely 111 mile ride from Sturgis. Formed by two basic geologic processes, deposition and erosion, Badlands National Park covers 244,000 acres with an expanse of mixed-grass prairie where bison, bighorn sheep, prairie dogs, and black-footed ferrets live today. The Badlands were deposited in layers. These layers are composed of tiny grains of sediments such as sand, silt, and clay that have been cemented together into sedimentary rocks. This happened during the late Cretaceous Period (67 to 75 million years ago, when dinosaurs roamed the Earth) and throughout the Late Eocene (34 to 37 million years ago) and Oligocene Epochs (26 to 34 million years ago). Different environments covering the area such as sea, tropical land and open woodland with curving rivers caused different sediments to accumulate during different times. The layers similar in character are grouped into units and are called formations. Logically, the oldest formations are at the bottom and the youngest are at the top, illustrating the principle of superposition. Erosion of the Badlands started about half a million years ago, when the Cheyenne River captured streams and rivers flowing from the Black Hills into the Badlands region. Once the Black Hills streams and rivers started seeping through, erosion dominated over deposition and the

modern rivers cut down through the rock layers, carving fantastic shapes into what once had been a flat floodplain. The Badlands erodes at a rate of about an inch per year. Evidence suggests that they will be gone in another 500,000 years, giving them a total life span of just one million years. Not a long period of time in the history of the planet.
This does make you think about human existence too.

We exploit the world and its resources to the max. Even though most people are aware of and acknowledge this, there is one thing standing in the way of further understanding and moving towards a more sensible approach. To find a solution we will need to look at the problems. Pollution, cutting down the rain forest, extinction of species, wars. The reason is greed. It is natural to put yourself first. The rat race for money has a tendency to push all rules and morale aside. I pollute the world too.

It is not just the uncontrolled consequences of deforestation that is regrettable. Animals are killed as a result of unnecessary reasons. But we have always done that. It is natural. I respect those who is against any sort of killing without compromise. They are on to something that can make the world a better place. But at the same time there will always be people who do not buy into that idea, so pacifism is weakly founded, even though the idea is sound.

Despite our superiority, adaption wise, we are basically animals. We should never forget that we are not alone. Our superiority should not hide the fact that we are very vulnerable in the global eco-system and can't survive on our own.
The Badlands were created through half a million years, humans has had more negative impact in just 200 years since the industrial revolution. Mankind is just a blip in the timeline of Earth.

The planet doesn't truly belong to mankind, we just borrowed it from Mother Earth.

Badlands National Park is truly unique, and if you're in Sturgis I highly recommend visiting it.

On the way back to Sturgis I noticed "Jack First" gun shop. The American Constitution is truly special. Besides all the negative effects as a crazy high murder and crime rate, school shootings and accidental deaths, it is hard to deny that shooting is fun. Having been a member of a sports shooting club in Denmark, I decided to check out what they had to offer. Talking to the sales guy I held up a couple of Smith & Wesson and Ruger handguns. Having small digits isn't a problem, there is a gun that'll fit anyone. South Dakota is the state with the most conceal carry permits and those liberal Californians were perceived as a threat to their lifestyle. Talking gun politics with the staff, they claimed that the opposition of the Second Amendment rights mainly comes from what they referred to as "Hollywood types" who want to be politically correct and shove their opinions onto others.

Some of my American friends are actually surprised of the restrictive arms laws in Denmark. To some extent I agree. When I grew up, a buddy of mine was fined around $180 for possession of a loaded weapon. Carrying a knife wasn't a problem, half the boys I grew up with used to carry a knife. We even had knife throwing contests at the playground. Then something changed in the early nineties. Everything was restricted to the max. Today you can't carry a knife with a blade longer than 2.75 inches, tear gas or even a sharpened screwdriver. Being caught with a loaded firearm now costs a year in prison and an illegal knife at least one week. It is even illegal to wear a bulletproof vest, unless you're a licensed security guard or a cop! Well, people are still being stabbed at the same rate as earlier, and criminals who wants to get a gun illegally can easily get them. So self defense is basically illegal. Danes are ruder than ever, and I think the country would have even more shootings per capita than the USA if the gun laws were the same. Compared with the United States, the two countries each have extreme arms laws, but from opposite positions. In my opinion, American gun laws need to include more control, and Danish laws need to be more relaxed. The Danish politicians actually made it legal to own tear gas spray for self-protection in your own home, but it is still a crime to carry it outside, and if you spray a burglar without him actually attacking, you can get punished for it.

When laws get too stupid, people stop caring about breaking them.

After an informative and entertaining chat with the owner of "Jack First", he was very interested in my Ducati. Without the pannier bags the S4 does look like a two wheeled porn star. Maybe I should have asked how many guns with ammo he would have traded for…

Passing through Rapid City I can't help but make a pit stop at Shotgun Willie's again. Not too much going on this afternoon, maybe the best dancers went up to Sturgis as more money could be made there during the rally. Some bikers have their girlfriends and wives with them, and they all chip in when tipping the dancers.

The trip to Badlands National Park was a 260 mile round trip, so I headed back to Rush No More Campground. Here, the guy with the wide tyre V-Rod had snapped the final drive belt on his bike. The motorcycle manufacturers spends fortunes on R&D to make safe and reliable motorcycles, so when owners starts to customize and modify their bikes, all sorts of shit usually goes wrong and breaks.

Outside the campground office I met Kit, a christian biker riding a Honda Magna VF750C. This is actually a very cool and interesting cruiser motorcycle as it has what I consider is the best motorcycle engine type possible, a V4, four cylinders in a V configuration. Like my Ducati it had a 90° "L" type angle on the cylinder position. The Honda Magna was discontinued by Honda in 2004. The most powerful bike I have ridden to date is a V4 Aprilia Tuono with 160 horsepower, way more than you'll ever need on public roads. And Ducati is now using V4 engines in their top range models pushing out around 200 bhp.

Kit was in Sturgis with his wife and pre-teen son. I can't remember his name but I think it was Carson. Being myself, I of course check out Kit's wife. She seemed super stressed. Kit later told me that she worked in logistics with the US armed forces. With the invasion of Afghanistan and the second Iraq war ongoing at time, it is no wonder she looked like one who really needed time off work. Kit was a super friendly guy and in case I dropped my wallet, I wouldn't worry about getting it back from him.

Sitting at a small campfire I talked with another Honda rider, another Bob. Talking bikes, Robert rides the "gold standard" for touring bikes, which actually has "gold" in the model name, an 1800 Honda Goldwing. His take was that Harley Davidsons touring models were way too overpriced and expensive compared to the alternatives. He paid $15,000 for his Gold Wing with all the gizmos fitted as standard. A Harley Davidson FLHT-CUI Ultra Classic Electra Glide with the same equipment had a sticker price of more than $28,000. So he was not gonna pay thirteen grand more for having a Harley logo on the tank.

At the time Gold Wings were even built in USA, at the Honda of America manufacturing Plant in Marysville, Ohio. Adding to this, the 2010 model year was the last to be produced in the United States, and no 2011 model year Gold Wings were produced as manufacturing was transferred to Japan in 2012. With a wet weight of 898 pounds (407 kg), you would think Robert's 1800 Gold Wing is a land barge that only can go fast in a straight line. But watching some videos online, there is a few showing fast runs on Gold Wings on the *Tail of the Dragon*.

I can say the bike isn't setting the limit, it all is down to the riders skills.

At the time Indian Motorcycles were basically Harley clones with an S&S motor and Indian badging. I thought that Polaris who manufactured the Victory motorcycle brand should buy the Indian name and rebuild the brand. I must be psychic, they did exactly that in 2011.

The Victory Motorcycle brand was discontinued in 2017. Having produced some very well performing motorcycles and I think Polaris should re-introduce the low and fat rear wheeled Hammer cruiser model as the Indian "Tomahawk".

Oil under the Ducati makes for some serious worries

Meeting new people is truly amazing and one of the greatest things about traveling. Meeting Kit the day before I talked with another Rush No More Campground patron, Tom Stone, who kinda looked like my cousin called Steen. Strange coincidence, Steen is actually a Danish variant of the German word for "stone". Tom had travelled from Texas with his girlfriend. Having been at the Sturgis Rally before, I got some riding tips about Spearfish Canyon and the surrounding area from him. So I rode into Sturgis again. Wanting to take a picture of Main St. from one of the platform towers that offers an overview of everything. It costs $5 so I decided that it was not that important.

A big queue had formed where the stars of the TV show Orange County Choppers held a fan poster signing. The queue was so long that it went around the block, and a guy waiting in line told me a poster was $10. This wouldn't survive the rest of my journey, so I made a pass on that too.

A staple of big motorcycle rallies are the bikini bike wash.
I ended up taking a different offer, as a christian biker group offered a free bike wash. These guys actually go to church, where "attending church" for 1%'ers is biker term for the weekly club meeting.

While waiting for my bikes turn I was handed some paraphernalia in the form of a pamphlet and a dvd. Of course I was asked if I had thought about Jesus lately. As is, I had not.

But I had to admit that I was and still am thankful for every day of my life, being blessed that with the options given to me. And thankful that I had the fortune not to be born or stuck in a "shithole" country as the orange swamp monster calls them. Getting my bike washed for the first time ever, the dirt ending up on the ground makes me think that it is the dust and grime collected all the way from Virginia, up to Chicago, around the big Lake Michigan and through the Mid-west, about halfway through my journey to the coast.

SONS OF SILENCE
MC
MINNESOTA
SONS OF SILENCE
MC
OPEN

WILD-BILLS-DEATH-CHAIR
SALOON NO. 10
Welcome
2004 Rally

Spiritual supplements comes in many different variations.
If you have found some goals in life, you don't need to rely
on any religion.

Far from despising, the most religions have a main commonality line
striving for "the ethical human". The Ideal is simple,
a good person doesn't take advantage at the expense of others.
The different faiths are based on a thought of a better world,
with differing opinions how to turn things in the right direction.
Some faiths come with a set of rules or laws of what is defining
right and wrong. These rules are often exploited and interpreted
by individuals who absolutely does not follow the general idea
of the good human. So whenever possible, look at other peoples' faith as
well as your own with equal criticism.

Some religions ask people to look for "the good" within their own
consciousness. This may come off as selfish but removes the idea
of forcing and beating an ideal into others.
The value of a religion you voluntarily have found and explored
is bigger than one you have been brought up with. So a voluntary
approach to religion is more open and appeals more to me
than any imposed faith.

New ideas and sects appear all the time. Faiths built around a close com-
munity. These usually has one flaw as a few individuals are getting a fat
bank account off of every single member.
This could be compared to the retail X-mas season, but most
cults are in my opinion too extreme to be acceptable.

With these views on religion I often ask myself if I have a faith.
The answer is both yes and no.
I used to be a member of the Danish state church.
When I need help (miracles or luck), I also look up at the clouds for some
divine loot box dropping from the sky.
But what is tangible is always better.

*The closest I come to gods is the thought that something bigger is every-
where, like energy. Energy is another miracle you can't hold it in your
hand. And thus it explains itself.*

*Energy is pure strength and force. Masculine. Therefore I would think
God would be male. But without the opposite there would be no balance.
So there might be more than one god,
and at least one of them female.*

*Other considerations concerning religion includes
the concepts of soul and fate.
The soul is in your consciousness.
It relies of your level of consciousness and ethical standards.
Fate is the most tangible confirmation of life:
You can look back at your own or others life and thus write about it.*

*The main pillar of all religion is the faith. A conviction that is
sincere often sets a fixed world view can be both positive or
negative, depending of the individual and its environment.*

*Faith can be many things, but first and foremost
should it be a belief in yourself.*

With a clean bike I went to Deadwood again, where I took another walk.
There was a Saloon No. 10, but this was a replica, the original is located
further down Main St., Deadwood. As a curiosity, they had Wild Bill's
"Death Chair" on display. I did spot some other Ducati motorcycles, an
S4R, a yellow 996 superbike. So while at the Sturgis Rally I saw a total of
six Ducati bikes including an ST on Lazelle St in Sturgis. Not a lot out of
half a million bikes. But it did make it a lot easier to find my scooter.

From Deadwood I went onto Highway 14A through Spearfish Canyon.
A very nice route, where the Harley riders cruise along at the 35 mph speed
limit. Continuing west through Hulet on Highway 24 I enter Wyoming.
With motorcycles all over the place, the Sturgis Rally is so big it has spread
out to other states.

My destination for the day was Devils Tower National Monument 80 miles from Sturgis. My National Parks Pass gives me free entrance, without it, entry costs $5. Devils Tower is a laccolithic butte composed of igneous rock in the Bear Lodge Mountains.

The name Devil's Tower originated in 1875 during an expedition led by Colonel Richard Irving Dodge, when his interpreter reportedly misinterpreted a native name to mean "Bad God's Tower". Featured in the classic Steven Spielberg sci-fi movie *Encounters of the Third Kind* from 1977, Devils Tower stands 867 feet (265 m) from summit to base and it does make you feel damn small. Some climbers looked like ants on a huge wedding cake. Walking around the base took 45 minutes. I still can't recommend hiking in the same footwear as you use for riding your motorcycle.

The Native Lakota and Kiowa tribes tell a different story about Devils Tower, a legend of a group of girls who went out to play and were spotted by several giant bears who began to chase them. In an effort to escape the bears, the girls climbed atop a rock, fell to their knees, and prayed to the Great Spirit to save them. The bears left deep claw marks in the sides, in an attempt to climb the rock which had become too steep to climb. Those marks gave Devils Tower its distinct shape. The Native American legend is a fair bit cooler than the facts, Devils Tower basically being a huge pimple on the face of the planet.

Returning to the parking lot, I spotted a big wet black pool of oil under my motorcycle. Fearing the absolute worst, I gunned it down Route 14 towards Interstate 90. Some idiot on an HD Ultra Classic wanted to race and sped up to overtake me. His bike might produce 20% more torque than mine, but the wet weight of the Ducati with me on top was around 560 pounds, compared to his ride totaling at least 1100 pounds. Owning a Harley may have you grow an attitude, but it makes you look like a chump when it counts. He quickly dropped keeping up with me, as the S4 has a top speed of 142.9 mph. Filling up at a gas station along Interstate 90, I managed to overfill the gas tank.

Great, one more fluid to make me jittery.

Finally back at the Rush No More Campsite after 80 miles of nervous riding, I sacrificed a white t-shirt and lay it under the engine to find out where the oil came from.

Talking with Tom Stone about yuppies, customizing motorcycles and life stories, Tom told me that at 18, he thought he knew everything, got married and had a kid. Learning that Tom is a deputy sheriff in Abilene, Texas is a big contrast to the outlaw image he was sporting here in Sturgis. Well, according to Tom, at 18 becoming a man of the law was the last thing he had imagined his future self as.

Tom's chopper is one of the most amazing motorcycles I have seen.
With all the Harley Davidsons that all look the same after a while, it does take a lot to stand out. What looks like a Softail Springer is a one off masterpiece. Equipped with an S&S motor, dry clutch, open primary and secondary belt drive, Panhead rocker covers, polished and clear coated polished tank and fenders it is a rolling piece of art. The truly unique detail is the modified rear frame and swing arm. It looks like a rigid frame like other Softail Harley Davidsons, but the custom framework on Tom's bike actually made even self-appointed experts think that it didn't have any rear shock suspension. The bike had participated in a custom builder competition once, but according to Tom, it lost to a bike that featured a lot of bolt-on catalogue parts and a five grand paint job. Some art is just understated and unappreciated.

Checking up on my bike I found absolutely nothing on the t-shirt under my bike. The big pool of oil must have been left from another motorcycle before I parked in the exact same spot! What a relief. Even with warranty you don't want to have serious engine failure on a newer bike, I have already tried that once. And the North American Ducati dealerships are far apart from each other, you can get a Harley fixed everywhere.

Putting our feet up for a bit, Kit offered everybody some drinks, a beer for the grown-ups and a root beer soda for his kid. Like many other christians Kit did ask me if I ever made thoughts about God. Nice to see that this aspect of Kits life didn't forbid him to have a cold one.

About forbidden stuff, if the muslims and jews are right about drinking alcohol and eating bacon will send you to hell, that is just a price I have to pay. I could have gone for a cold root beer instead.
Maybe I'm not that grown-up.

Tom and I decided to take a ride to Main St. in the evening. Even though Tom has the coolest bike in Sturgis, his tiny peanut style gas tank only gives him a range of around 80 miles between fill ups. So Tom ran out of gas on the way from the campground and into Sturgis. Fortunately, this happened in front of the local fire department, who were very helpful with a bit of monster juice.
While people watching on Main St., Tom told me that the party used to be crazier and the real wild party has now moved to the Buffalo Chip and Glencoe campgrounds. The Buffalo Chip amphitheater can hold around 50,000 spectators and is one of the nation's largest music festivals. So I definitely want to book there if I get the chance to experience another Sturgis Rally.

As mentioned earlier, the cops do have a heavy presence during the Sturgis rally, so as Tom put it, "Some people think Sturgis has people fornicating on the sidewalks, but they got no idea as they haven't been here". Being a Texan deputy sheriff, Tom actually fits the popular culture stereotype well, as he enjoys chew tobacco. Using a plastic bottle as a spittoon this looks pretty nasty. But it sure is better than pestering your surroundings with secondhand smoke.

At this point nine people had died at Sturgis 64th, as two were killed on a racetrack on Tuesday. With so many people not wearing helmets when riding, some won't survive.

I guess some people just have to learn things the hard way.

Motorsport and the world's biggest biker bar

The Sturgis Rally and Races is also known as "the Black Hills Classic", referring to the events roots, starting as a single race with nine participants and a small audience on August 14, 1938. Arranged by the Jackpine Gypsies motorcycle club. The club still owns and operates the tracks, hillclimb, and field areas where the rally is held. Jackpine Gypsies was founded in 1936 by Clarence "Pappy" Hoel, the same year he became the Indian Motorcycle dealer in Sturgis. The Jackpine Gypsies were inducted to the Motorcycle Hall of Fame in 1997.

Parking at the JackPine Gypsy Grounds, a guy almost laid down his Ultra Glide as the entrance driveway has two big tyre grooves with different depths in it. To his luck another biker saw this coming and managed to rush over and help keeping the bike upright. It is always costly to lay down a bike, unless you are like me and don't care about small dings and scratches. Watching the AMA Hillclimb, the crowd really rooted and cheered for the only two Harley powered motorcycles competing.

As with all other sporting events, it starts with a pledge of allegiance and a prayer that no one gets hurt. The hillclimb is a contest of getting up a hill the furthest and fastest. A lot of participants don't make it to the top, and part of the spectacle is people coming off their bikes.

I sat next to a couple of bikers from Spain who had come to Sturgis without motorcycles, so I told them that I had come across a place in Sturgis that offers motorcycle rentals. A lot of long distance travelers fly in from all over the world, and Sturgis is just not the same without a motorcycle, you'll be missing out of about 50% of the Sturgis experience. Paying dearly to get there you'll want to ride. Renting an HD Sportster cost $200 per day and three days was $500. The big twin models were $250 a day and $675 for three days. Pretty steep, but that is supply and demand for y'all.

After an hour in the hot sunny weather I went back into Sturgis. Walking around Sturgis, I checked out Lazelle Street, the street running parallel with Main St., this is also blocked off to allow for motorcycle parking. While at the Yamaha booth, they sold and mounted new tires that would fit

WEST COAST CHOPPERS
ASSHOLE'S GARAGE
SMOKING IS MANDATORY
FULL THROTTLE SALOON

the Ducati. My rear tire is really close to worn out, so I definitely wanted to keep them in mind. Checking out West Coast Choppers, Jesse James is another motorcycle builder turned TV celebrity. Today he is famous for being the most hated man in America, having cheated on his third wife, Hollywood star Sandra Bullock. His stand had some custom motorcycles on show. Most choppers suck in my book, and many of them are high maintenance trailer queens that is best as art on wheels for show use only. Most bikes with long forks, raked out triple trees and the popular wide rear tires have awful corner handling. It is like driving an old car without power steering. The worst test ride experience I ever had was on a Lauge Jensen, a now defunct danish manufactured custom brand. With the foot controls too far forward I melted a hole in my riding pants touching the air intake.

In the same area there was a number of different manufacturers and customizers present. Here, the prototype Dodge Tomahawk motorcycle is a true showstopper. A motorcycle that make the Chevy V8 powered Boss Hoss motorcycles look small, the Dodge Tomahawk is equipped with four wheels paired close front and rear, and a V10 car engine, this sadly never made it into production, a production model would probably cost 100K.

Later that night Main St. was filled to the brim. Again I spot some more Sons of Silence MC members. Some said a Bandido had killed a member of the Hells Angels in a neighboring state recently and that is why I hadn't seen members from either club. Well, bikers love to tell stories, so this remains unconfirmed. Besides that, Hells Angels MC got a property on 3rd St. just off Main St. selling "Support 81" merchandise and further down a tattoo shop. Hell's Angels own land near Sturgis so the club has a presence at every rally. The outlaw clubs do tend to keep to themselves.

As it is getting dark, I follow the flow east out of Sturgis and turn left onto Highway 79. 10 miles north I stop at "the World's biggest biker bar", the Full Throttle Saloon. This is basically a compound with bars, restaurants, merchandise stores and my favorite, pole dancers.

The sign shop offered half price on some really cool signs for your garage or man cave. I decided they wouldn't fit on the bike, so maybe another time. Well, these could probably be found on eBay too. Full Throttle Saloon is big on the classic biker sport of making burnouts until your tire goes pop. Not sure if the tire guy had rubber that would fit anything but a cruiser, I left my bike outside on the parking lot.

Biker culture is very macho oriented and some would say that there is a lack of equality within the biker subculture. Women who constantly nags about differences seem unaware that it'll take time to break down the walls of tradition. Equality is far from black and white. As a main point and condition, men are usually physically stronger. The physical superiority men possess often leads to the thought of further natural dominance, which often shows in real life. The problem with inequality is not just visible in salaries, but also the general acceptance of women taking on traditional male roles. I got the feeling that women slowly but eventually will get equality. One thing I do disagree with, call it old fashioned if you want, is women in the armed forces being present on the battlefield.
I do not think women belong in frontline fighting.
What I do love is the fact that women enjoy riding motorcycles themselves. Compared to riding yourself, sitting on a pillion is a totally different and far more boring motorcycle experience. And riding with a passenger is like having a huge touring load on the back of your bike. It is great for dating, though, as the correct position for a motorcycle passenger is close up to a rider. I have never complained about having a good pair of tits leaning up against my back. Ever.

In 2009 Full Throttle Saloon got their own American reality television series on the truTV network. This gave an insight into the inner operations prior to the rally opening and for the duration of the rally each year. At the end of the summer of 2015, the Full Throttle Saloon unfortunately burned down. A pinched power cord to a keg refrigerator overheated and sparked a fire in a nearby cardboard box. Full Throttle has since been rebuilt, but the fire put a halt on the television show. Full Throttle Saloon had the finest women I had seen in Sturgis yet. So a pro tip: Don't go to Sturgis without going to Full Throttle at least once.

Genuine biker party in Sturgis

Tom packed up before noon, the distance to Abilene, TX is 980 miles. Even though he could do an "Iron Butt", a thousand miles in 24 hours, I wouldn't want to convince the missus that was a good idea. Wishing them both a safe ride home, I thought that was a true biker. A guy who actually ride to Sturgis on his motorcycle. I am not sure if they are a majority, but a lot of bikers trailer their bikes or roll them onto the beds of their pickups before going to Sturgis. The motorcycle crowd is getting older and more comfort oriented. This includes myself. The longest ride I have ever done in one day is 1,026 miles (1652 km), from Bologna, Italy to my home in Denmark. My bike broke down and needed to be repaired, while I had to be at work the next day.

Did you know that you can come to Sturgis and actually ride a Harley Davidson for free? Well, it'll be a limited experience as you will have to follow a fairly short route, but the Harley Davidson dealer in Sturgis do have a range of bikes you can test ride. While signing up the test ride staff had a serious laugh and an extra look at my driver's license. Besides it being foreign, the expiration date was in 39 years and it is valid until 2043 when I turn 70 years old. After that I have to renew it. In the USA, licenses are generally valid for eight years. You may renew in person, and every other year by mail or online. If your license has expired for more than one year, you will need to have your vision screened/pass the applicable knowledge and skills tests. Aloun actually had to retake his motorcycle license as he hadn't renewed it after returning to the USA from his Korean teaching gig in 2008.

Once again found myself riding on a Twin Cam HD Low Rider. This time the ride wasn't as good as the one I had on this model in Milwaukee, since it was accessorized with forward foot controls for the "heels in the wind" riding position. Being a short-ass, I couldn't reach the gear lever and brakes properly, making braking a crap experience. A Harley Davidson Low Rider does look sweet in blue. And grinning ear to ear, I was riding on a big Harley in Sturgis. Mission accomplished, bitches!

Having talked to Kit the day before, he was actually working as a volunteer, collecting the $5 charge from the view platforms on Sturgis Main St. The profits from this go to charity, the Sturgis Rally actually support more than 50 charity organizations. Kit having the Saturday off, we agreed to take a ride through Needles highway. Having done this already, it still is so fantastic that I didn't mind going on the same route twice.

Not exactly sure where we were heading, Kit wanted to experience the Jewel Cave National Monument. Declared a national monument in 1908, this is the third longest cave in the world, after Mammoth Cave System in Kentucky and Sistema Sac Actun at the Yucatán Peninsula in Mexico. Cave explorers recently mapped the 200th mile in Jewel Cave National Monument. The name originates in the year 1900, when the brothers Frank and Albert Michaud discovered a cave lined with calcite crystals which led them to name it "Jewel Cave". Most of the cave formed within the Mississippian Pahasapa Limestone deposited 350 million years ago. The later limestones, sandstones, and shales deposited in these Paleozoic and Mesozoic seas were eroded with the geologic uplift associated with Laramide Orogeny and the formation of the Black Hills. Again you are reminded of the two seconds mankind represents in the timeline of planet Earth.

Riding behind Kit, at the Jewel Cave National Park entrance driveway and waiting in the left turn lane for oncoming traffic to pass, a pair of bikes zips past. The last guy narrowly escapes a collision with his Ironhead Sportster and I manage to hear the rider yell for me to "get off the fuckin' road". Riding like a Moto GP racer without a helmet at the Sturgis Rally, I could only shake my head.
Using proper protective gear is a must for me, gloves, back protector, helmet and footwear that offers at least some protection. I am so used to wear a back protector that I feel naked riding without it. Breaking your arms and legs is something that you can live with, breaking your back can have such severe impact on your health and mobility that it is irreversible. Having come off my motorcycle at speed several times I have learned two things: The laws of physics don't discriminate and they don't forgive.

Jewel Cave is 69 miles out of Sturgis. Taking the scenic Needles Highway we got to Jewel Cave National Monument with too little time to go on a tour. These take between an hour and a half and up to four hours. So instead we went to Mount Rushmore.

Having been there four days prior, I still had my valid parking ticket in my wallet. I did get some more pictures taken. Asking another biker to take a photo, he is so eager to help he lays down on the ground to take a low-angle shot capturing myself and the four presidents in the same photo. It is nice to meet genuinely friendly folk.

Having covered 200 miles, Kit and I headed back to the campsite. Kathy and Sarah had also been out riding, one of them looked incredibly funny as the sun had given her a "panda eye" sunburn, her sunglasses had spared the area around her eyes, but the rest of her face was red from not wearing sunscreen. As a gentleman, I didn't say anything. But absolutely hilarious to look at.

Kathy and Sarah chose not to wear a helmet when riding. A lot of people I talked to about wearing a helmet argue that helmets don't save you properly anyway so they don't want to end up in a wheelchair. If people think their heads can take it, riding without a helmet is their choice and I have stopped trying to convince anyone about rethinking their position on this. You can't help people who don't want to be helped.

I decided to go to a pretty packed Sturgis Main St. where I spot the hottest ass on a bike in Sturgis, a girl on a Yamaha R6 sportsbike. At the auditorium I write myself into the visitor guest book. On a world map there, six of my fellow countrymen had marked their attendance with a pin, two of them from my hometown of Esbjerg. Looking for a happening place, I had a drink at the Broken Spoke Saloon. Not impressed, I got on the bike to the Full Throttle Saloon.

Outside they had a quarter mile race dyno bench set up. A dyno bench is a rolling road where you can measure the horsepower and torque on your bike. This one was a twin unit where you would race another bike in a standard quarter mile race. A chance for letting the Ducati rip, this was too good to pass up on.

Before fitting a bike the owner had to sign a waiver in case you manage to destroy your bike or engine. Watching a guy get his Honda CBR 600RR to punch out 108 hp on the rear wheel, I was pretty impressed. Honda CBR 600 was the one motorcycle model that sparked my interest in this two-wheeled hobby, and in the meantime Honda had increased the crank performance on their 600 cc sport model from 100 to 117 bhp.
Two female riders did a dyno race just before me. One of them didn't shift gear and registered going 200+ miles per hour. A Sportster has a top speed of around 100-120 mph. At least her bike survived being revved completely out in first gear.

Getting my bike set up against a Honda VTX 1800, the other guy managed to win 3 out of 3 races. Being 0,5 seconds slower, my fastest run was 11.3 seconds. Racing with a snapped clutch lever isn't optimal. The performance measurement on my Monster S4 was 78 horsepower on the rear wheel, the motorcycle manufacturers use the power output on the crankshaft for performance measurements. But 78 horsepower is a bit disappointing compared to the factory indicated 100 hp. However, dyno rolling roads differ too, many being poorly calibrated. Correct chain tensioning and tyre type and wear also has an impact of performance readouts. As I did not go to Yamaha to fit a new tire, I also didn't do any burnout to warm up my tire before racing.

Before entering the Full Throttle Saloon, some drunk ass tool tried to ride his bike off the Full Throttle parking lot but instantly laid it down on the side, it basically tipped over at standstill. Some of his buddies helped him up and he dumped his bike for a second time. Again, without a helmet. I hope his friends took the keys from him. The problem being this is the USA and you don't want to get shot trying to prevent stupid people doing stupid shit. In situations like this you're better off notifying the cops. Fortunately, this guy was so drunk he couldn't even hold his bike upright.

Later there I discovered some broken glass on the parking lot,
no prizes guessing who managed to ride over this…

Alcohol is an integral part of many peoples everyday lives.
Besides riding motorcycles, a legal and fun way of shortening your time
on Earth. An emotional catalyst, alcohol can be all you need or all you
don't want. You loosen up and become more free spirited and open.
Or too stupid to be around.

It is okay if you lose your dignity. But when you lose your sense of
responsibility you won't find any support from me.
Here I especially think of drinking and driving (DUI). I will not claim
to be innocent in this. I am happy to say that no one but myself has been
hurt in me riding under the influence. Since upgrading from moped to
motorcycle I have never been drunk driving, and I can assure you that
you won't find me riding rat-faced.
My life is simply too valuable to me.

Inside the Full Throttle Saloon, the party is on at, er, full throttle. The former professional cheerleader squad "Perfect Angels" was hired to get the party into high gear, and the female bar staff sports chaps, tight shorts and g-strings.

On stage, the 80's rock band Skid Row played a concert. Not a Skid Row fan, I do have a theory about music. The music and artists you enjoy in your late teens sticks with you for life. Guns'n Roses is my all time favorite rock band and along with ZZ Top, Queen, Aerosmith, AC/DC, Bon Jovi and Bruce Springsteen, I'll listen to a lot of different music genres including pop, hip hop and country. But you can't top 80's and early 90's classic hard rock.

Some of the ladies eventually got drunk and ended up dropping their tops, a true outlaw style biker party! Though it was tempting to get completely wasted in this live "girls gone wild" environment, I settled for just a few beers. Heading out before I became unable to operate my motor vehicle legally, I rode through Main St. around 12 pm. Plenty of space, the 2004 party in South Dakota was coming to an end.

Sunday, August 15th 2004

In the TV show I saw as a teenager, Sturgis shut down and packs up in just hours. Everyone has to show up for work the next day. I wanted to see this for myself, so I rode into Main St. for one last time. Talking to a couple of locals, it was with a sign of relief that they said that "it's finally over". Yup, the 64th Sturgis Rally and Races was dead by noon on Sunday. It actually kicked off about a week before the official opening, so it does affect the local community. Bringing in money, but also much annoyance for 10 to 14 days.

A total of nine was killed at Sturgis 64th in 2004. Seven in traffic and two on a racetrack. 405 individuals were jailed this year. The police didn't kill anyone and the rally had been fairly peaceful until two years later in 2006, where two men affiliated with the Hell's Angels shot and wounded five Outlaws MC members in Custer State Park.

Approximately $250,000 worth of motorcycles are stolen annually in conjunction with the Sturgis Rally. With the customizing culture and the 50% market share in the USA, a stolen Harley Davidson motorcycle can easily be chopped up and sold as parts. The situation in other countries are similar. In Europe, Harley Davidson motorcycles tends to be stolen for export to eastern Europe and can be difficult to insure.

Some vendors are still open and are eager to off-load the remaining merch, especially the items printed with the year on it. I bought a cool t-shirt for $5, just hours prior it was $18.

The official stats tallied up 514,951 attending the Sturgis Rally in 2004. And as mentioned the rally grew in the following years. Unfortunately, price gouging has become rampant in recent years, a contributing cause to a decline in visitor numbers. A room at the Holiday Inn, for example, typically goes for $94 a night but runs upward of $600 during the event. So Main St. is full of *RUBs*, a mocking acronym for Rich Urban Bikers. Shifting demographics of bikers means the rally needs to change or adapt. Young people riddled with student debt don't go buy $20,000 motorcycles, making grey hair the new normal in Sturgis.

On the topic of supply and demand, I think there is a good chance of buying a cheap used Harley Davidson in the future, as baby boomers reach their seventies and get too old to ride. Unlike motorcycles, hot women and cold beer will always remain in high demand.

Checking on the raffle, a guy from South Dakota won the Harley Davidson Heritage Softail. Damn, I would have loved to win that one. Raffles and lotteries are different depending on countries. At World Ducati Week, Italian lottery rules states that you have to be present to claim your prize at the draw, so in 2002 I saw a guy from Holland miss out on a Ducati 916 Superbike.
Packed up and ready to continue west, I got the lamest farewell dad joke possible from Kit, telling me "Don't to talk to strangers". Super cool dude, with a hint of Ned Flanders mixed in.

Out of Sturgis I ride through Spearfish Canyon with just a bit of traffic. Reaching Interstate 90, I stayed on this until Buffalo, Wyoming. The roads have plenty of riders heading home from Sturgis, so while refueling I talked to a guy called Douglas on an HD Heritage Springer. He recommended me to visit Irma's in Cody, 176 miles west, so I followed him until reaching Highway 20. On Route 16 Douglas decided to gun it at a sweet 80 mph. Following behind, it is always nice to have another rider get zapped or pinged by the cop radar instead of yourself being laser tagged.
Route 16 passes through Bighorn National Forest. Once again I was gobsmacked of the beautiful and varied nature views the USA has to offer. While trying to take in the vistas riding next to the Meadowlark Lake, I end up going downhill while engine braking in too low a gear, so the rear wheel stepped out. With a total of 5,200 miles on my rear tyre, I found this a bit too exciting.

Speeding on highway 16 I did contemplate where the line of acceptable behavior goes. This should be set by a mix of sense logic and your own personality. Looking at how other people behave, we should not forget to look at ourselves too. Maybe you unconsciously do things that is not really acceptable. Or on purpose. In that case moving the limit of what is acceptable, you put your conscience away.

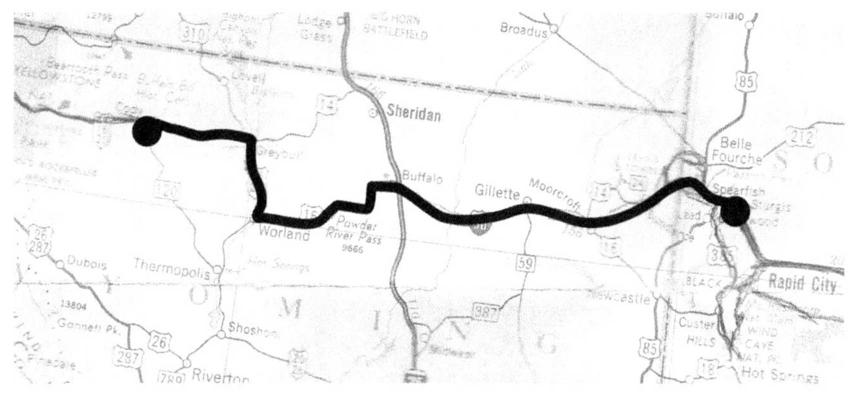

Conscience is the confirmation of your consciousness.
Doing "the right thing", to take responsibility for your actions and
thinking before acting. Feeling guilt after making a mistake, you have
normally taken a step in the right direction.
There can be misunderstandings when you feel guilty without
actually having done anything wrong.
You may have lost grasp of the situation
and be parked by the wrong explanation.

When conscience is another individual boundary,
a feeling of guilt can be hard to suppress
and comes with pain and frustration.

Done is done
-Learn from your mistakes so you don't repeat them.

Wrong may not be changeable to right. But right can turn wrong.
Much can be turned positive if you try to think about it.

This could be called an easy way out. I see it as an emergency
procedure when the road dips or bends too sharply.

After 320 miles I reached the city of Cody on Highway 16. Looking for accommodation, I ended up at Econolodge for $115. The Irma Hotel is just three minute walk from Econolodge, so I go to Irma's to eat dinner as recommended by my riding buddy Douglas. This is "Buffalo Bill's" Saloon Hotel, built in 1902 and named for his youngest daughter, Irma. The Irma is listed on the National Register of Historic Places by the National Park Service in recognition of its contribution to the cultural foundations of America. The Irma's famous cherrywood bar was a gift from Queen Victoria, dating to the period of construction and is one of the most photographed features in all of Cody.

Not to be confused with "Wild Bill" Hickok, William Frederick "Buffalo Bill" Cody was a pony express rider, scout, bison hunter and showman. As such, Willian F. Cody eventually created "Buffalo Bill's Wild West Show" which even toured Europe eight times. One of the shows stars were the sharpshooter Annie Oakley, "Wild Bill" Hickok even had a part performing in some of the earliest shows. While waiting for my order I talk to a local guy. Heaving for air when eating, he was very curious about me traveling across the USA.

Wyoming is the ninth largest state but has only around half a million people living there. In the early days farming, logging and cattle breeding was the major industries. With more livestock cattle and sheep than people, Wyoming is also called "the cowboy state". So of course I had ordered a real cowboy meal, beer, steak and fries.

A bit later the waitress asks if I need anything else, so I ask if they had any dessert as I felt like drinking a milkshake. The stern answer was that they didn't serve milkshake, and I needed to find that elsewhere.
Basically, I could fuck off to Dairy Queen if I wanted that.

Not being thin skinned, I found this answer pretty hilarious.

If the world is going soft, these folk ain't going with it.
Genuine shit kicking wild west attitude for y'all !

Ride to Yellowstone

Monday, August 16th 2004

Drinking a morning coffee on the porch outside my motel room at Econolodge, I had a chat with my neighbor, a fellow biker calling himself "Big D". Talking about the rally in Sturgis Big D had a different attitude to exotic dancers and strippers than me, he wanted strippers to drop all their kit, so he could see genitals. Well, tastes are different and I think if you leave nothing to the imagination, you might as well find a hooker to get a full service package. Big D handed me his personal business card which states his stances on life, citing one in each corner. "Gun owner", "Tax Payer", "Voter" and "Motor cyclist". Well, it sure does give you an unmistakeable idea of who he is. And the size of his ego.

While near a computer, I sent some e-mail to my sister and uncle, still no baby pictures of my favorite, and at the time only, niece. Luis did time his e-mail message well, as he had to cancel his planned trip to Colorado. Colorado is bordering Wyoming to the southeast, so I decided to head for Yellowstone National Park instead. Checking out of Econolodge, I made some error with my travelers cheque, signing it in the wrong spot. The clerk eventually chose to accept it after noting down my passport information. Cody is just 59 miles away from Yellowstone National Park east entrance, a one hour drive on highway 14.

Yellowstone has five entrances of which West, Gardiner and Bozeman is in Montana and the fifth is Grand Teton NP in Idaho.
My National Parks Pass provided free entry.

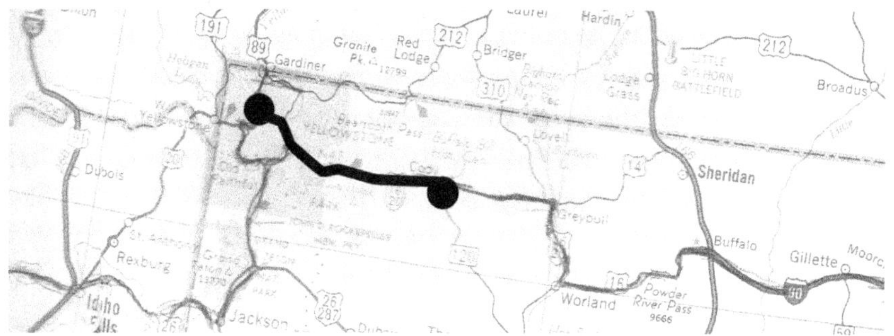

Founded in 1872, Yellowstone is the world's first National Park and it spans an area of 3,468.4 square miles (8,983 km2) over three states. With lakes, canyons, rivers and mountain ranges it is a part of the Rocky Mountains and contains the headwaters of the Yellowstone River, from which its historical name originates. Yellowstone National Park is also home to the largest supervolcano on the continent, Yellowstone Caldera. This is an active volcano having erupted several times in the last two million years but as it is collapsed it functions as a cauldron or boiling pot, hence the name Caldera. As a result of this ongoing underground volcanic activity, half of the world's geysers and hydrothermal features can be found in Yellowstone.

Known for its wildlife such as grizzly bears, wolves, and free-ranging herds of bison and elk living in this park, the Yellowstone Park bison herd is the oldest and largest public bison herd in the United States. Hundreds of different mammals, birds, fish, and reptiles have been documented in Yellowstone, including several endangered or threatened species.

Every year forest fires occur in Yellowstone National Park. The largest forest fires took place in the summer of 1988 where 793,880 acres (3,213 km2) was burnt, nearly one-third of the National Park. Starting as many smaller individual fires, the flames quickly spread out of control due to drought and wind conditions combining into one single huge conflagration which burned for several months. Only the cool and moist weather in the late autumn brought the fires to an end. The marks of this fire was still very visible in 2004.

Riding around Yellowstone Lake right into the center part of Yellowstone NP, I inquired about accommodation options. Everything is booked, so my only option is camping. No problem, camping is a part of motorcycle culture and for $48 I whip up my tent at the Bay Bridge camping. This is very basic without any running water or electricity but does offer toilet facilities. Yellowstone has a total of ten camping grounds, with Bay Bridge being the closest to the marina office.

With five million visitors each year there is a good amount of traffic.
My first stop was 20 miles away from the campground and is the first thing a lot of people associate with Yellowstone National Park, the big "Old Faithful" cone geyser. Called "Old Faithful" for its highly predictable geothermal feature, it was the first to be named in Yellowstone. Old Faithful erupts on average every 90 minutes, and eruptions shoots 3,700 to 8,400 US gallons (14,000 to 32,000 Liters) of boiling water up to 185 feet (56 m) up in the air, lasting from 1½ to 5 minutes. The average eruption height of Old Faithful is 145 feet (44 m). A lot of people had the same idea so there were plenty of spectators. Fortunately not so many that it was overcrowded. I just had to wait five minutes before the show started.
There is always some numb-skull who ends up going too close to the attractions and this time was no exception. Well, the guy did realize his stupidity before any accidents happened. Freshly steamed tourist could be a wildlife favorite.

Riding back to Yellowstone Lake, I decided to see West Thumb Basin. A part of Yellowstone Lake, it is the largest geyser basin on the lake shores. West Thumb is a caldera within a caldera. The sulphur fumes is not for everyone but growing up with a family of mink farmers I am hard to faze. The West Thumb is about the same size as Crater Lake in Oregon, but much smaller than the great Yellowstone caldera which formed 600,000 years ago.

Walking on the West Thumb Trail I walked behind a young woman with a pretty huge ass. Having travelled for a month in the USA now, I initially took notice of how big everything was, including cars and restaurant servings. A this point I had become oblivious to the fact that people also are bigger. But this one woman had me contemplate the American attitude to food and exercise. I had started to make side orders and by this point I knew I had gained some weight since arriving. There is a few issues to consider when it comes to eating right.

I live a rich life and when I eat I repress the thought of the World's less fortunate who are starving. I don't always eat healthily but do think about food quality and have a set limit of how much

fatty food I consume. I will change diet when enough is enough.
I have my own method for gauging this, a certain pair of pants.
If they feel too tight it's time to adjust the diet and start exercising.

While it is a joy to look at Kate Upton, the ideal is beautiful but
unrealistic. However, it does provide a goal to strive for.
While a goal that is not always worth the effort, I don't think I should be
allowed to set higher demands to others than I do to myself.
I would rather be labelled "chubby, but happy"
than a total lettuce head.

We have been inculcated a form of health ideal. It seems to me that the
health nuts takes this too seriously. It is their choice to strive for better
health. Some prioritize health over anything else, living by the phrase:
"You are what you eat". But that doesn't give them the right to judge
others. If you eat too much fat you get fat yourself.
A little extra from time to time won't harm.
You just need to remember to burn energy later.
I know there is a limit for "a little extra body fat" and I do have a hard
time understanding why some people let themselves get so big that the
sight of their own genitalia becomes a sensation.
But the chain comes off when the health nuts sets the standard.
I have never seen a jogger who looked happy.

Another group that is fun to have a go at when it comes to food,
is obviously vegetarians. But somehow they seem to show the right way.
Vegetarians should be met with a bit of respect as "You should not kill"
is morally correct, but doesn't fit in my real World view.
Animals are first and foremost deliberately killed for food.
Fair enough, no animal on my menu would hesitate to
feast on my dead carcass if they got the chance.
We have always killed and eaten other animals, and we're not
going to stop anytime soon. The important issue to me is the method used
when animals are killed. There are many options and some are cruel.
It should be as painless and quick as possible. Anything else is torture,
and without discussion simply wrong.

The roads in Yellowstone are well maintained, but it is worth noting that the speed limit is 45 mph. Without any groceries I ate a hot dog at the cafeteria by "Fishing Bridge". Not very good, actually pretty crappy. The guy next to me looked like he hasn't slept for a while. Shortly thereafter the waitress asked me if I had seen where he went. After eating half of his meal the guy had slipped out without paying his bill. Classy. Talking to the cafeteria staff I learned that young people from all over the world have summer jobs in Yellowstone NP.

On the four mile ride back to the Bay Bridge campground it started to rain, this continued throughout the night. My tent didn't stay completely dry, but my swag saved the day - and night.

"Big D"'s business card

Tuesday, August 17th 2004

As it had been raining throughout the night, the weather was cloudy. The plan for the day was to ride around Yellowstone to see as much as possible. Having the hard bags and luggage off the bike, it is way more nimble to maneuver around. My first stop was Grand Canyon of the Yellowstone, sharing the name but different in size, it is the first large canyon on the Yellowstone River downstream from Yellowstone Falls. The canyon is approximately 24 miles (39 km) long, between 800 and 1,200 ft (240 and 370 m) deep and from .25 to .75 miles (400 meters to 1.21 km) wide. Not too impressed I took a few snapshots and continued.

Basically just riding around, I stopped by an area that sixteen years later very much showed the aftermath of the 1988 fire. Looking at this, there is no doubt the firefighters were stressed to the max.

A bit later the road got blocked by a herd of bison, so I stopped and got off the bike to take some pictures like pretty much everybody else. I did worry that the Termignoni mufflers and the bright red color on my bike could provoke or trigger some aggressive behavior. An American male bison can weigh from around 880 to 2,000 pounds (400 to 900 kg). Parked next to a car, a grumpy bus driver stops and opens his door to complain. Dumbass could just drive around, he still had to navigate past the bison herd.

A cager tries to muscle his vehicle past the traffic queue and manage to piss off another biker in Mammoth Hot Springs. So he ended up receiving the classic "motorcycle boot meets car door".

Shouldn't we be allowed to dish out a little kicking when there's
a good reason? In my opinion would this be all right –in theory.
It just isn't possible as the law would contradict itself.
And doesn't really work. The problem arises when the law cannot punish
the criminal, but you can. You are just not allowed to,
otherwise you become a criminal yourself.

The solution must be to let a hog become bacon.
If others can lie, so can you.

You decide how sour the grapes need to be.

*The above incident shows how the law is one of the biggest limitations
we'll meet in life. A set limit for what society allows you to do.
Taking the law into your own hands is cool until you receive a
subpoena accusing you of assault.
When right is wrong and wrong is forgotten, we must decide
if we want to take an eventual penalty. The question remains,
whether you want to be a passive victim or strike back.*

Caught up in some dense traffic and unsure where to go, I briefly wound up in Montana up near the north end Gardiner entrance. Turning around and finding the right route, my next stop was Tower Fall near Tower Junction. Tower Fall has a stunning 132 feet drop. The unusual rock columns north of the fall were created by lava flow that cracked as it cooled. Because of severe erosion, hikes to the bottom of the falls is no longer possible. You can walk three-quarters of a mile past the Tower Fall overlook to see Tower Creek flow into the Yellowstone River. But Tower Fall is quite beautiful and a nice stop in Yellowstone.

With my socks being moist in my Caterpillar boots, hiking wasn't a part of the program. These were barely dry when it started to rain again.
Heading south to Yellowstone Lake in the rain I spotted some elks on more than one occasion. The rain just kept coming down so I made a stop at a resting area alongside the road. Not following Kit's advice I find myself talking to a stranger here, George Iu from California. George is an American-Chinese IT guy, who also happened to own a Ducati. Like Big D, he gave me his phone number and business card with the note that he would be back on Monday, August 23rd if I was in the area. I decided not to use it.

I do find it surprising that some people will give their contact information to a random stranger with whom they have just spoken to for around fifteen minutes.

Covering 200 miles within Yellowstone NP this day, the Monster was getting close to needing the mandatory 6,000 mile service, so I called up the Ducati dealership in Boise, Idaho. Explaining my situation, touring the USA, we made an appointment for me to come by Wednesday or Thursday morning.

Most of the other campers in Yellowstone are in RV's or camper trailers. Waking up around midnight for a nature call to the men's room, I heard wolves howling as the skies were clear and it was almost a full moon. I think my tent was just like a candy wrapper with a human snack in it. Not much you can do, but I decided to keep my multitool within reach before dozing off again.

Wondering about life and if Ida was a hoe...

Wednesday, August 18th 2004

The first order of business was to fit the new temporary tag. Since it had been dripping from the skies, I needed the tent to dry out for a bit.
The bike alarm system started to act up too, it might have been all the moisture. Blowing the 30 amp main fuse I was just about to call Stubbs at Ducati Richmond. Fortunately, I bought a sparc at Advanced Autoparts in Indianapolis. So it was 10:30 AM before I headed out of Yellowstone NP. Because of roadworks, getting out of Yellowstone took one and a half hours. Heading south through Grand Tetons National Park on Route 191, I ended up in Jackson. This is a super touristy Wild West style village. Making a stop here to fill the tank I talked to some tourists from Norway. On Route 26 westbound, I ride up mountainous roads through more rain.

After five hours and 205 miles I made a pit-stop in Idaho Falls for lunch and decide to try Jack in the Box, yet another a fast-food chain I only heard about but never tried. The burger and fries combo offer came with a pretty good milkshake. I don't think I ever had a burger served with milkshake before. Well, I have seen people eat some weird fast food combos.

In China I was very surprised to see a woman use her ice cream sundae for dipping her french fries at a McDonald's. Thanks to the Internet, this since became a trendy fad.

Continuing on Route 20 I again found myself in a prairie type terrain with no shelter from the gusts of side wind or turbulences. Letting the Monster stretch its legs, I averaged 75 mph. Riding can be a very adrenaline pumping and exciting experience. In the right weather it can be very stress relieving on your mind too.

Reaching Interstate 84 I am once again cruising through
the great wide open, thinking about life.
Why was I born? What is the meaning of life? What shall I do?
Where am I going? There are plenty of questions.
And another: Where are the answers?
Don't look for "what" but for "where".
From this point of view the answers appear closer.
The questions of life seems to me as a search for a sense of security in the answers, which hopefully does not exist. We float around searching for roots we don't need. The 100% certainties is not in the past but in the future. It all ends one day.

Even with today's technology, we can't live forever. Instead you will want to base your life on quality. It is not an appealing thought ending up unconscious on a life support system.
Successfully searching and finding a solution for eternal life would probably see yourself in an eternal haze, unconsciously rigged up to a machine. An ironic thought.

When on the subject of chance, a lot of people hope to be reborn, often holding a belief that there will be a form of "salvation".
Many of these base their life on different religions. Their choice, fine with me. However, I do not believe that I get more chances at living than this one current lifetime. To me, it is irrational to believe otherwise.
This makes it easier to live with the consciousness that life ends someday.

I got one single guaranteed chance,
so I will do what I can to get as much possible out of it.
Convinced in this belief it reassures my stance.

When in doubt I keep my opinion to myself, not pushing my agenda
on others. I will allow myself to take certain reservations, as I could be
misunderstood.
I used to be scared of death, especially without reaching
certain goals I would like to reach and experience.
If you find yourself in doubt, that can be a help to stay grounded.
Just set goals which are achievable. My shining example:
To write a book! If you have a direction, it is just a matter of putting one
foot in front of the other. Or typing one more word.

Some people get frustrated when they try to find ultimate and
universal answers, making this more complicated than necessary.
You only need to look within yourself.

Life should be lived while you can. My limits are set only by of sense and
strength. My strength is my sense, and my sense is my strength.
With that in the back of my mind, I know that I shouldn't waste time
on doing nothing. It is ok to think and do some fine thinking for a while,
but then you have to act, get shit done, take care of business.

Allowing myself to dwell too long in thoughts, my goals become
indifferent. As I am typing this, I feel I am getting closer to my goals,
making me feel alive.

Don't let life pass with you as a bystander.

Before reaching my end destination for the day, I overtook a car where the driver was wearing an unusual hat. While passing I noticed the Sheriffs logo on the side of the car. The speed allowed was 65 mph, he was driving 55. A little further on I find out he was on the way to a pretty bad accident at an intersection ahead. Two cars had collided and the outcome looked pretty brutal. Fire and rescue was already on the scene.

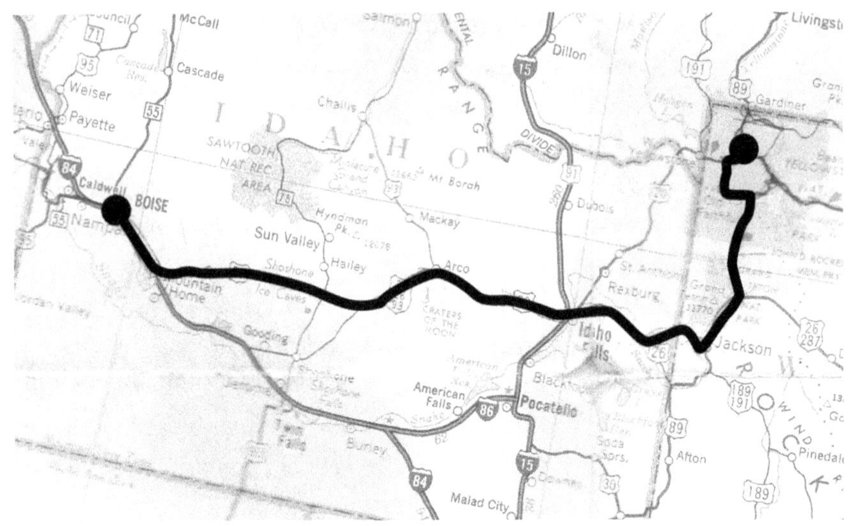

Arriving in Boise, Idaho at 7:30 pm I stopped at Motel 8 who charged $85 a night. After riding 457 miles it felt good having my first bath in 3 days. I have noticed that there is a ton of particles in the air around built-up suburban areas. Riding with the visor open lets a shitload of this crap hit your face, causing irritation, this feels different in European cities. It may be because American fuel often is a lower octane grade, lowering the temperature and not combusting fully, pumping unburnt particles out of the exhaust. With harsher emissions standards in the European Union, I think there is a noticeable difference. For the better.

My new best friend Wendy sold me a burger with a square beef patties. I had tried Wendy's once eleven years before, actually at the time when I was living in London where my book project was initiated.

Every fast food chain has a signature item that distinguishes them from their competitors. Wendy's is that they use square fresh beef patties which hasn't been frozen. The Wendy's experience is similar to McDonald's, the experience is of a varying quality from restaurant to restaurant. In April 2007, Wendy's launched a new sandwich, The Baconator. Two beef patties layered with cheese slices and bacon, Baconator is such a cool name and Wendy's trademarked it in 2008 and contributed to an increase in store sales of approximately 11%. I have not tried it yet, but it sounds too good to miss out on given the chance.

On foot in Boise, Idaho

Handing in the Monster for service at "Big Twin Motorcycles" on West Victory Rd in Boise, Ducati are notorious for being expensive to service. Having to get a big 6000 mile service done cost $980 as the desmodromic timing belts both have to be replaced as part of the service. The Monster S4 has eight valves, four per cylinder, and this part of the service also make up a big part of the high maintenance costs. You can't skip this as you don't want to void the factory warranty.

My real tire was completely worn down and the new replacement cost $170. Rubber rings for bikes are more expensive than car tires as a lot of research, development and technology goes into the production of these. Motorcycle tires have different rubber compounds in the middle than the sides. The center part usually has to have durability to last longer and have less wear than the sides. The tyre side walls have a softer compound for better grip when riding leaned over in the turns. With many different types of motorcycles such as cruisers, touring bikes, sport bikes, race and track bikes, there is a tyre for each purpose.

The Ducati Monster S4 is a detuned 916 Superbike, so fitting a sport or race tyre is the natural choice to fit. But I was doing long-distance riding, and sport-touring tires usually offer the best compromise for most riders. So that is what I replaced my rear tire with. Rear tires usually get worn down one to two times faster than the front tire. You don't want to ride with a worn front tire or with wrong tire pressure in this. As noted earlier, if the front end lose traction, you cat asphalt.

My jacket had annoyed me for a while. A cheap crappy bargain bin offer I managed to find a good waterproof black and red textile riding jacket with zippered vents and a removable inner thermal jacket for $290. So out with the old, in with the new.

Motorcycles are a hobby that can lead to you spending a lot of money you don't really take into consideration when starting out.

Just like boating or RV camping, they get you on the accessories.

I was not impressed with the "Big Twin Motorcycles" sales guy who seemed a bit grumpy. Looking around the shop they did have a showstopper, a Triumph Rocket III. This huge motorcycle was launched to the press in 2003 and has a 2,294 cc (140.0 cu in) three cylinder engine. The factory specification claims 163 pounds (221 Nm) of torque and 148 horsepower. This was the first time I saw one of these in real life, and standing next to it, I felt really small. With all that torque the Rocket III pulls so hard the rear wheel basically tries to overtake the front end.

A BMW RT 1150 Police motorcycle was parked outside. This had been in for service and was waiting to be picked up. That is one cop bike I would not try to outrun.

The service would take three to four hours so I had plenty of time to kill. So I decided to take a city-walk around Boise, the capital and the most populous city of Idaho. Around 210,000 of the states 1.7 million inhabitants lives there.

Heading towards downtown Boise, I stop by "Cutting Crew" on the way. Not having a haircut done in three months, the timing was excellent. With just one customer before me it is just a five minute wait for my turn. Fifteen minutes and fifteen bucks later I was on my way. Actually, this was only my fifth visit to a hairdresser since moving out of my parents' home. Once when studying for my graphic design degree, my mother thought I needed a haircut, two times were when I lived in London, and the fourth was while on holiday in Thailand. I own a machine cutter and have trimmed my own hair ever since I had an argument about a haircut by some numbskull who couldn't even do a simple crew cut. Thinking I could do that better myself; I have cut my own hair since 1994. With 25 years of practice, I think I am pretty good at it.

And maybe I just found the answer to why I never got married.

The weather was fine, not too hot. With clear skies, the sun was sharp on this day. Finding it pretty harsh on my face I go into a Walgreens pharmacy and buy some chapstick. A big difference between motorcycle touring in the USA compared to Europe is that your lips really dry out going through the open parts of the United States. Having heard a lot about the legendary snack, I got myself some Twinkies too.

On the way downtown I noticed a store displaying vintage Commodore 64 computers. Maybe some folks in Idaho are twenty years behind the rest of the world. I found it unbelievable that there would be a market for these twenty years after their heyday. I have owned a Commodore 64 and have fond memories of turning a small screwdriver to adjust the cassette tape drive. Today, Commodore 64 computers has become cult retro among nostalgics. Computer games has come a long way and those old games were probably closer to reading a comic, where video games today is getting near to motion picture quality.

Walking five miles to Ann Morrison Park, I checked out Main St., the 8th Street pedestrian zone and 9th St. which is the restaurant area.
The Idaho State Capitol is also located in Downtown Boise. This area appears to be a very caucasian dominated. Not sure what I wanted I end up getting a Frappuchino at Starbucks. Coffee has become a huge business and is a huge earner for self-service outlets a gas stations. I love a great cup of coffee, cold or hot. Nescafe Gold instant coffee is fine with me, also after it gets cold. And it is great with Thai food. I had a girlfriend who couldn't understand how I could sleep after drinking coffee shortly before going to sleep. And no, she wasn't that boring.

Returning to "Big Twin Motorcycles" my bike was ready and with a fresh rear tyre it felt sharp. The issue with the alarm wasn't solved as the main fuse blew once more when I activated the alarm system, I suspected the free wire coming off the alarm system was causing a short.

COMPUTER CENTER
COMMODORE
Quasar
PARKING
EITHER SIDE
Commodore
Computer Center
33

No fuel left for the pilgrims

Friday, August 20th 2004

After a full day in Boise I estimated that it would be just two days before I reached the west coast. Staying on Route 20 westbound, I rolled through more beautiful mountainous landscape. One oncoming driver got close to wiping me out making a hazardous overtaking maneuver. Again a matter of luck rather than skill. Making my first gas stop of the day 127 miles out of Boise, in Juntura, Oregon, the fuel economy seems to have improved after the service and adjustments. The tach reached 160 miles before the fuel warning light came on.

Once more, I found myself in an old cowboy movie, prairie desert as far as the eye could see. After a little more than two hours of riding, the tiny place of Brothers came up on the horizon. Seeing there was a gas station, I checked the trip meter. I had done 146 miles since my last fuel stop, so I decided to just wait and take the next gas station that came up.
In hindsight everyone gets wiser, but man did I forget about making any deep thinking about life after this. The fuel warning light came on 14 miles later as expected. The next little group of houses were a place called Millican which did not have a gas station. Well, they had one, but it had gone out business at what seemed like a very long time ago...

With two options, I could have turned around and filled up in Brothers. Mr. Brain had to choose the exciting option and continue west. As it was getting close to sunset, I had the most nerve-wrecking 20 miles of riding in the USA yet. Getting stuck in the Oregon desert without gas was not something I wanted to try. I could camp with no problem, but I would still be waking up in a desert with an empty gas tank. So it was with a sigh of relief I 25 minutes later turned the bike into the first gas station on the outskirts of Bend, Oregon. Of course there was an abundance of gas stations in Bend after refilling the tank.

Running completely out of gas has only happened to me once, when my Triumph started to cough and stutter at an intersection just across from a gas station. Crossing the intersection after the lights turned green, I ran completely out of fuel in the turn lane into the gas station, so pulling the clutch I could roll on to the pump with the very last engine cycles providing propulsion.

This was my first taste of true range anxiety and it sure takes the fun out of riding. The future of transport may be full of EVs (electric vehicles). But until there is an adequate amount of charging stations available, you will have to deal with range anxiety. I have test ridden a Brammo Impulse electric motorcycle, and I just love electric vehicles.

Just like the deep exhaust notes of a v-twin reaches your soul, zipping silently through traffic like a ninja is an amazing experience. Having had a ride in a Tesla S too, this is just as amazing as riding in a supercar. EVs can deliver the maximum torque from standstill and accelerate on level matching a muscle car or a race motorcycle. The market pioneer in electric motorcycles is Zero Motorcycles. Like Tesla, another California based company. I haven't had the chance to try a Zero Motorcycle yet but will jump at the first opportunity. Harley Davidson launched their first electric powered motorcycle, the Livewire, in 2019. With a claimed range of 140 miles (225 km) in city traffic and 88 miles (142 km) of combined stop-and-go and highway range, this is primarily useful for urban areas. Well, a lot of Harley Davidson owners are hauling their bikes on trailers to the motorcycle rallies anyway, so an electric Harley Davidson will get you some attention if you park it on Main St. during the Sturgis Rally.

At a starting price of thirty grand, there won't be a lot of people on a Livewire in Sturgis either. It'll most likely some hipster scum with too much money - or myself after winning the lottery.

Some cynics call playing the lottery a tax on the stupid. That is a bit of a harsh statement, playing the lottery is more like a tax on hope and irrationality.

But life sucks without hope.
And being stupid ain't free.

Not exactly sure where I wanted to go and just making a plan on the fly, I headed towards Crater Lake National Park going south out of Bend on Route 97. At Mount Thielsen I turned off at byroad 138 and turn in at the Broken Arrow Campground. A bargain at just $9, it did come with a lot of bugs as it sits right next to the south shore of Diamond Lake.

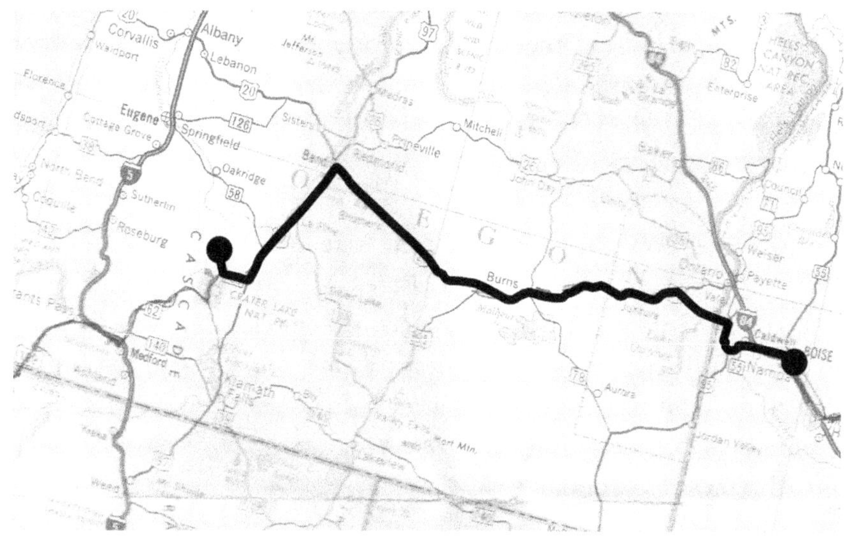

With 390 miles on the bike this day, I raised the tent without hammering any tent pegs into the ground. Discovering a metal splint in my brand new rear tyre was definitely not what I wanted to see. Fortunately, no puncture. Pulling the splinter out is always taking a chance. If the splinter has gotten too deep in you got a flat tyre without air inside. If not you can just ride on. Leaving the splint in, there is a high risk of a puncture later, but you might luck out and be able to ride on until the rubber layer is flush and wear the splint down. The latter is not recommended. I once picked up a two inch nail with my wheel. When I discovered it the head was ground down flush. Taking the chance I pulled it out and immediately ending up with a flat rear. Fortunately, it happened in my garage, so I wasn't stuck in the middle of nowhere. Modern sport touring tires are so solidly built that I actually have ridden three miles on a completely flat rear from a friend's house and back home. Not recommended, but possible if you go really slow.

The Ducati still blew the main fuse when activating the mounted alarm system, so I think had to be moisture causing an electrical short within this unit. So for now I had to leave the alarm system unarmed. Alarms have always been a source of problems for motorcycles. Today a lot of motorcycles have immobilizer chip systems built into the ignition and key, but anyone who really wants your motorcycle can get it. An alarm system just deters the casual amateurs who hasn't understood the meaning to "no touchy", the pros don't give a fuck and will come prepared and haul of your bike into a van. Criminals are the most creative people you'll ever meet, the ideas and methods they'll use to get money or valuables are infinite and never ceases to surprise.

At the Broken Arrow Campground there were some other bikers. They are from Seattle and members of Border Riders MC. They did seem to prefer not talking to others. The Border Riders Motorcycle Club were founded in 1969. The members are mostly from Washington, Oregon, and British Columbia. Finishing the day with a cold Miller Lite, I realize that "Lite" beer in the USA means low calorie content, whereas in Denmark "Light" beer this means low or non-alcoholic contents.

My first thought of Border Riders MC was that they were a 1%er club, preferring to keep to themselves. Doing a little research later, I learned that the Border Riders is the largest and one of the oldest gay motorcycle clubs in North America. At the time I had no clue. My attitude toward gay men was like today, and I don't swing that way. I would think their club parties are a bit different than what I had seen in Sturgis.

Coast to coast

Packing up the next day, I left Broken Arrow Campground to experience Crater Lake. Internationally, this is one of the lesser known National Parks in the USA.

Crater Lake National Park is a crater lake in south-central Oregon. The lake partly fills a caldera, nearly 2,148 feet (655 m) deep. Formed around 7,700 years ago by the collapse of the volcano Mount Mazama after a massive volcanic eruption. It features two small islands. Wizard Island, a cinder cone and Phantom Ship, a natural rock pillar.
There are no rivers or other inlets flowing into or out of the lake, so evaporation is compensated for by rain and snowfall. 1,949 feet deep (594 m), Crater Lake is the deepest in the United States. It looks absolutely stunning, the water clarity looking almost flawless with its deep blue color, so I decide to make a ride around the 21.8 mile (35.1 km) shoreline. Meeting several small groups of Border Riders MC cruising on their bikes, the speed limit is 35 mph around the lake, these guys were going 30. I didn't know anything about the Borders Riders MC at the time, but their riding style sure was pretty gay. Later I met a group of ten Chevrolet Corvettes, dang a cool sight.

Oops, I did it again. Forgetting to fill the gas tank before entering Crater Lake NP, I got very close to running the tank level down to empty. The trip meter hit 177 miles before I found a fuel pump in Prospect, 25 miles south on Route 62. This shouldn't become a habit. A little further south I entered Interstate 5 heading towards highway 101/199. After 155 miles and three hours I was in Crescent City, CA.

The weather was mix of cold, moist and hazy, and my lips had dried out. But at this point all that doesn't matter. Passing through the city I reach the west shore, sticking my hands into the water of the Pacific Ocean.

MY OLD DREAM OF RIDING COAST TO COAST IN THE USA HAD BEEN FULFILLED!

Talking to a guy called Everett, he helped by taking a few photos to capture this monumental moment of my life. Another one crossed off the bucket list! A bucket list is a number of experiences or achievements that a person hopes to have or accomplish during their lifetime before the Grim Reaper comes to call. Death is the one thing we all need to face. Especially embraced in biker culture, it is better to burn out than fade away. "The other side" of life. The end of the road where no u-turn is possible.

You got only one guaranteed attempt at life. But what then?
The earthly remains are buried in the ground and the person is gone.
While we can't change that, I do think you can have a life after death.
Once you've bit the dust you can't do shit.
But as long as your actions and person is remembered,
you live on in memory.

One of the worst consequences with death is the sorrow over the loss of
someone dear. That has to come with an acceptance of an end.
Having said farewell to more than one pet dog.
I find it easy to put feelings aside after a short period of mourning,
accepting that life must end.

Death can happen in many ways.
One of the most known is the light at the end of the tunnel.
I guess we'll see what happens when I am out of time.
The most important for me is if the leap to the other side will be painful.
I am hoping to go in my sleep, "dead, fed up of days",
simply forgetting to wake up.

Death is far from negative. A confirmation of time.
It is the Yin to the Yang that is life.
Death gives every day of your life value.
If you could live forever the world would be a worse place than now,
and we would float in an eternal state of indifference.
Value the time you have been given and get yourself a bucket list.

Highway 199 goes through forests and mountains to California Highway 101. Half an hour south I reached Redwood National State Park (RNSP). This is actually a complex of four state and national parks along the coast of northern California, Redwood National Park and Del Norte Coast, Jedediah Smith and Prairie Creek Redwoods State Parks. The combined RNSP contain 139,000 acres (560 km2).

Located entirely within Del Norte and Humboldt Counties, the four parks together protect 45% of all remaining coastal redwood. These are the tallest and one of the most massive tree species on Earth. *Sequoia sempervirens* is also known as coast redwood, coastal redwood and California redwood. It is an evergreen, long-lived, monoecious tree with a lifespan of 1200 to 1800 years or more and includes some of the tallest living trees on Earth, reaching up to 379 feet (115.5 m) in height and up to 29.2 feet (8.9 m) in diameter at breast height. Redwood trees are also among the oldest living things on Earth.

Before commercial logging and clearing began in the 1850s, these massive trees were spread out over an estimated 2,100,000 acres (850,000 hectares) along the southwestern corner of coastal Oregon and much of the coastal north of California. With preservation efforts, the Redwood National and State Parks became a United Nations designated World Heritage Site in 1980. In addition to the Sequoia forests, the parks preserve other indigenous flora and fauna, including 37 miles (60 km) of coastline and a rich variety of wildlife.

Making a stop here to see these fantastic forests is a must if you are in the area. The park has served as a filming location for numerous films. Tall Trees Redwood Grove in the northern part of Humboldt County was the set for the scenes on the forest moon Endor in *Star Wars episode VI: Return of the Jedi*. One attraction they didn't mention was a young lady with pigtails, the cutest park ranger I have ever seen.

Even though my travels had accumulated some big expenses, an experience like this unique part of the USA made it worth it.

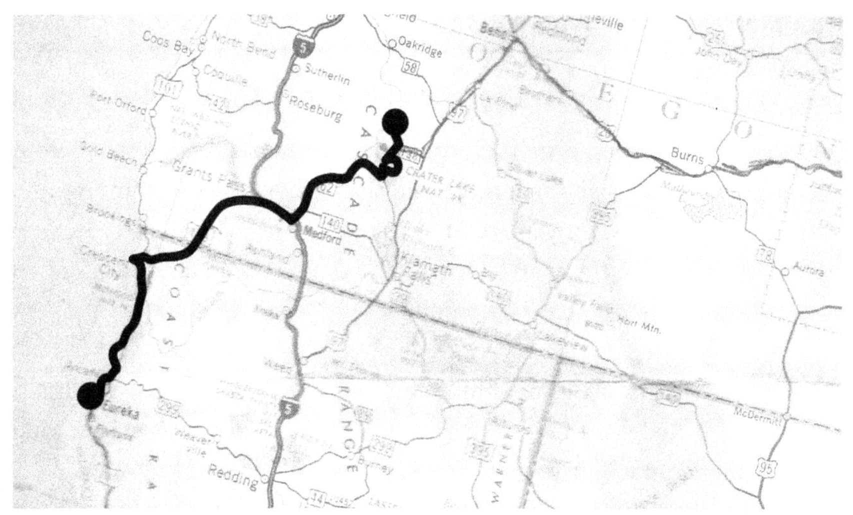

Another 50 miles south I decided to check in at Econolodge for $87. This was run by another Indian family. Having driven through moist and foggy conditions earlier, I really needed a hot bath. California does seem a fair bit more expensive and talking to a guy traveling with his family, he told me that a rodeo was in town so motel prices were jacked up.

Some people do make a lasting impression. Having what seemed like a lightly disfigured face, I thought this guy had been injured serving in the armed forces. Wife looked pretty nice, but I don't think she appreciated me eyeballing her.

Some latino kids in the area were being pretty noisy, and it somehow felt a bit unsafe and creepy. So I made sure to chain the bike to a rail.

Eating dinner I noticed that I had begun to add side orders again.

Sunday, August 22nd 2004

The weather was still moist and crappy when I rode out of Eureka. Before passing the city limits I saw a motel offering a room for $67. Finding the best price is tricky, when you are tired you just want to crash into the first option you find. With smartphones, it has since become a lot easier to scope out the best accommodation offers.

Riding down highway 101 is fun, four lanes becomes a twisty mountain road through Redwood Highway. Turning off at Leggett. I wanted to ride through the famous "Drive thru three".
The Chandelier Tree in Drive-Thru Tree Park is a 276-foot (84 m) tall coast redwood tree with a 6 foot (1.8 m) wide by 6 foot 9 in (2.06 m) height hole cut through its base to allow a vehicle to drive through. The base measures 16 feet (4.9 m) diameter at breast height. The Chandelier Tree is around 315 feet high and 21 feet wide. It is estimated to be up to 2,400 years old. The name comes from its unique limbs that resemble a chandelier. The carving is believed to have been done in the early 1930s by one Charlie Underwood. That name does sound like a bit of a pun.

There is a few "drive through" trees in the USA. Carving big holes into the base is not healthy for a tree. Another drive through tree was the "Pioneer Cabin Tree," a sequoia in Calaveras Big Trees State Park. This collapsed in January 2017 as what might be the biggest winter storm to hit the region in more than a decade slammed into California and Nevada. Drive-Thru Tree Park in Leggett is an absolute tourist trap, but who cares. Some things are once in a lifetime so the $2 charge was fine with me. Another visitor was kind enough to help take a couple of pictures. So yeah, been there, done that. With less than a handful of trees that offers this experience you might want to check this out if you get the opportunity.
The Forest protection and World Heritage Site designation will probably prohibit anyone else carving into the existing trees.

And waiting 2400 years to grow your own tree is not really an option.

OPENING IS
6' WIDE
6' 9" HIGH

Forty-five miles down route 101 I went a right on highway 20 towards Fort Bragg. Here I took a left and found myself on the legendary California Highway One. After 18 miles I failed to turn right and ended up on route 128. Not a bad error, this is a nice 55 mile winding road with some sweet curves. So in Cloverdale I am back on route 101 where I got myself stuck in a traffic jam for an hour while going through Santa Rosa, Peta Luma and Novato. I did figure out to place my feet on the crash pegs I fitted on the bike. This is ok at low speeds but incredibly stupid and dangerous if going beyond 30 mph.

After 82 miles I reached the Golden Gate bridge at around 5 pm.

When opened in 1937 after more than four years construction time, it remained the longest bridge in the world until 1964. The main span is 4,200 feet (1280 m) and the total height 746 feet (227 m). The Golden Gate is so iconic for San Francisco that riding across its one mile span at the 45 mph speed limit was a letdown and a pretty tame experience. The most exciting part was not being prepared for paying the road toll. With a cost of more than $35 million when constructed, it would cost more than half a billion today. Maintenance isn't free so it costs a fee to cross it. This varies with the amount of traffic, so congestion affects this. I didn't have $5 ready at the south end, so the woman in the toll booth told me that I would be let off with a yellow slip with a warning citation as it was my first time crossing. I think they want to avoid big discussions with people crossing as this immediately would turn the bridge toll booth bottleneck into a traffic jam. Fumbling around I remembered where I had stashed my wallet, handed the citation back and paid with minimal delay. Toll booths are a pain in the ass when you are on a motorcycle as you wear gloves and your wallet is in a pocket.

The Golden Gate Bridge is the second-most used bridge used to commit suicide in the world. The deck is about 245 feet (75 m) above the water.

After a fall of four seconds, jumpers hit the water at around 75 mph (120 km/h). Most suicide jumpers die from impact trauma. About 5% of the jumpers survive the initial impact but then drown or die of hypothermia in the cold water. The only upside is that it won't hurt until you hit the water surface. With an estimated 1500 deaths, installation of suicide barriers began in 2017.

The thought of suicide has probably crossed most people's mind in times of adversity. My family has experienced suicide and I can tell you it is horrible for the people left behind. I am too stingy to throw away my only shot at life. If you have not found values in life or you can't find any, it is understandable that the thought look appealing. Therefore, it is important to be conscious and avoid letting feelings of indifference take over.

I got a curc for that. Being a smart ass 18-year old me, I had to try bungy jumping. Leaping off a platform 196 feet (60 meters) up, I got scared as fuck screaming my fear out until I could start feeling the bungy cord stretching to stop me smacking down into the concrete below. What happened is that I met myself and learned I wasn't ready to die.

So if you ever think of ending it all, go bungy jumping first.

Don't kill yourself.
For those left behind,
the pain remain.

Just across the bridge I took the first exit and ended up in the Presidio. This is an old military fort established by Spanish colonists in 1776. This was handed over to the National Park Service in 1994. All I knew about this place was that "The Presidio" was the title of and old not very memorable Sean Connery movie. Not being prepared I did manage to become lost and confused trying to find a road out of the area. ending up on the western shoreline I got the chance to take some pictures of the Golden Gate bridge at sunset.

Aloun told me his brother Vila lived in Oakland and that I should give him a call while I was there, as I could probably stay at his place. Well, while it was super nice of Aloun, I thought that would be a bit too intrusive as I never had met Vila before. I did meet him a few years later. Like his brother, a really cool and friendly guy.
Oakland is a bit of risky place, with an overall crime rate in Oakland 165% higher than the national average. For every 100,000 people, there are 19.95 daily crimes that occur in Oakland. So I was pretty content not having to go there after dark.

Instead, I decided to find a motel not too far from Downtown SF.

The Geary Parkway Motel was $75 a night, a tram ride away from downtown and had parking facilities where I could park my motorcycle out of sight. In my room I found that the TV picture is blurred and the colors distorted. Complaining about this at the reception the Indian guy just looked back at me as if I was stupid. What an arrogant shithead.
I ended up getting a new room after insisting on a fix or a discount.

Being happy with my first visit to Jack in the Box, I went for a "Diner Melt Combo". Crunchy coco shake, fries and a beef'n cheese toast sandwich, not as good as my first impression. For dessert, I decided to buy some beer at State Market minimart across the street. The Chinese lady owner didn't want to see ID as Asians knows Asians.

Monday, August 23rd 2004

Before walking towards downtown I checked the lock and chained the bike to a pillar at the motel. Getting a ride on one of the city's famous cable cars is also one of those things you must do. An icon of San Francisco, the cable car system is the last manually operated of its kind in the world. A local character had a conversation with the cable car operator. Talking about restaurants closing just a few months after opening, this guy seemed like a loud mafia type smart-ass. Well, smart mobsters are discreet, so maybe not.

Every larger metropolitan city has a Chinatown, but I had never seen a Japantown before. Having Japan on my travel itinerary, I had recently tried sushi for the first time. Since the restaurants weren't open at the time of day anyway, I just took a look at the characteristic architecture. The internment of Japanese Americans into camps during World War II has probably not helped the assimilation among immigrants of Japanese descent, so sticking together as a group would be a logic consequence.

Pier 39, with its 110 specialty shops and 10 restaurants, has over ten million visitors a year. One big tourist trap, but a nice place if you like a festive marketplace. Next to the market is the West Marina. Here a big group of California sea lions are chillin' in the sun. What they don't advertise is the smell these fat mammals have. You may want to think about whether or not to eat before checking out the sea lions.

Like in Chicago, I get a seat on a guided bay cruise. For $20 I went for "Golden Gate Tours". Sailing under the Golden Gate with its "international orange" color, the Presidio, the Palace of Fine Arts, and Fort Point can be viewed to the south and Lime point on the north side. The weather was a bit hazy so the photo op conditions weren't optimal this day. As previously noted, I recommend boat rides in order to see the most in the shortest time possible. The unobstructed views from the waterside are better and you get much closer to the 22-acre rocky island in the middle of the bay that houses Alcatraz, the prison famous for detaining inmates as Al "Scarface" Capone and "Machine Gun" Kelly. In the 29 years this was used as a federal prison, no successful escapes were registered.

Four prisoners are unaccounted for, they are believed to have drowned attempting to escape. Alcatraz is also known as "The Rock". Which is the location of another movie starring Sean Connery…

The boat ride offered a nice view of the San Francisco skyline as the weather cleared up on the way back to the pier. San Francisco is a diverse place and I did notice a lot of ethnically mixed couples. On foot I wanted to get some of the single use cameras developed, $25 seemed a bit steep, but I wasn't sure what this was supposed to cost. I can recommend getting your images transferred to CD-ROM, having to scan these later was an absolute pain in the ass. Waiting for the photos to be developed and printed, I decided to check out Chinatown which is cantered around Grant Avenue and Stockton Street. Besides being the "original" Chinatown, it is the oldest in North America and also the largest Chinese enclave outside Asia. San Francisco actually has three other Chinatowns, the others are located on Clement St, Irving St and Noriega St. Walking through, I spot ted the Transamerica Pyramid skyscraper in the financial district. Plus a video store selling the new home video starring Paris Hilton.

And a bus on fire. No joke, the rear end had gone up in flames.

In the area near the cable car stop I got eye contact with a pretty girl sitting up against a rail fence. Smiling at me, I was not sure what her situation was, but I had a notion that she was unemployed, homeless or both. So I regret walking past without talking to her. Being unemployed isn't much fun, I have tried this numerous times myself. It is an unpleasant social ailment that just won't go away. It's just there. And no one is immune. Get in a traffic accident and your career can end faster than a snap of your fingers. Like STDs, a lot of people convince and delude themselves into thinking it can't happen to them. I have had this optimistic attitude, until reality struck first. Fearful of the future I felt depressed.

I found myself entered in a public social security program designed to "scare" people into working, as if the unemployed don't want to work. I became a social burden on society. So I opted out. Saved whatever money I could and got a job doing housekeeping in a London hotel for $4 an hour. While possible for a limited period, but then you have to move on. Whining doesn't make your problems go away and it clouds the horizon to

where you can find actual solutions. So I found some new goals.
Travel while young. Started writing this book. Get a motorcycle.
Take control and initiative. Dead fish flow with the stream.

Unemployment can strike anyone. Not at least the young.
It is obvious that one will need qualifications and experience,
otherwise, you will be much less likely to get far.
Complacency is bad for you. Personal values should not be
forgotten and being without a job you got time to work with these.
If you are on social security it is easy to adapt to not working.
To be unemployed wears you down mentally, so most people don't create
anything and don't get wiser or smarter on welfare.
I believe everyone deserve the chance to work their way up in life.

The difference of an unemployed and a lazy person is often
not visible. But it is clearly there.
A lot of people affected by unemployment often feel powerless
and give up. I do not want to defend this position
but do understand the reasons why some give up.
It's neither fun or eazy to be without a job.
To some degree there is always something you can do.
Stick to a schedule and stay active. Get inspired, collect
information about your options and alternative options
to being unemployed. You can't expect that the state,
county or others carries your ass. That is up to you.
Nothing is for free and there is no guarantee.

Back at the motel I bought some more beer from State Market across the
street. The little sweet Chinese lady looked happy to have my business.
I did get riled up as those lazy Indians running the motel had only made
the bed. The bathroom had not been cleaned and the towels were dirty.
If it wasn't for their location they would be out of business.
Before going to bed I watched the news, two couples camping was found
murdered, shot dead in a remote area in Arizona. This seemed as nothing
out of the ordinary by the anchorwoman. So I wasn't going to be doing any
camping in Arizona outside designated campgrounds.

Tuesday, August 24th 2004

The Geary Parkway Motel got a farewell gift as I decided to drop the towels on the floor and piss on everything that wasn't the bowl. Having worked as a hotel room cleaner in London 11 years earlier, I knew the guy with the attitude in the reception wouldn't appreciate it. Besides the ability to operate a clutch operated manual transmission vehicle, revenge is the only thing that make humans different from other animals.

Going on Geary St. to 47th, I wanted to experience the city hills of San Francisco on my motorcycle. Made famous by Steve McQueen racing his Ford Mustang in *Bullitt,* these are so steep the local laws demand that you park with the wheels turned toward the curb so your vehicle won't roll into traffic. I think electric bicycles is a big hit if you decide to live in San Francisco, those hills are steep. Not aware about this at the time, I did miss out on going down Lombard Street with its 27-degree incline. This unique street features landscaped flowerbeds and eight hairpin turns.

Out of the city, I took Route 35 southbound until I made a detour on Skyline Boulevard. This is Route 92 and it offered some fun curved tarmac towards the California Route 1, also known as the legendary Pacific Coast Highway. I followed this for 52 miles until reaching Santa Cruz. Eating some lunch at Burger King, I couldn't help noting that the guys there is the hardest working staff I have ever seen in a fast food outlet. Teamwork, speed and courtesy coming together perfectly. Respect.

Twenty miles after Santa Cruz the day ride went all to hell, I basically got lost again and again trying to reach Yosemite National Park. Riding through Watsonville I missed turning left to Highway 152 and take 156 onto 101. Looking at the sun's position on the sky and checking the time on the clock on my dashboard, I realized that I was facing south. Using the sun is actually the way I have used to navigate a lot, but in California you want to get a GPS. So I made a u-turn and end up driving in circles in and around Aromas, ending up back on 101 eastbound towards Hollister.

I thought perhaps I should make a stop and see the town that was the scene of the famous biker inci-dent. But having wasted an hour pulling out my Road Atlas every ten minutes I decided to give this a miss and find Highway 156 and 99 to Merced 96 miles away.

On the way to Merced I made a stop at "Auto Save" in Los Banos to fill the beast and buy some spare fuses as I had fried the two 30 amp mains bought way back in Indiana. Another customer told me he likes the bike and looking and my touring gear on the back he couldn't help but ask how far I have ridden. Just to get a reaction I point to the license plate. "Whoa, you are far away from home". Auto Save in Los Banos is probably able to save you if your vehicle is broken down and need fuses, they can't help you save money as the fuses are so pricey that I only bought two.

In Merced I missed the intersection ramp to Highway 140. Going around in an arch I ended up on a road I believe is Highway 140. Lucky me, finally catching a break from this horrible day of going in circles. Finding this road to Yosemite was worth the hassle, the ride through Sierra National Forest is absolutely beautiful.

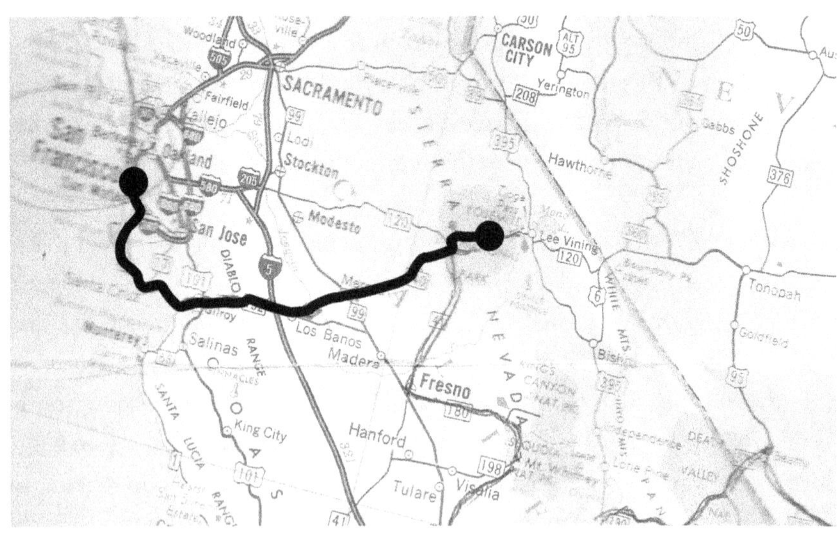

Yosemite National Park is located 180 miles east of San Francisco.

Riding down to Santa Cruz on Highway 1 was part of the plan for the day but tooling around in Aromas had the trip meter running up to 275 miles. Arriving just before sunset, I talked to one of the Park Rangers. Once again I got some value out of my National Parks Pass, as this allowed me free entry. I got the impression that the Park Ranger on duty really loved his job, which is neat as I have heard their paychecks are pretty low.

Following the instructions given, I passed El Capitan on the three mile ride to the campground. Everyone with a 2008-2016 Macintosh computer will most likely know El Capitan in Yosemite National Park, as Apple Inc. decided to use the name for version 10.11 of their operating system. El Capitan is huge monolith with a vertical side composed almost entirely of a pale, coarse-grained granite. It is approximately 100 million years old. The height is around 3,000 feet (900 m) from base to summit along the tallest face, so it is popular among rock climbers.

I managed to find Camp 4 without any issue. This is a walk-in camping for visitors without a reservation. About four million people visit Yosemite each year, making reservations prior to arrival is a good idea. The charge for my tent is a measly $5.

Going to National Parks is a great opportunity for a crash course in the German language. There was a lot of German tourists in Yosemite, many of them are into hiking, for which Yosemite offers plenty of trails. Having had my last German lesson twelve years earlier, I was a bit rusty. But the father and his grown-up son whom I talked with were a bit surprised as I don't look particularly German.

Taking a quick stroll around the campground, some young noisy American guy received a $350 fine. Not sure what had transpired, it seemed like he had been smoking pot, which was illegal in California at the time. Weed is a problem that needs to be tackled at the root level (pun intended). Previously, I had a less hostile attitude to weed and it is not hard for me to understand the joy people find in using it. To me, stoners have a tendency to have a harder time learning, while procrastinating setting goals and achieving these. Weed just act as a brake on your life, a brake that easily can lock up and send you tumbling into a ditch.

Besides weed, I am not keen on tobacco either. Dried plant leaves rolled in paper. Ignite one end and you got smoke to choke on, not the healthiest pleasure around. I am well aware of the addictiveness of tobacco but lack understanding of the reasons to start smoking. Community? Wrong role models and idols? A mix of both?

Growing up with my father smoking, I have been breathing second hand smoke for twenty years. I of course tried smoking as a teen. Tobacco taste like crap. And smells like crap.

Well, people can smoke all they want as long as I don't have to inhale it, or end up smelling like an ashtray.

My first impression of Yosemite is that it is way more beautiful than Yellowstone. But my with my late arrival, I had to set up for the night in darkness. Having camped out quite a bit more than I had been before, I was getting pretty good at quickly whipping up my tent.

My 2004 National Parks Pass

Wednesday, August 25th 2004

Arriving a bit later than expected, I didn't see much of Yosemite National Park on Tuesday. Campground 4 is a 12 minute walk from Yosemite Village where the visitors center post office, tourist shop and lodging service are located. Here I found and picked out where I want to go. Packing up the Monster, I took the 32 mile ride to the northeast entrance and back, making a few breaks to take in the sights.

Yosemite was originally the name of a Native American tribe which was driven out of the area after 1851, to no surprise this was a consequence of the California gold rush. Just like in Richmond, Virginia and the Black Hills in South Dakota, American history has some dark moments that should not be forgotten, lest they will be repeated.

War and conflict is a constant here and there, people getting tormented and tortured. I often ask myself why the world hasn't improved with the technological progress and advancement.
Whatever the means there are people not subscribing to the idea of living peacefully alongside each other. Things have always been, and they seem to stay like this. Understandable when thinking about yourself as the first priority. What can you do?
You just go along but do not make a difference.
The rest of the World may be as rotten as usual
but starting with yourself is the first step on a new path.
Is there more to this? I can't answer for you but only for myself,
I do try to follow the ideal of constant self improvement. At the same time I feel it is a waste of time if I care too much about others.
I am aware that thinking this way isn't optimal.
I will not apologize for this but do regret my errors.
I can be very egoistic and conservative.

To this I will add that my expectations of others aren't high.
The world does not become a better place this way, but he core message is that I strive to avoid being selfish at the expense of others, making the

Opened in 1890, Yosemite covers an area of 1,168.7 square miles (3026 km2) in the western Sierra Nevada mountains and is famous for its high concentration of waterfalls in a small area. Featuring granite cliffs, clear streams, giant sequoia groves, lakes, mountains, meadows, glaciers and a rich biological diversity, Yosemite was designated a World Heritage site in 1994.

Glacier Point was my second stop. It is located 31 miles from Yosemite Village in the center of the National Park. The drive from Yosemite Valley up to Glacier Point takes little over an hour. Glacier Point sits at an elevation of 7,214 feet (2199 m). If you want to hike to Glacier Point this can be done on a trail from Half Dome Village. Glacier Point offers a superb view of several of Yosemite National Park's landmarks, including Yosemite Valley, Yosemite Falls, Half Dome, Vernal Fall, Nevada Fall and Clouds Rest. This day the weather was sunny and clear so all I can say is "wow".

Characteristic for Yosemite is the deep and narrow canyons. These started to form 10 million years ago, when the Sierra Nevada was up-lifted and then tilted to form gentle western slopes and the more dramatic eastern slopes. This uplift increased the steepness of stream and riverbeds. Around one million years ago, accumulation of snow and ice formed glaciers at the higher alpine meadows that moved down the river valleys.
I know I am spending too little time at some of the National Parks, as they have so much to offer besides the spectacular vistas, such as hiking, fishing, river rafting and climbing. Yosemite is home to 300 to 500 black bears. But primarily riding through, I didn't spot any of these. So I would definitely like to take another trip to Yosemite, it is truly special.

Heading out through the south exit, I encountered some more Redwood trees. Southbound on Route 41, I pass through Sierra Forrest. This is a fun twisting road, but it only offers a few viewpoints.

Getting into what must be my tenth close call on this journey, I narrowly missed wiping out as I hit a gooey lump of roadkill. In Fresno, fifty miles south I missed turning left onto Route 180 towards Kings Canyon. Realizing my error, I turned around at the first off ramp. Due to road work I ended up seven miles north of Route 180. Here I found the most amazing dome shaped hills and beautiful sunset. This is the one view I wish I had taken a picture of at the time, along with a later incident in Las Vegas. Eventually I found my way back onto Route 180 and head to Kings Canyon National Park. At this point my National Parks Pass must be saving me money as showing this at the entrance, entry was once again free.

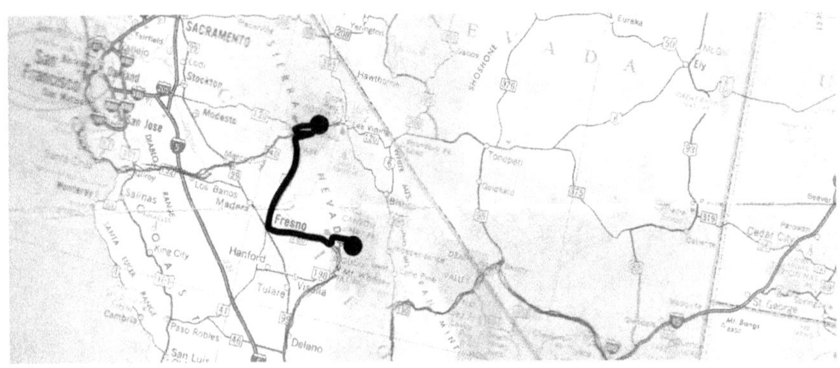

Camping at the Sunset Campground cost $18. I got to practice the fine art of pitching a tent in the dark and again I bumped into a shitload of Germans. They are very talkative, and once again my German skills is a great icebreaker. Even though you get far with English, learning other languages is a great tool when traveling. I also talked to a couple from California, a retired teacher and a real estate agent, traveling in an RV. They found my trip amazing, but they wouldn't swap their RV for a tent. Well, the price of an RV is much higher than buying a motorcycle. And a $30 tent…

Kings Canyon and Sequoia National Park

Thursday, August 26th 2004

For some unknown reason I woke up at 10:30, a lot later than usual. I guess some riding days are just more exhausting than you realize. While I was sleeping a park ranger had put a note on my motorcycle, just letting me know he had been inspecting the campground.

Kings Canyon is a rugged valley carved through time by glaciers drained by the Kings River over the last 2.5 million years. Kings Canyon is more than one mile (1,600 m) deep. The western section is centered on Grant Grove where most of the visitor facilities are located. Grant Grove is also home of many of the park's sequoias. I think the terrain provides some nice protective conditions for these big threes. The larger eastern section accounts for the majority of the park's area and is almost entirely wilderness. Less than 1.5 miles from the campground in Grant Grove is the General Grant three. This is the second largest tree in the world, second only to the General Sherman three. General Grant three is a giant sequoia (*Sequoiadendron giganteum*) which is estimated to be around 1,650 years old and it is 267.4 feet (81.5 m) tall and has a diameter of 28.9 feet (8.8 m) at chest level. It is named after Union army general and 18th president, Ulysses S. Grant.

King Canyon NP and Sequoia NP are contiguous located next to each other. The entry fee was covered by my National Park Pass. If you don't have such a pass, the entrance fee covers both King Canyon NP and Sequoia NP. The road from General Grant three to the General Sherman three in Sequoia NP is a 29.3 mile ride down Generals Highway 198. Sequoia National Park was established in 1890 to protect 631 square miles (1,635 km2) of forested mountainous terrain. Mount Whitney, the highest mountain in the contiguous United States, is located here. It stands 14,505 feet (4421 m) above sea level.

General Sherman three is named after the American Civil War general William Tecumseh Sherman. Like General Grant three, this is also a giant sequoia. The height is 274.9 feet (83.8 m) and the diameter is 25.1 feet (7,7 m) at chest level, and the estimated age is between 2,300 to 2,700 years. General Sherman Three is not the tallest, widest or oldest three in the world, but measured by wood volume it comes out as the biggest single stem three in the world. At this time there weren't a lot of other tourists present, but I did get a family guy to take a picture of me in from of this massive three. And of course I offered to help them get some shots for their photo album too.

The 24 mile stretch of road from General Sherman three to the Sequoia National Park south entrance in Three Rivers is so twisty that the speed limit is just 25 mph. A fun piece of asphalt, but some of the RVs just go incredibly slow. After 60 miles, I reached highway 99 to Bakersfield, my ass was pretty sore from averaging just 20 mph for one and a half hour. Damn RVs are so big you can't pass them. The last time I went this slow was in Italy going through the Dolomites, 18 miles in one hour because of tourist traffic. The locals are easy to spot, while on my 600 cc Ducati, I couldn't keep up with some kid on a 125 cc on an open bit of mountain road.

To make up for time spent in a slow caravan of RVs, I got on Interstate 5 through the Tejon Mountains at high speed. No need to get too much police attention so I didn't go more than 5-10 mph over the legal speed limit. The traffic was getting denser the closer I got to Los Angeles. I am happy that I decided to keep a little distance, a customized metallic-orange Nissan pickup truck driving in front of me had a tire blowout with dust and tire debris flying right in my face. Had I not been wearing a helmet and keeping my distance I am sure my trip could have ended right at this point.

Some idiots spend a lot of money individualizing their vehicles with cool paint jobs and chrome but end up without being able to afford some decent tires.

GENERAL SHERMAN

This reminds me of my buddy who had a side gig doing car repairs. I have noticed the customers with the nicest shoes often had a problem paying as agreed, and the customers with the nicest cars, such as BMWs, couldn't afford new tires and basically drove on slicks.

Narrowly surviving a blast of flying shrapnel, I met a Harley enthusiast from Maine at the next gas station. Hauling a huge black and orange trailer with a 100th anniversary Road King, he was touring the USA for two months like me. He had three weeks left of his trip. What made him a bit unusual was the fact that he was deaf but still able to communicate on a level as if he didn't need the ability to hear. I guess he wasn't in the market for a set of loud pipes. A lot of motorcyclists use earplugs while riding, this include myself. If you fuck up your hearing, it is permanent.

At the gas station I bought a bottle of A&W "Vanilla Cream" soda, another treat I decided to try for the first time.

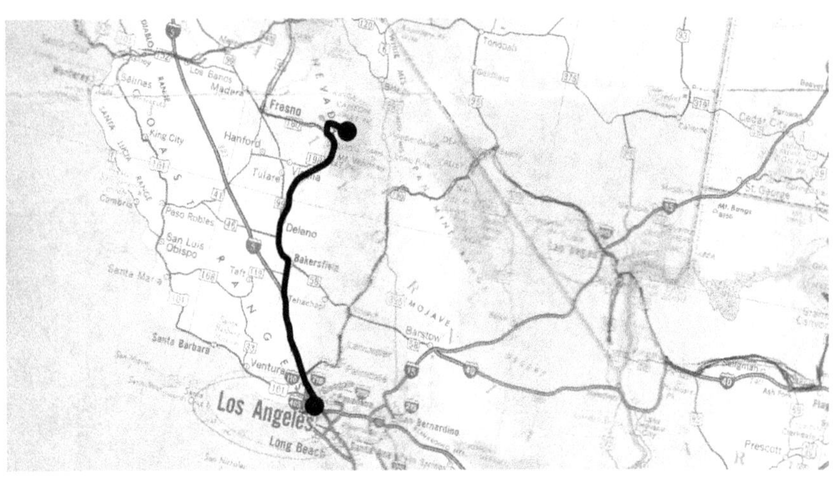

Taking the I-5 off ramp to Glendale, I got lost for gawd knows which time. Ending up on Hollywood Boulevard at 6:45 pm, I checked in at Motel Hollywood Inn Express for the very fair price of $55. The toilet wouldn't flush but I managed to fix this issue myself.
Throwing my gear into the room, I could finally put my feet up after 260 miles in the saddle and pop open the A&W Vanilla Cream soda. Yuck.

Friday, August 27th 2004

Even though the Indian reception guy at the motel didn't recommend it, I took the bike to see the world famous Mann's Chinese Theater. It was just 2.2 miles west on Hollywood Boulevard, the same road as the motel, so I guess he thought I was going to walk there.

Seeing Mann's Chinese Theatre is a must when you are in LA, being a home theatre enthusiast I wasn't going to miss this. The movie playing at the time was Anacondas, the sequel to the movie that ruined Ice Cube's street cred. Ice Cube did star in a biker movie called Torque launched earlier in 2004. With a lame plot, a trait for most biker movies, it is an iffy CGI fest with Jaime Pressly providing some much needed cleavage. Both Ice Cube and Jaime Pressly are pretty good actors, but some of the roles they have played has been less than stellar.

The Hollywood Boulevard sidewalk is a classic tourist trap with celebrity impersonators trying to make a living and I made sure to watch my pockets. Looking pretty scruffy in my weathered boots I might have looked like a homeless person, none of these hustlers approached me.

In front of Mann's Chinese Theater some iconic hand- and footprints has been cast in concrete. So you can compare digit size with Harrison Ford, Sean Connery, Eddie Murphy and Sylvester Stallone there. Even R2-D2 and C3PO, the two gay robots from Star Wars, had dipped their feet on a slab too. As mentioned I am a bit of a germaphobe, so I wasn't going to do that.

Fifteen blocks of Hollywood Boulevard and three blocks of Vine Street is where you find the Hollywood Walk of Fame. It includes more than 2,600 five-pointed terrazzo stars with brass inserts embedded in the sidewalks. Just checking out who had a star in close proximity of Mann's Chinese Theater, I found the stars of Hollywood legends Bruce Lee and Jack Nicholson. I never wanted to become an actor or singer myself. Can't act. Can't sing.

On my bike it is easy to get around and all the interesting places are actually pretty closely located. Just riding around taking in the city from the bike, I ended up on Sunset Boulevard, legendary for the 80's hard rock music scene. On Sunset Boulevard I parked my bike in a booth with a parking meter next to a guy selling "Maps to the stars homes" at Sierra Drive. The classic Eddie Murphy comedy Beverly Hills Cop 2 made the brown Beverly Hills sign famous, so I had to get a photo of one of those. The map vendor calls for my attention as within minutes, a parking control inspector had rolled up and was taking a long close-up look at my bikes temp tag. As I had put money in the meter and parked within the booth lines there shouldn't be any problem.

Most jurisdictions have a long string of rules about how motorcycles must be parked in parallel and angle parking bays. In parallel bays, most statutes stipulate that bikes must be parked at 45 degrees to the curb. While only the most fascist parking inspector or police would ever fine you for such a tiny offense, it happens. The reason 45 degrees is stipulated is so that it makes the bike visible to passing traffic but it doesn't stick out too far into the road. Not wanting any discussion, the parking inspector leaves when I come towards him. Private parking and towing companies are in my book mafia scam artists who deserve to die screaming.

The stars' homes are properties with tall fences and hedges, so going around the residential area of Beverly Hills was pretty pointless.

Known around the world from Julia Roberts breakthrough movie *Pretty Woman*, the shopping street of the rich and famous is Rodeo Drive. Many of the top luxury brands as Cartier, Prada, Ralph Lauren and Bang & Olufsen had a flagship store here. Ducati is considered a premium motorcycle brand and I spotted a fellow Ducati rider while taking a quick stroll around Rodeo Drive on foot. And I see the local cops ride BMW 1150 RT boxers too. By the way, parking on Rodeo Drive was 50 cents for twenty minutes, the problem is finding a vacant booth. A permanent resident guy from England was very interested in my S4 and stops to have a chat about it. He could "only" afford a Honda 900 priced at $8,000. Rodeo Drive is the place to put your success on display and excellent on the weekend if you love supercars, as owners come here to show off.

Different lifestyles. The visible difference shows in affluent peoples cars, motorcycles, toys and homes. Poor people may look the guy on the cool bike with envy. Expressing envy being a poor person, you may need to rethink your mindset.

Locking yourself into unfounded prejudice, will make you susceptible to the very same, exhibiting different class through material possessions or lack thereof. With no thought or knowledge of how the other person acquired his possessions, thus being less open to anything but a preconceived opinion, placing oneself into a negative mindset.

Having a lot of material things may be a result of being buried in debt beyond the ability to make payments on time, causing stress and sleepless nights.

Showing high class is naturally having respect, ambitions and being open to new impulses and input, yet staying critical.

Everything depends on the eye that see.

So don't forget to look both ways.

The locals drive very fast on Wiltshire. So I took a wrong turn on Pacific Coast Highway 1 and end up in a one way entry to a pay parking lot adjacent to Santa Monica Pier. This is a $7 trap once you accidentally turn into the entrance driveway. Santa Monica Pier is a Los Angeles land mark attraction, so not really a big issue. Checking out the amusements there is a rollercoaster and candy shops. Nothing particular, but a good place to bring your kids or a date. A panhandler near the parking lot had some success holding a sign stating "Why lie? Need money for beer". While funny some people fall for it, this was a bit too smart for my liking. Being lazy won't earn you any money, nor respect, from me.

Walking onto the beach I check out the ladies in bikinis. With no swimming trunks, I paddle my feet in sea, this time properly touching the water of the Pacific Ocean on this eventful lifetime coast to coast ride. Not having my jeans rolled up high enough I managed to get these well soaked too.

From Santa Monica Pier to Venice Beach there is less than two miles. Finding a parking lot, the parking attendant pockets $5 for the bike, instead of the $8.5 stated on the sign. I don't think his boss saw any of that money. On the beach I checked out the Muscle Beach Venice Beach Weight Pen, operated by the Los Angeles Recreation and Parks Department. It is an open playground with a gated area that encloses weight-lifting equipment. The second area is a sandbox with gymnastic, rope climbing, and acrobatic bars. Not a lot of people present at the time. Exercising in the hot sun may attract the ladies. I can only say: Been there, haven't done that. Venice Beach has a number of shops and restaurants on the concrete path running along the beach with people roller skating and riding bicycles along this. I find it more interesting to people watch here, even more so than in Sturgis.

Starting my trip at World Ducati Week 2004, I had talked to Bill on May 22nd. Bill is the owner of Pro Italia, the Ducati dealership in Glendale. At the time they were the second most successful Ducati Dealership, selling about 150 bikes per year. With Ducati growing in popularity, I think sales are even better today. Finding 3319 North Verdugo Rd. in Glendale was an absolute nightmare with me constantly getting lost. Going through Culver City I pass the big iconic Space Age structure Theme Building at LAX, Los Angeles International Airport. I found this pretty wild as I was pretty much back where I started my trip in the USA with some fond memories of my first arrival on July 10th. A five hour flight to Newark and returning 46 days later traveling on the road. Mind-boggling in the moment.

Well, I was still lost so driving through Inglewood I realize that I am riding on Crenshaw on a red motorcycle in wearing a red jacket. The signals you send or choose to send can have unintended consequences. Right can be interpreted wrong. And the other way around. Not being sure which gang area I was in; this isn't the safest place to be lost so I didn't stop here to tool around with my Road Atlas accidentally provoking the natives. Inglewood is Bloods territory where red is the right clothing color, while Compton is dominated by Crips who prefer people wearing blue.

Getting away from Inglewood I get on Interstate 110 northbound. LA traffic is just crazy and lane splitting on a motorcycle, riding between the rows of cars, is allowed in California. On I-5 I finally find Highway 2 and Pro Italia. Talking to Marcus, I find that Bill is attending a dealership meeting and he wouldn't be back before Tuesday. That really sucked, but at least I didn't get mugged in the hood, as Dr. Dre say; *Inglewood is always up to no good.*

With Bill not home I wanted to see the famous and iconic landmark Hollywood sign on Mount Lee. Here "HOLLYWOOD" is spelled out in 45 foot (13.7 m) tall white capitals and it is 352 feet (107.3 m) long. Originally created in 1923 as an advertisement for a local real estate development. Due to increased recognition, the sign was left up. The Hollywood sign is actually trademarked by the Hollywood Chamber of Commerce. My guidebook recommended I ride to Griffith Observatory in Griffith Park to get the best view of the famous sign. On a curious note, Griffith Park was the place where paparazzi found Brigitte Nielsen, one of the most famous Danes in the USA, drunk as a skunk. Married to Sylvester Stallone in the eighties, and later rapper Flavor Flav from Public Enemy, she played the role of Ivan Dragos wife in Rocky IV and starred as Red Sonja in the movie of the same name.

Entering through the wrong entrance to Griffith Park, I rode around for a bit. Using a $3 map of LA I bought, I managed to find the correct entrance, but the Griffith Observatory was undergoing renovations so it wasn't open for visitors. So the view of the Hollywood sign I got was pretty poor but did get a great view over the city.

Back at Hollywood Inn Express, I discovered this is located in the LA area known as Thaitown. I love Thai food, so just across the street on the other side of Hollywood Boulevard I eat some spicy dinner at Vim Thai Restaurant. I wasn't prepared for the Thai Iced Tea though, it was insanely sweet and tasted like it was eighty percent sugar.

One way to easily visit the most places just described is to play the video game GTA V. Los Angeles has been very well reimagined in this virtual version. The Sierra towers near the north end of Sierra Drive has been recreated as the Eclipse Towers. Sunset Plaza on Sunset Blvd, Rodeo Drive, Griffith Observatory and Mann's Chinese Theatre are all in this massive digital piece of entertainment. Americans are world champions at entertaining, with Hollywood and LA being the epicenter of popular culture. My many movie and TV references are probably a good indicator of the influence this has had worldwide as you probably know, recognize or remember these when reading about them.

Fascinating and scary at the same time.

"I'm going to Disneyland"

Saturday, August 28th 2004

Denmark is the birthplace of LEGO toys and LEGOLAND.

But the big dog in amusement parks is Disney. It is time to go to the Magic Kingdom. Yes, I'm going to Disneyland! This phrase is actually went on to become a fun tagline for anyone asked about what their plans are after accomplishing a significant achievement. It stems from a series of TV ads by Disney starring NBA star Magic Johnson, MLB player Frank Viola and other athletes and sportsmen. In 1987, Disney CEO Michael Eisner's wife Jane Eisner thought this would make a great slogan in an advertising campaign after hearing it at dinner party and she has been credited for inventing this classic catchphrase.

Riding from the motel, I was back on Highway 101 looking for signs going to Anaheim. Taking exit 111 on I-5 I got off at the Paramount intersection, so I got to scoot around for a bit before finding Disneyland Drive. Being absolutely tired of getting lost in California, I managed to find the house of the mouse around 11 AM. Parking was $9 and admission for one $49.75. Traveling around the world to get here, the entry fee doesn't matter. They did offer a "Day-tripper Pass" for $69 including Disney's California Adventure section, but I wasn't feeling it.

Disneyland Park opened on July 17, 1955. It is the only theme park designed and built to completion under the direct supervision of Walt Disney. Disneyland Park consists of eight themed sections or "Lands" and covers around 100 acres. The park opened with Main Street, U.S.A., Adventureland, Frontierland, Fantasyland, and Tomorrowland, and has since added New Orleans Square in 1966, Critter Country in 1972, and Mickey's Toontown in 1993.

The first thing to greet you is one the first Disney movies, Steamboat Willie from 1928. A black-and-white animated cartoon by Walt Disney Studios it is considered the debut of Mickey Mouse and his girlfriend Minnie Mouse. Steamboat Willie is special as it is the first Disney cartoon with synchronized sound, including character sounds and a musical score. This is a good piece of history to start with as the Disney Corporation is an entertainment juggernaut today.

Checking out "Main St. U.S.A.", this is where you get the direct view to Mickey's Castle at the far end. But as with the Washington monument in D.C., the damn castle was wrapped in blue tarp as it was undergoing refurbishment, getting a fresh coat of paint. That was a bit of a disappointment, to say the least. Main Street, U.S.A. is patterned after a typical Midwest town of the early 20th century. It has a train station, town square, movie theater, city hall, firehouse with a steam-powered pump engine, emporium, shops, arcades, a double-decker bus, horse-drawn streetcar, and jitneys. Main Street is also home to the Disney Art Gallery and the Central Plaza functions as a hub to the other sections of the park. Main Street, U.S.A. uses the design technique of forced perspective to create an illusion of height. Buildings along Main Street are built at 3⁄4 scale on the first level, then 5⁄8 on the second story, and 1⁄2 scale on the third, reducing the scale by 1⁄8 each level up. With my graphic design background I just love these trivia factoids.

Growing up with Star Wars and being old enough to have seen *Return of the Jedi* when it had its first run in cinemas, I am a sucker for science fiction. My love for Star Wars as a kid made me want to learn English so I could understand what the characters were saying. So my first stop was of course Tomorrowland and "Star Tours", a Star Wars ride where the entire seating section moved and tilts wildly in sync with the on-screen action sequences. This was action filled, super fun and everyone loved it.

Bringing a backpack was a bit of a hassle, as it had to be stowed user the seat not to go flying all over the place. The Tomorrowland monorail was a bit of a dud. To get on I this needed the "Day-tripper Pass" as its destination was Disney's California Adventure.

Instead, I had my first 4D movie theatre experience on the "Honey, I shrunk the Audience"-ride. Unfortunately, with only vision on one eye I can't see 3D movies as they are supposed to be experienced. Based on the 1989 comedy "Honey, I shrunk the kids" starring Rick Moranis, this sure was a new experience as the audience were required to wear protective eyewear. The title explains the story, a scientist at the Imagination Institute holds a lecture and accidentally shrinks the audience. The end part is the kicker, as he manage to re-size the audience, he simultaneously turn the dog Quark into a giant. Quark walks out onto the stage and the curtain closes while you hear the Imagination Institute's crew trying to stop him from crushing the place. He then finds his way through the curtain and sneezes on the audience for the finale, which triggers hidden water sprayers in the back of the seats in the row in front of each rider. This ride is no longer available, but I recommend the movie as it is another true classic 80's flick.

Under CEO Bob Iger, Disney has bought a long line of intellectual properties in the last few years, most notably Pixar, 21st Century Fox, Marvel, Muppet Show and in a $4.05 billion deal, Lucasfilm. Lucasfilm means Star Wars and hearing about this acquisition, my first thought was that I hope they didn't screw up Star Wars. And they did. Big time. Even with the merchandise, the quality has dropped since this Disney took over.
I really like the director J.J. Abrams reboot of the Star Trek universe in 2009, didn't even care about Star Trek before this. But *Star Wars Episode VII: The Force Awakens* is absolute bantha crap. A lame remake of the first movie from 1977. Unoriginal beyond belief, I could have written a better story myself.
Why Disney didn't create a coherent storyline for the new movies instead of making the story on the fly was just idiotic. The universe is well established, so all they had to do was make the full script for the last trilogy before filming a single second. Introducing new characters who don't resonate with anyone, the loyal fan base were rightfully disappointed. Having to please an audience that has grown up having their imagination taken to a galaxy far away is not easy. Some of the dialogue from the old movies is hammy and stilted, but it doesn't matter as the Star Wars universe offers a truly immersive experience.

George Lucas understood that Star Wars is a kids universe. So in my view, Jar Jar Binks is a comedy character who delivers a well-deserved slap in the face to those grown-ups who are taking Star Wars way too seriously. Another good example is the Ewoks in *Return of the Jedi*, cannibal teddy bears is just a ridiculous concept when you think about it. The Star Wars universe would actually be a pretty shit place to live in for real, with oppression, genocide and slavery all over the place. I must admit, even today, Carrie Fischer still looks incredibly hot in that gold bikini.

After a good time in Tomorrowland, I walked to Fantasyland, the one with the teacups. The wait time was around 15 minutes, not too bad as there weren't that many people this day. This actually puzzled me a bit as it was a Saturday. With love for speed I went on the "Matterhorn bobsleds". I was bit baffled of what looked like a group of four 13-14 year old's in front of me. One girl casually discussed whom in their school she had slept with, bet she was popular among the boys. If you really want respect you shouldn't advertise who got lucky with you. The kids went on the ride on the run before me so I got seated behind a family of four. During the ride I looked up and noticed that if you don't crouch a bit, this ride could actually rip your head off. No kidding, you do not want to test this theory. But it was a cool ride as everyone loves speed.

Having no specific plan besides seeing and trying as much as possible while here, I ended up on the sick boat ride, "It's a small world". If I hadn't tried brainwashing before, that is another one off the list.

Adventureland had an Indiana Jones Adventure ride. Pretty cool, but the CGI snake looked super fake. Every attraction has its own store for you to buy some merchandise, this is worth checking out as I bought some "Rebel Alliance" and "Galactic Empire" shot glasses at the Star Wars ride that would be hard to find elsewhere. In Mickey's Toontown there was a 45 minute wait for Roger Rabbit Car Toon Spin, even though I could easily fit, it was a kids ride. So yeah, I would need to borrow a kid from someone to go on that. Kids are fun to make, less fun to raise.

You can't go to the happiest place in the world without meeting the rodent in person, so I had to go to Mickey's House. At 5 Ft 3 In I really like the dimensions of Mickey's Toontown.

There was a one hour wait to go on "Splash Mountain" in Critter Country. So I got a fast-pass ticket. Unlike LEGOLAND, this is not a way to pay to get ahead in line of the less affluent. You pull a ticket and on it there is a time printed at which you have to be back to enter the shorter fast-pass queue. So you don't have to stand in line for hours but are free to do spend money elsewhere in the meantime, buying merch or something to eat. Waiting in line to go on the ride I talked to Mindy and Dan, this couple were having a blast here regressing to childhood wearing a plastic tiara and some Mickey Mouse hands. Learning that I planned to go to Las Vegas they did give me some tips on saving money there. Splash Mountain was a mixed experience. With all the water, I couldn't see shit. The park takes a picture of you and gives you an option to buy this after the ride. The snapshot with me in it was crap, so no sale.

Frontierland is like a miniature Deadwood, a wild west town theme. They have a coin-op shooting tent and the Big Thunder Mountain Railroad ride was enjoyable too. They have park employees dressed up as different characters and Frontierland of course had a sheriff. Spinning a lasso, the Sheriff challenged a young lady to give it a try. What he didn't know was that she was a high school cheerleader. So she surprised him with some unexpected skills. At this time it is 5:30 pm and sensing the crowd had increased somewhat since noon, I thought that maybe I should eat early so I don't end up in the dinner rush. Well, there is a lot of jokes going around about Disneyland being expensive, and a double cheeseburger at the Golden Horseshoe was $7.21 - without a drink!
From New Orleans Square I got on the Disneyland Railroad back to Tomorrowland. Here I watched Sandbox, a cover band playing hits from P!nk and other popular artists, and did some shopping. I didn't shop just after arriving as I would have to lug my purchases around all day. So I bought a Mickey Mouse t-shirt and a key ring for Mindy.

At 9 pm Mickey's Imagination Show is held with fireworks, song and music. Here I experienced the greatness, magic and impressiveness of Disneyland. It is hard to explain, you have to have been there yourself. Expensive, yes, but Disney has the ability and skill to positively reach you on an emotional level that truly makes the Magic Kingdom deserve its designation. A new 14-acre Star Wars-themed land named Galaxy's Edge just opened. If this matches the "Star Tours"-ride, it would be an absolute must to visit if I get the chance to go to Disneyland Park again.
Leaving the parking garage the Termignoni mufflers on the Ducati set off every car alarm I passed. You never get too old to find that amusing. The ride back to the Hollywood Inn Express went without a hitch and I managed to avoid getting lost at all. I was a bit surprised to see the number of cars on Interstate 5 at 10 pm, just a fraction less than during daytime.

Death Valley

With a fair room cost and a plethora of Thai restaurants right next door, I would not hesitate to choose the Hollywood Inn Express if I ever return to Los Angeles. Getting out of the city was no problem either as I had made sure to extensively study my Road Atlas before heading out on Interstate 5 northbound, onto Highway 14 to Mojave and Highway 14/395.

Heading to Sin City, I had the choice to go through Mojave National Preserve or Death Valley National Park. The latter would be a more than 400 miles, where the Mojave route would be around just 275 miles. Death Valley is a super cool name for one of the hottest places on Earth and not having been there while having the chance would just be missing out on another unique once in a lifetime experience. So Death Valley it was.

The name Death Valley originated from a group of travelers who found themselves trapped in the valley in 1849, while trying to find a shortcut to the California gold fields. One of their group died there, so the name may be a little dramatic. Nearly coming off the bike being dehydrated on Interstate 95 to Washington D.C., I wasn't going to let that happen again, for sure not in Death Valley. And having a sense of humor won't help in case of a tire puncture. So I bought an extra half gallon bottle of water to supplement the 12 oz. bottle I usually carried on the bike.

The highest ambient air temperature ever recorded at the surface of the Earth was registered in Death Valley by the United States Weather Bureau on July 10, 1913. A record high temperature of 134 °F (56.7 °C) at Greenland Ranch (now Furnace Creek). Daily summer temperatures of 120 °F (49 °C) or higher are common here. As a contrast the nightly temperatures often drop below freezing in the winter. The hottest month is July with an average high of 115 °F (46 °C) and an average "low" of 88 °F (31 °C).

On the roads towards Death Valley I saw numerous signs advertising "home-made beef jerky". I think Death Valley is a great place if you need something to dry effectively and these signs were basically making a countdown to the beef jerky shop. By the time I got there these signs had started to annoy me, so I made a pass and rode on.

Death Valley became a national park in 1994, and has a diverse environment of salt-flats, sand dunes, badlands, valleys, canyons, and mountains. Sticking to highway 190 that goes through, I mainly saw salt flat and dunes. As I got into Death Valley NP I got a tangible understanding of why the name describes this place well. Death Valley is the hottest, driest and lowest of all the national parks in the USA. Besides that, it is the largest national park in the lower 48 states. Using a full face flip-up helmet and riding with the visor up, but still with the chin piece closed, this felt like someone held a hairdryer right in front of my face. It was considerably more comfortable riding with the visor closed but still pretty dang hot.

In the middle of Death Valley, in Furnace Creek, there is a gas station. I decided to stop there to top up the tank and drink some water, but the fuel level was only about a quarter down so I changed my mind. So I chugged half a liter of water instead. While there a car pulled up. The driver got out but the price per gallon here was a dollar higher than gas prices outside the National Park, so with the comment "that's too much" he quickly got back in his air-conditioned cage and drove off.

Before Corn Creek on Highway 95, around twenty miles outside of Las Vegas, I passed the Southern Desert Correctional Center located on the right side of the road, which is a part of a larger prison complex. During the research for this trip I had read another travel story with a group riding motorcycles turning right onto this driveway and having the guards go on high alert and running out with their weapons drawn. I wasn't going to repeat their error, but when you're heading to Las Vegas southbound on Highway 95, you can't miss it.

I have gotten close a few times, but have never been to jail
and have never been arrested. (Interrogation doesn't count. I generally
do not talk to the police and stick to my right to remain silent.)
But when errors are made you cannot change what has already
been done. You can only see to that you don't repeat them.

As said earlier, don't get caught. And admit nothing.
Snitches gets stitches.

Justice is also a way to say, "reward for your efforts".
If a criminal is jailed for his bad deeds, it does give him time to think if
his actions make the stay in "reformatory lockup" worthwhile.
The preventive effect is based on a good principle which unfortunately
doesn't work in the long run and dissipate with time.

While I try to "do the right thing" myself,
of course you really shouldn't take justice into your own hands.
But justice can be defined and bent. It is easy to get away with
doing wrong without any consequence. Justice is a weak in itself.

Driving past the Southern Desert Correctional Center made me think of a Danish repeat offender. I am not going to dignify him by mentioning his name here, but everyone in Denmark knows who this asshole is. Convicted of murdering his American mother in 1993, he was jailed in North Carolina. Gaining fame after appearing in a TV documentary, he got transferred and deported to Denmark in 1999. Here he was released pretty much immediately. Within a year he had murdered three more people, the woman he was living with and her two kids. He is serving a lifetime sentence in Denmark now, but life usually means serving 16 years in Denmark. The West has gone soft and some prison cells in western Europe are comparable a room at Travelodge. Adding insult to injury, this piece of human garbage has fathered several kids himself while incarcerated. Some women are attracted to bad boys, the worst of those will eventually kill more than once. Not being politically correct, I believe that some people simply deserve the death penalty, especially if your only achievement in life is murdering women and children.

With the exception of Japan and the USA, most of the western world has abandoned termination of convicts. Speaking against capital punishment is the risk of killing people who are innocent. This is the reason I do find abandonment of capital punishment understandable and reasonable. But with the great improvement of forensic technology I also understand why Americans rightfully want to keep this as an option for punishment.

Heading east on the Ducati it dawned on me that I was on the last leg of my fantastic journey across the United States and this once in a lifetime trip around the Blue Planet.

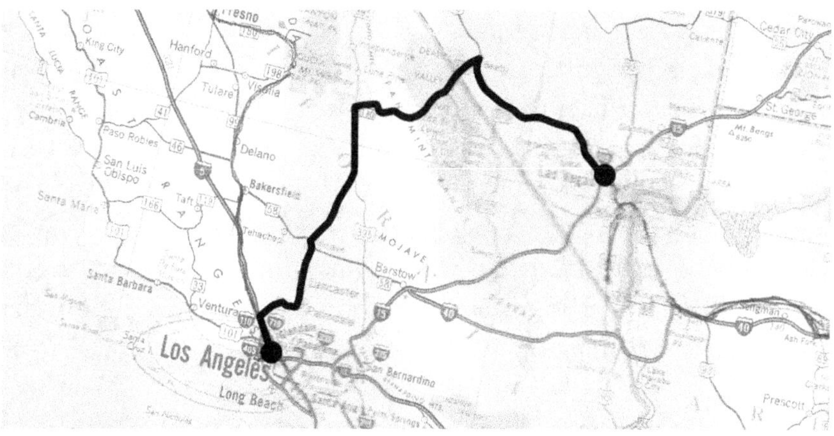

Entering Las Vegas around 5 pm, I found the Strip without any problems. Taking a right into the Boardwalk Hotel and Casino I kicked out the side stand on the bike and went to the reception to ask for room availability and prices. Being dusty and sweaty I didn't have enough patience to wait as there was quite a few other guests queued up in front of me.

So I went back to the bike, where one of the valets told me, "Mister, your motorcycle is leaking fluid". Not really what you want to hear, but I had to find out what fluid we were talking about. Swiping my finger across the small puddle that had dripped on the asphalt I couldn't tell for sure what it was from the viscosity. So without recommending this to anyone, I made a quick taste test. Thank the motorcycle gods and bacon it was only engine coolant and not oil. The engine had gotten so hot from riding through

Death Valley that the coolant had gotten so near boiling point that it had started to expand to the point of overflowing while I was going too slow through Las Vegas city traffic. In have never experienced anything like this before or ever since.

Still in search of a hotel, I asked at the MGM Grand at the other side of the Las Vegas Strip. I got an offer for a super nice room for $89 plus taxes. For this price it is not worth wasting time to find anything cheaper. Being right on the Strip with all the other big casinos, the money potentially saved following the advice from Mindy and Dan in Disneyland would probably be spent on transportation.

Throwing the bags and camping gear into the room, I got back on my bike to take a ride up and down the Las Vegas Strip after dark when all the neon lights have been turned on. At the MGM Grand's motorcycle parking area, a heavily customized Ducati 996 Superbike had been parked next to mine. You can't park or stop on the Strip, so I made a u-turn at the Stratosphere, cruising here is crawl speed like Main St. Sturgis -but primarily with cars. Rolling back into the MGM Grand parking garage is like leaving Disneyland, setting off a row of car alarms is free and pure unadulterated fun.

I am not a big gambler and I have hated card games ever since two of my friends ganged up on me as a kid, collaborating in cheating while playing cards. My first thought about Las Vegas is that one should never forget that the city is built by the money from people who did not win there. So when you enter a casino the odds are stacked against you and everything you bet is basically lost. So I had decided to spend no more than $200 on gambling.

The classic Vegas legend is people selling everything they own and putting it on red, and you haven't been to Las Vegas unless you have played some chance game. Exploring the MGM Grand after a much needed shower I get $10 worth of chips and put it on red at the first roulette table. Repeating this success twice, I changed my bet to black. Well, my gain disappeared as quickly as it came. My lucky number is 16, but with the speed money disappears on a roulette table, 1:35 odds isn't worth the return unless you are willing to spend $10 bills on each spin.

Throwing my money away was more fun at Shotgun Willie's than here. And the fun bit lasted longer.

Going out of MGM Grand, I took a long walk going through Paris Las Vegas, Caesars Palace and the Venetian, a Vegas version of the Italian canal city. Having visited the original location a few times, this is pretty corny. Well, both places do qualify as genuine tourist traps. At New York, New York I get my face 3D scanned and laser pointillized into a cube, a great gift for the family. Bet this was exactly what they didn't want.

Crossing the foot bridge from the Excalibur to the Tropicana, a young african american lady is very friendly small-talking with me. Tropicana has been known for being a mob run casino and the Las Vegas sequence of *The Godfather* was filmed inside this casino. Today, I still am unsure if she was a soliciting escort or just being friendly.

Back at the MGM Grand I decided to play the slots. Growing up these were known as "One Armed Bandits" where you had to pull a mechanical lever to spin the reels. This nickname was used because of their ability to empty a player's pockets and wallet like a thief. The modern version has buttons and a winning line. This was new to me, the pictured symbols had to hit the winning line to count, yet another way of decreasing your chance of winning. Playing on the $1 "Megabucks" the grand jackpot was 10 million dollars, and the second optional great prize is a Dodge Viper. As I needed a Harley Davidson Heritage Softail in Sturgis, I didn't need a Viper as I didn't have a driving license allowing me to drive a car at the time. You don't need a license to own 10 million dollars.

The upside of playing in the same spot for a prolonged time is that the casino will comp you with free drinks, so at least I got some beers for the $45 spent. Winning what amounted to a pittance, I stopped when the amount that I won and set aside for playing was reached.

Repeating myself, your money is lost when you decide to enter a casino. Not being a dick like the guy who sat next to me, I decided to tip the waitress a buck for each beer she brought me.

Monday, August 30th 2004

First order of the day was to pick up the 3D Cube portrait I had my face scanned for the day before at the New York, NY casino. Walking around I took some mandatory touristy photos of the Las Vegas Strip.

Founded in 1905, Las Vegas is the biggest city in the state of Nevada. Legalizing casino gambling in 1931, Las Vegas is the 28th-most populated city in the United States today with a population of around 642,000 people. Famous for its legalized prostitution, gambling, shopping, fine dining, entertainment and nightlife, Las Vegas markets itself as The Entertainment Capital of the World and in 2004 Las Vegas attracted 37.4 million visitors. Later this number has passed 40 million annually.

In 2004 stick figure singer Celiné Dion was performing a three-year, 600-show contract to appear five nights a week in an entertainment extravaganza called "A New Day...", at The Colosseum at Caesars Palace. Having performed in a 4000-seat arena modeled after the Roman Colosseum since March 25th the year before. "A New Day..." is the most successful Vegas residency of all time, grossing over $385 million ($465.2 million in 2018 dollars) and drawing an audience of nearly three million people to 717 shows. Like Whitney Houston, Celiné Dion can sing. So even though I don't consider myself a fan, this would be the best option as Elvis Presley had been dead for almost 27 years. An average ticket price being $135, these were very expensive. But this wasn't a problem as Celiné Dion didn't perform on Mondays. Beside Celiné Dion, Elvis Presley and Britney Spears both have held residency performing in Las Vegas. You can't go to Las Vegas and not see an Elvis impersonator, so instead I bought tickets to the show "American Superstars" starting at 7 pm at the Stratosphere Casino located at the north end of the Strip. This show cost just $19 and featured Christina Aguilera, Michael Jackson, Ricky Martin, Elvis Presley and Britney Spears impersonators.

Without any other specific plans for the afternoon I stopped at Treasure Island and the Mirage. The pirate show was just weird to me, but the fountain in front of the Bellagio is pretty impressive. The Bellagio Fountain is an 8.5-acre lake which with 1,214 spritzers shooting water up to 460 feet in the air. This show starts every half-hour between 3 pm and 8 pm, and every 15 minutes from 8 pm until midnight.

At Walgreens, I got four single use cameras transferred to CD-ROM for $50. Waiting for these to get finished, I decided to get a cold drink at the McDonald's on the Strip, as being outside in the daytime is hot as hell from June through September. On average, 134 days per year reach or exceed 90 °F (32 °C). Most summer days are consistently hot, dry and cloudless, but the North American Monsoon sporadically interrupts this pattern and brings more cloud cover, thunderstorms, lightning, increased humidity, and brief spells of heavy rain.

After leaving McDonald's I realized I had forgotten my backpack there, including my guidebook and travel diary. So I made a 200 yard dash back, fortunately everything was still where I left it. Had I lost my diary, you would not be reading this right now !

*My diary,
on which this
book is based*

To get to the Stratosphere casino I decided to go on the Monorail. Trying to find the MGM station I took a wrong turn inside the MGM Grand and find myself a bit lost inside the damn hotel!

Las Vegas is a top three destination in the USA for business conventions and a global leader in the hospitality industry, so I end up in a wide hallway being asked for my visitor badge to some business event. At $6 I found the monorail a bit pricey, but still cheaper than a taxi. Arriving a bit early and waiting for the "American Superstars" show I am tempted to play "Lucky 20", $50 worth of playing for $20. This is a bit different as the prize are gifts exchanged for points won. Not wanting to miss the full show, I chose to pass on this.

Taking a seat a woman ask if she could sit in a vacant seat next to me and behind a family with kids. The show wasn't disturbed by anyone's phones going off, but instead this stupid cow had to yell, whoo and holler so loud it really made it hard for everyone around her to hear the performers sing. What a stupid bitch. After the show I told her that I was glad I didn't sit in front of her, and if she realized that she had ruined the show for the poor girl sitting in the seat in front. She quickly disappeared without comment. The show itself was pretty good especially with the Christina Aguilera and Britney Spears impersonators being talented singers and performers. With some hot dancers displaying some cleavage and ass too. The show ticket included an elevator ride to the top deck of the Stratosphere Tower, offering a view of the Strip and enticing you to stay and spend more money at the Stratosphere casino. The only downside was that loud dumbass.

Down on the Strip after dark I got approached by plenty of Latinos handing out flyers to clubs, strip joints and escort services. Here I see what is pretty much the only violent conflict on my journey. Two Latinos swinging wildly at each other. Not much fighting skills left as they were pretty drunk. So some in their group broke up the fight by pulling their buddy away from the other guy.

While inside the Paris Las Vegas to enjoy some free chilly recirculated air, this version of the French capitol does come off as a bit tacky. Instead I should have studied my guidebook and gone to Freemont Street, guess that has to be another time, just like taking a ride in a stretch limo. I have been inside a stretch limo, but actually never as a passenger while it was moving. So I'll save that for an eventual future honeymoon.

At the Luxor I played the slots again. Not having any travelers cheques on me I withdrew some cash from an ATM, this is the pricey option as it comes with a $5 fee. The jackpot price here is a black and orange Ford F150 pickup truck Harley Davidson Edition with a matching motorcycle on the bed. Black and orange are Harley Davidsons race colors. The casinos are constructed so you can't see daylight outside. This is deliberately designed to make players forget about the amount of time and money spent. It is a typical Vegas thing that some other players stand around and watch you play. After dropping $30 here I headed back to the MGM Grand. Without a lot of people playing I walked around for a bit and saw a small group play on a mechanical horse race machine. One girl is especially enthusiastic and looks like she is having a great time. This is with a cost of a quarter per race, so this is a huge contrast to what high-rollers drop here.

It felt good sitting down after walking from the Stratosphere. Playing the slots at the MGM Grand I was $120 up from my total set aside for gambling. This is nothing, so cashing in didn't matter. Playing the Mega Millions slots a full jackpot spin costs $1. A cheaper option is playing for the second grand prize for 50 cents per spin. So I went for the cheaper loss.

Then that "oh fucking no" thing happens. This is the second incident that I wish I had taken a picture during my travels. But unsure of casino photography policies I didn't. Here goes:

At 1 am the rollers stop at "Jackpot", "Jackpot", "Jackpot". But the last roller just misses the winning line by a hair! Un-be-fuck-ing-lieve-able. Poking the guy next to me on the shoulder he is speechless too. I think the chance of hitting the slots Jackpot is 1:49,000,000. So close, but yet so far, this instantly cured my desire to spend more on the slots.

Still having credit left in the machine I played until this had been spent and went back to my room at 2:30 am. At this time hotel security checks if you are a guest before letting you enter the elevators.

Death Valley
National Park
MGM
THE CITY OF
ENTERTAINMENT
GRAND
998

Tuesday, August 31st 2004

It is a good idea to decide a limit or budget your expenditure when going to Las Vegas. I overspent $50 on gambling as my initial budget for this was $200, so no horrific damage. I guess I am a lousy gambler. Las Vegas offers some great opportunities for you to part with your money, however, having fun in Las Vegas doesn't have to cost a fortune. I got some stories for life and as expected, I didn't win.

On the other hand I didn't lose more than I could afford. For a better Las Vegas experience I would definitely plan another trip to Sin City before arrival, letting me get the most out of it, instead of primarily ending up playing slots. Well, risking your life riding a motorcycle is a different form of high stakes gambling too.

Leaving the MGM Grand I went north towards Downtown as I would like to see a bit of old Vegas. Here I ended up behind a couple of motorcycle cops, a pretty sweet gig if you ask me, riding a bike in sunny weather, taking pictures with the tourists and getting paid for it. On top you get to harass and beat up people too as a part of the biggest gang in the world. Not remembering which highway I had to go on and as there were no places to make a u-turn on this double lane highway, until I reach a US Postal office, I end up going 33 miles the wrong way on highway 95 instead of staying on Highway 93. While there, I decided to mail home all the items I had bought that and didn't want to drag around for the rest of the ride. And I got the bike facing in the right direction to the Hoover Dam about 30 miles (48 km) southeast of Las Vegas. Again. Sixty-six miles wasted time in the saddle, this was one of the longest stretches I had gotten myself lost in America. At this time I had also lost count of how many times I had needed to double check my Road Atlas.

Hoover Dam is a concrete arch-gravity dam in the Black Canyon of the Colorado River, on the bordering state lines of Nevada and Arizona. Standing 726.4 feet (221.4 m) high and 1,244 feet (379 m) long, Hoover Dam is named after the 31rd President, Herbert Hoover.

Built to control floods, provide irrigation water and produce hydroelectric power, Hoover Dam impounds Lake Mead. Lake Mead gets filled by the Colorado River and is in volume the largest reservoir in the United States. The dam's generators provide up to 2,080 Mw of power for public and private utilities in Nevada, Arizona and California. Via two controlled drumgates up to 400,000 cubic feet (11,000 m3) can flow through at maximum productivity. Constructed during the Great Depression between 1931 and 1936, Hoover Dam was the result of a massive effort involving thousands of workers, and the loss over one hundred lives.

The first of its kind, a concrete structure of this scale had never been built before. This engineering marvel is 660 feet (200 m) wide at the base, and some of the techniques used to build it were unproven. So it does impress to note that Hoover Dam actually was finished more than two years ahead of schedule.

Going south on Route 93 the road runs atop the dam's 45 Ft (14 m) wide crest, 1,232 Ft (376 m) above the lowest point where the Colorado River continues. Here I encountered another parking trap. The parking garage cost $5 but a little further I found a free parking booth along the road. In October 2010, the Hoover Dam Bypass opened, redirecting traffic onto Mike O'Callaghan–Pat Tillman Memorial Bridge arch over the Colorado River, connecting Arizona and Nevada. Taking some pictures of this impressive piece of construction and engineering, it is a long day trip just to see this when you're in Las Vegas. But traveling through, you will want to make a stop here. Hoover Dam attracts nearly a million visitors each year. Crossing the Hoover Dam and thus entering Arizona, I had travelled back to the future and was now on mountain time.

The landscape down Route 93 could be the set backdrop of a John Wayne movie. But driving or riding though a desert easily becomes monotonous. Having tried this on the way to see Ayers Rock in Australia, you easily can become drowsy going 55-65 mph. I actually knew a girl who got killed in Australia because of that. So I whipped the Monster up to 80-90 mph continuing east on Route 93 and just button my jacket to increase airflow. Not a smart move as I got onto I-40 my jacket blew open at 75-80 mph. In hindsight, I should have used the zippers at least halfway.

After 180 miles in the saddle since leaving Las Vegas, I reached King-
man. Here I noticed a sign to the Historic Route 66. U.S. Route 66 is also
known as "the Mother Road" and is one of the most famous roads in the
United States. I did think of making my journey from Chicago to Los Angeles on this road, but wanting to experience the Sturgis Rally it wasn't the
best route. Established in 1926, road signs were erected the following year
and Route 66 became the first highway to be completely paved in 1938.
With a length of 2,448 miles (3,940 km), Route 66 originally started in
Chicago, Illinois, through Missouri, Kansas, Oklahoma, Texas, New Mexico and Arizona before ending in Santa Monica in Los Angeles, California. US 66 served as a primary route for people who migrated west during
the 1930s droughts in the Mid-west, also known as the Dust Bowl.
Having undergone many improvements and realignments over its lifetime,
Route 66 was officially removed from the United States Highway Sys-
tem in 1985 as this had been replaced by the Interstate Highway System.
The removal of US 66 is often seen as the end of an era of US highways.

Today, several states have adopted significant bypassed sections of the former US 66 into their state road networks as State Route 66. The road
supported the economies of the communities through which it passed and
many people doing business along the route became prosperous due to the
highways growing popularity. Those same people later fought to keep the
highway alive, but to no avail. So what remains of the original road are Na
tional Scenic Byways of the name "Historic Route 66", using the name on
maps and road signs. Riding through one section of the Historic 66 isn't
very exciting. But people still earn a bit off this history selling touristy tat.
Filling the gas tank in Seligman I bought a "Historic 66" patch to sow
onto a jacket. Seligman is located in an area between two Native American
Reservations. My first impression was that they look on outsiders with, er,
reservations. A couple of Native American kids in the car filling up at the
pump in front of the Ducati seemed very fascinated by it. Their mother
didn't appear very talkative, not even acknowledging a friendly nod from
me. Maybe she didn't like the store clerk. A bit of a character, he had
the weirdest hairdo I had encountered yet, surpassing the Sturgis party
people bonanza. A puff-perm with the sides hedge trimmed vertically!

I guess corporate dressing codes were pretty relaxed there or maybe he was related to the owner.

I might have been a little under hydrated as I felt drowsy again while on Interstate 40. Overtaking three Harley Davidson touring bikes fitted with apehangers going 60 mph where 65 is legal, they looked pretty stupid in my opinion. Apehangers are handlebars with the controls positioned high, so you hold on to these like an ape hanging off a branch. This riding position is tiring for sure, and combined with forward foot controls, it make a lot of people feel like they're skydiving when they try it for the first time. Apehangers do come with a cool story, I am not sure if it is true. To stop American Army dispatch riders during World War II, the Germans hung up wires across the road to injure or kill these. As a countermeasure the riders mounted high bars on their bikes, so the wire would hit the bar before the rider. Many of the first bikers were returning veterans who stripped their bikes of unnecessary weight, that's how we got chopper motorcycles, and retaining the high ape hanger bars as a styling element.
Having tried several bikes with ape hangers since, riding on a bike with ape hangers does feel pretty cool as long as you're leisurely cruising and don't go fast.

Stopping in Williams located next to I-40 at 7:45 pm, I checked in at Motel 6. I have noted that this motel chain is good value for money. The damage here was a fair $47. Making some preparations for the next day, I booked a flight with Papillon Grand Canyon Helicopter Tours for a price of $129 plus $16 tax. Williams is situated just 30 miles south of Grand Canyon NP.

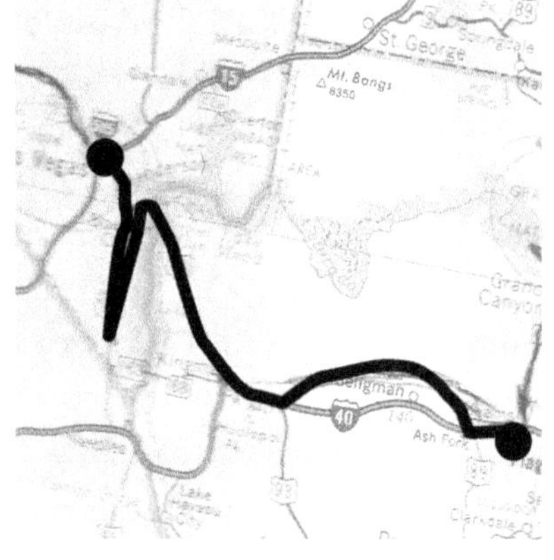

This day I had covered 300 miles, including my idiotic 66 mile detour down route 95. On TV the evening news showed pictures from Virginia. Downtown Richmond had been flooded with water.

Wednesday, September 1st 2004

The road to Grand Canyon is on the third exit at Williams. I decided to find out by wasting an extra 25 miles on Interstate 40 eastbound.

Finding Highway 180 from Flagstaff to Grand Canyon National Airport, I got to see the Ponderosa pine forest, but turned off to early, getting lost twice is a great way to start the day. At the airport I discovered that my temporary tag was dangling freely, attached with just one single plastic screw instead of four as it was supposed to. Looking at my picture of the bike taken in Las Vegas and at Hoover Dam the tag was fine, so somebody had tried to fuck with it while the motorcycle was parked overnight at Motel 6. If I hadn't noticed this, I don't think it would have been there at the end of the day.

I had never flown in a helicopter before so I was super excited. Along for the ride was another passenger, Michael from Australia. The pilot flying us over the Grand Canyon was an American married Japanese chick, Yoshiko. To my luck I got to ride shotgun in the front next to the pilot. (Riding shotgun was an American term used to describe the guard who rode alongside a stagecoach driver, ready to use his shotgun to ward off any attackers. Today, it refers to the practice of sitting alongside the driver in a moving vehicle.) Our flight was a half hour trip, and just hovering while waiting for another helicopter to pass ahead was pretty damn sweet. The Grand Canyon has a depth of over 6,093 feet (1,857 m) so we were approximately 1.25 miles (2 km) above the river. Sitting up I got a much better view out of the front as the lower part of the nose section is transparent. Me being me, I checked out Yoshiko's legs too. Nice.

I should have booked the slightly more expensive "Imperial Tour" for $169 + tax. I have since had the chance go on a helicopter ride with the side door open making for an adrenaline filled experience. If there is a next life, I want to be a helicopter pilot. I am a bit too short, vision on only one eye and a terrible swimmer, so getting a helicopter license in Denmark is not going to happen. So I had to choose the second best option, motorcycles. But if you ever get the chance to get a helicopter ride, don't miss out.

Anyway, I have noticed a lot of wealthy people and politicians tend to get killed in helicopter crashes. This especially seem to happen to politicians in the former soviet bloc countries, such as former Russian air force general Alexander Lebed who got killed in a helicopter crash in 2002.

Back at the airport, Yoshiko had the helicopter mechanic help me re-attach and secure the temporary license plate with some fresh bolts. I wonder how far I could have ridden without a license tag before getting stopped by the cops and getting my vehicle impounded.

Entering through the South Entrance on highway 64 my National Parks Pass again provided free entry. After buying a single use camera in Grand Canyon village, I was ready to check out Grand Canyon National Park. Grand Canyon is carved by the Colorado River, a process that started around 5 to 6 million years ago, simultaneously deepening and widening the canyon. The Yavada Point facing the North Rim is just 8.3 miles from the airport. Here I looked at nearly two billion years of Earth's geological history exposed as the Colorado River cut through and eroded the many layers of rock while the Colorado Plateau was uplifted. The Grand Canyon is 277 miles (446 km) long and up to 18 miles (29 km) wide, stretching through three states, Utah, Nevada and Arizona. The colors from this viewpoint are absolutely amazing as the sun shines onto the North Rim from the south. Standing here even the fattest American can appear small. The scale of this place is just massive and overwhelming at the same time.

Continuing on highway 64 I stopped by several more viewpoints. My guidebook stated that around 3 million visitors go to see the Grand Canyon each year, but this number has more than doubled as 6.38 million wen there in 2018. Grand Canyon offers many activities and going south on highway 89 was in hindsight a mistake as I missed out on Horseshoe Bend. This has become famous for tourists coming too close to the edge and falling 1,000 feet (300 m) to their deaths, as the law of gravity does not forgive foolish or risky behavior.

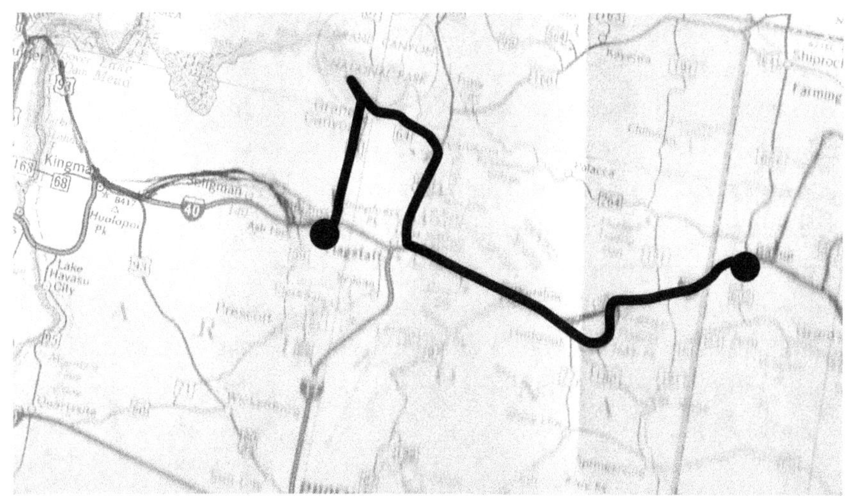

On highway 89 I was back in 30 miles of desert and prairie; and loving it. Reaching I-40 again, I gunned it for 55 miles keeping the speed at 80-85 mph until Winslow where I ate an early dinner. Should have waited as time was spent here that I needed later. From Holbrook, another 50 miles east, I went 18 miles to Petrified Forest National Park. This place is very significant to my dream of touring coast to coast, as a travel article about this place was the first time I read about motorcycle traveling in the USA.

Petrified Forest National Park is located in Navajo and Apache counties and known for its fossils of fallen trees that lived around 225 million years ago. Petrified Forest NP was declared a national park in 1962. The name originates from the many large deposits of petrified wood. The region was a low plain flanked by mountains to the south and southeast and a sea to the west. Streams flowing across from the highlands deposited inorganic sediment and organic matter, including trees, other plants and animals that had drowned or fallen into the water. While most organic matter decays rapidly or is eaten by other organisms, some were buried so fast that they remained intact, becoming fossilized. By eating dinner earlier, I lost one hour of daylight, and arrived just one hour before sunset and closing time. So this visit became an absolute rush job.

For the second time this day, my National Parks Pass lets me enter waiving the entrance fee. The fee area covers around 230 square miles (600 square km), encompassing semi-desert shrub steppe and highly eroded and colorful badlands. The park is about 30 miles (48 km) long and up to 12 miles (19 km) wide. Typical visitor activities include sightseeing, photography, and hiking. Having only one hour of daylight left I only got to experience a tiny bit of this national park. With less than 650,000 visitors in 2018, this is much less crowded than the viewpoints in Grand Canyon NP. With minimal time available I took a walk on the Giant Logs Trail which is less than half a mile in length and located right behind the Rainbow Forest Visitor Center.

The main attraction is "Old Faithful". Sharing the name with the famous geyser in Yellowstone, this is a massive petrified log that was named by the wife of the park's first superintendent. Along with this I just get a quick glimpse of the other sights within walking distance. The northern part of Petrified Forest NP extends into the Painted Desert, and the park ranger recommended watching the sunset on the Painted Desert Rim Trail as the color changes during this. Not unlike what I experienced looking at Ayers Rock (Uluru) in Australia at dawn.

Petrified Forest was a bit disappointing due to my late arrival, but an essential stop for me personally. Getting back on the Monster, it is close to pitch dark, so the headlamp from the bike is the only light source in vicinity. Interstate 40 is less than a mile from the Painted Desert Visitor Center, so I rolled a further 49 miles east to Gallup. It is chilly to ride in Arizona after dark. After 380 miles ridden, including a 25 mile detour in the morning, I checked in at Motel 6 for the handsome sum of $46.

The left turn signal on the Ducati had started to act up, not working every single time activated. And I was now in New Mexico.

Ah, Italian electricals…

Thursday, September 2nd 2004

Waking up early, I talked to a guy towing his Harley Davidson Ultra Glide on a trailer. I can understand people hauling choppers as many of them are super uncomfortable, but it has always puzzled me when people trailer touring bikes instead of actually having fun riding them long distance. I know it happens, but I don't recall seeing anyone trailering their Honda Gold Wing on my journey. If you want street cred as a biker, you need to ride your bike on a street. Talking to this guy, he told me that he had never seen a Ducati before.

Firing up my L-twin beast at 8:45 am, I realized that I had ridden past Red Rock State Park yesterday, so instead of going 220 miles back west I turn and continued east. It was too hot for hiking in motorcycle gear anyway. I must have been tired from yesterday's ride as I came close to laying the bike down for the third time.

Going down Interstate 40 for most of the day, a Ford Explorer was keeping the speed at the allowed 65 mph limit, so I ended up riding close behind this guy for a while. Getting annoyed with looking at his tailgate and the turbulence the truck bed created, I overtook right away. Some people don't like to be overtaken, so he started to tailgate me too. If he wanted to race, fine with me.

In Clines Corners I missed the route 285 off ramp to Roswell because of roadworks east of Moriarty. Roswell is of course the home of Area 51 and stories of UFO crashes. I love a good conspiracy but expecting a bunch of loonies trying to sell alien merchandise and tin foil hats, I decided to pass on this. I have actually seen what I would describe as a UFO right in the suburb town I grew up in. On a clear day I observed a black object high up in the sky and simply couldn't figure out what it was. Looking away and looking up again this thing was still there. With an airport nearby I knew how the usual air traffic looked like.

So yeah, I actually respect people who claim to have seen a UFO.

Besides the conspiracies concerning the Kennedy assassination and Roswell alien activity, I do not believe the moon landing was faked. Had this been the case the commies would have been slapping the USA in the face with the embarrassing proof for years. So the concept of a faked moon landing may have been the ultimate successful Soviet conspiracy.

The conspiracy to plant the theories denying the moon landing.

Maybe is it possible to go crazy while looking for sanity?

Sticking to I-40 for 250 miles, I took a right at Santa Rosa, going 50 miles south on highway 84 to Fort Sumner. With Red Rock out of the picture, I had read a flyer at Motel 6 about William H. Bonney aka. the famous outlaw Billy the Kid being buried in the local cemetery.

Having killed eight people himself, Billy the Kid was shot dead in 1881, just 21 years old. Fort Sumner isn't a big place, around a thousand people reside here. Finding the cemetery wasn't an issue but getting in posed a problem. The cemetery was closed and it took me a while to figure out why. Mr. Brain had forgotten to set the clock on the bike, so being on mountain time I had arrived one hour later than what I thought. Easy Rider my ass. I need a GPS that can show the time too.

With nothing to stick around for, I hopped on highway 60 east and after riding through Clovis I was in Texas. Texas has a certain vibe to it and I imagined pictures of the stereotypical redneck sheriffs conducting speed checks all over the place. There must be something to it as I saw plenty of cop cars on the highways and the following day on Interstate 40. I even saw a cop car parked at a school when I drove past. Thinking it would be dark at 7 pm, I whipped it to Lubbock. Texas is in the Central time zone so the sun sets at 8 pm. The damn time zones got me bamboozled twice in the same day.

In Texas everything is bigger, and the wind gusts are brutal on highway 84. I fact so hard I got close to get hit by a moving box flying off a truck. In Lubbock, I found my way to Super 8. I am not camping after more than five hundred miles and at $48 there was no need to look elsewhere. And yeah, an Indian family owned the motel.

Before putting my feet up I went to the nearby 7-Eleven. Buying some Slim Jims, a thin sausage snack in plastic and some root beer, two scruffy looking guys were sitting outside. Asking for some small change, I dropped the few pennies I got inside the convenience store. As usual I did not walk around alone after dark unless I had to, so I returned to the hotel making sure those guys weren't following me. Not being paranoid, but I am also not dumb enough to put myself at risk.

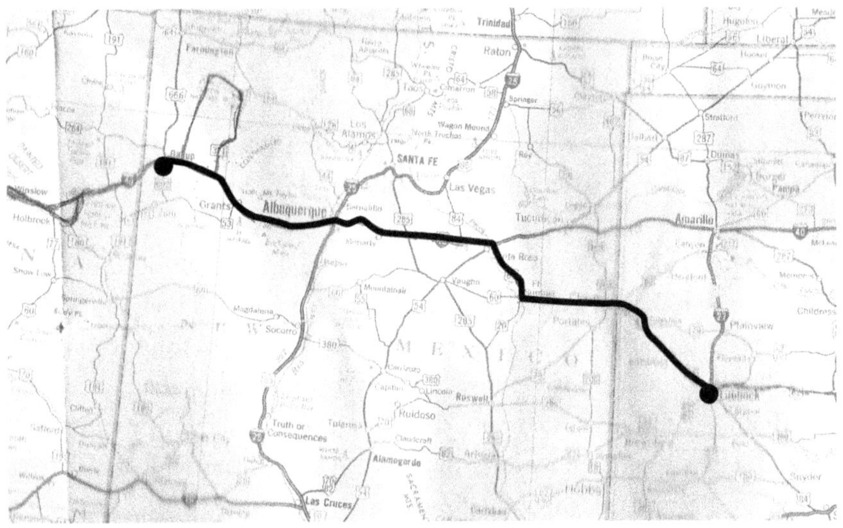

Lubbock is 160 miles from Fort Sumner, so this is the day where I covered the most distance on this trip, a grand total of 510 miles. The longest ride I have done in a day in the USA was in 2011 on my Harley 883 Sportster, going 600 miles to Minneapolis. Having ridden 480 miles I decided I would do the extra 120 miles to my final destination so that I didn't have to fork out for a motel.

Checking my Road Atlas, it was just 160 to Abilene where Tom Stone was from. I got his e-mail in Sturgis, but trying to meet up with him before noon the next day could be a hassle, as he most likely would be on duty for the sheriff's department.

I have never tried Slim Jim's before.
I am not going to again.

Dallas

I rode out of Lubbock at 8:45 AM, or so I thought. The clock on bike was still on Mountain time as I set it at the Fort Sumner Cemetery. Texas uses Central time, so yay, an hour of daylight less for me today. Eastbound on highway 82, it was a chilly start to the day, so I closed the vents in my jacket. Later, approaching noon, this became too hot.

Texas partially remind me of home as has many smells and is very flat. You don't notice that in a car, but on a bike you are not boxed in a sealed cage. And I like to ride with the flip front open feeling and sensing the environment around me.

At Henrietta, I should have turned off at highway 287 to Fort Worth/ Dallas, so having missed the intersection, I continued on highway 82 through Wichita Falls to Sherman, more than fifty miles extra on the road. Here I turn south on highway 75 to Dallas.

Dallas is the third largest city in Texas, and the ninth largest in the USA. Around 1.3 million people lives in the city, which is the largest in-land metropolitan area without any infrastructural connection via waterway. For me Dallas means two things, a presidential assassination and an 80s TV show starring Larry Hagman as Jr. Premiering in the USA in 1978, the first episode aired in Denmark on December 26th, 1980. With the amount of TV channels limited to four, this was a piece of Americana that had a big impact in Denmark at the time. Portraying an image of the lifestyle of wealthy Americans, it had a big audience and tied in nicely with Ronald Reagan becoming the 40th President of the United States.

Arriving in Dallas, it had become a habit for me to find something to eat before reaching a destination -or find that I am lost. Sitting down and studying my Road Atlas, I might as well eat too. So hello Burger King. The triple cheeseburger I bought was a bit gross, all I could taste was meat and cheese. Looking for accommodation, I got back on highway 75. Without spotting any motels from the road, I decided to look for Elm Street instead.

Having studied Main and Elm St. the day before, both run parallel in downtown Dallas. Parking on Main St. was not a good idea with my luggage strapped to the bike. I thought if I left it on the bike, it wouldn't be there when I got back. So I decided to lug the swag and tent with me as I went to see Elm. St. What a pain in the ass having to carry this around. On the way I gave some small change to a really dirty homeless African American guy. He did come off as dope head addict. In return he gave me some directions. I later discovered that I easily could have found a parking spot much closer.

Just like the 9-11 attacks in New York, everyone alive at the time knows where they were on November 22, 1963, at 12:30 pm. At this point in time, the 35th president John F. Kennedy was shot and killed while seated in an open top convertible Lincoln Continental, riding in a presidential motorcade going through Dealey Plaza and onto Elm St. Kennedy was rushed to Parkland Memorial Hospital but was pronounced dead about thirty minutes later. The assassin, former U.S. Marine Lee Harvey Oswald ambushed the presidential motorcade from the nearby book depository. Dealey Plaza has two plaques describing the historical event, including a map showing where the projectiles struck.

In front of this book depository a guy standing on the other side of the crosswalk yells at me if I was taking a picture of him. Looking for a fight or not I just say no. Either he must have been cheating on his wife with the woman next to him, or else he had an ego problem. Who the fuck cares what some random stranger thinks? Some people just have a bad attitude and I see no reason giving these types an inch. The same goes for people jumping in front of me in a line, I have no problem getting physical and staking my claim. I believe you should not automatically let other people push you around. Getting into a fight is not usual for me, the last time I was decades ago way back when I was 18. But I have never shied away from getting into a conflict if I deemed it necessary. I am also pretty indifferent to threats of being sued, and my auto reaction is to end any talks and negotiation as soon as anybody mentions the words "lawyer" or "lawsuit". People act like assholes when they can get away with it or think they can.

So never give an inch.

To show consideration is healthy and enables you to act correctly, with courtesy, sense and reason. So one of the other tourists at Dealey Plaza helped out taking a few pictures of me in this historic spot. Like Abraham Lincoln, John F. Kennedy was shot in the back of the head. Two white "X" markers have been placed on Elm St. in the exact spots where the bullets struck. Having watched a few documentaries about the JFK assassination and the Oliver Stone movie starring Kevin Costner, I also checked out the parking lot and the grassy knoll.

Something doesn't add up and the FBI files has been classified to an extent that does leave plenty of room for numerous conspiracy theories. If you are in denial of the truth you'll just end up lying to yourself. And concerning Kennedy, somebody is not telling the full story.

Or Lee Harvey Oswald was one of the most amazing shooters in history.

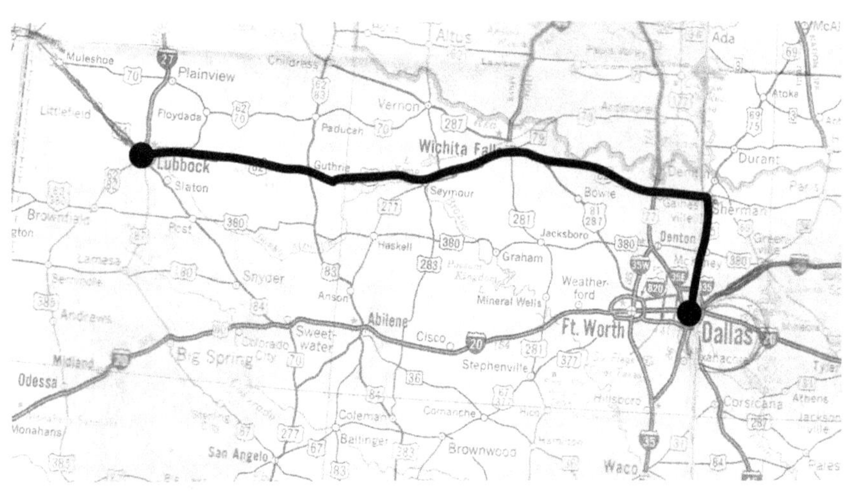

Interstate 30 runs south of Dealey Plaza and going 40 miles to Greenville, the landscape becomes greener and more lush. Going from Lubbock to Greenville via Dallas, I covered 450 miles this day. I was traveling east at a fairly rapid pace.

Checked in at another Motel 6, school had started again and low season for the motels had begun. So I got a room for just $38 + tax. Again, those Indian folk seem to dominate the American motel industry…

Saturday, September 4th 2004

With a goal of reaching Memphis today, I had a 400 mile ride ahead. Checking out of Motel 6 at 10:30 AM, I think the changes in time zones was affecting my sleep and ability to wake up early. Wanting to get to Memphis before sunset I took I-30 to Texarkana. Interstate travel is effective but you don't see nearly as much as you do on highways, so after 131 miles I found myself in Arkansas. No day without getting lost, missing an exit or taking a wrong turn. So for some inexplicable reason I ended up on Route 82 west to El Dorado, where I should have turned off in Magnolia onto highway 79. When lost I don't turn around unless it is an obvious advantage, this ensured that every day become an adventure.

So I punched on to El Dorado and 167 miles northeast up highway 167. The speed limit is 55 mph. I was going 55-65 mph. but tried to avoid attracting attention. I must say I always drive sensibly within city limits. Approaching Memphis the weather is very hot and humid, so I began to lose concentration and felt drowsy. Once again I found myself dehydrated, so I down a 17 ounce bottle of water. After 450 miles on the road, I checked in at Motel 6 West Memphis for $48. This is on the west side of the Mississippi River. Not knowing anything about the area I chained the bike to a banister, unsure if I was partially blocking a handicap access ramp. This might have been the least eventful day of this trip. Talking with another motel guest about what to do in Memphis, he recommended Beale St. near downtown. This is also known as the birthplace of Blues music. Not too much into blues, but blues and soul was the base for rock'n roll. And yeah, I love rock'n roll.

Arriving late afternoon and with a bit of drizzle from above, I was not going into downtown Memphis at this time. So in order to get the most out of the next day I did a little study in my guidebook to prepare for it. Watching the weather forecast on TV, there was a storm warning over my intended end destination, Florida. Hurricane Frances had triggered the largest pre-emptive evacuation in the history of the state of Florida and was coming ashore within the next few days. This would turn out to have a great impact on my intended route.

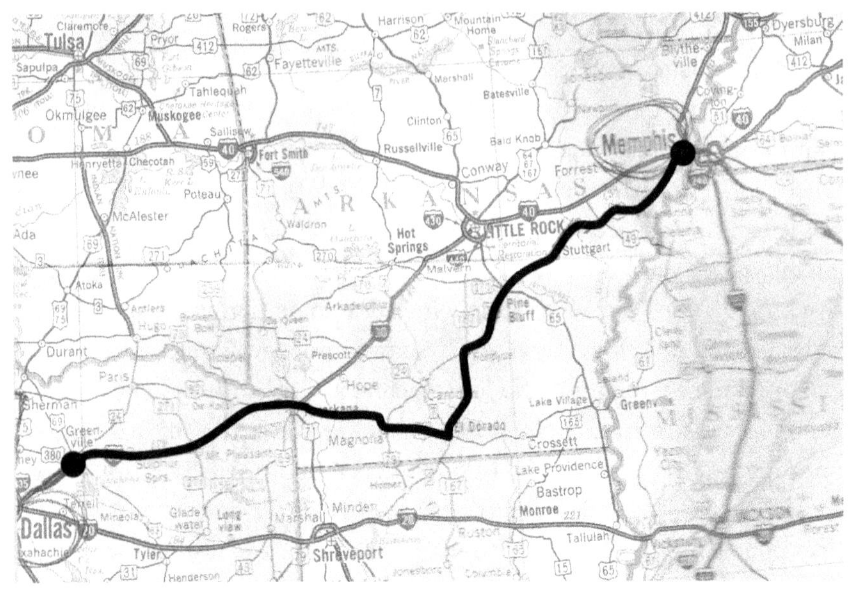

I guess we all have done some thinking about the future.
Where will I find myself in ten years? Besides the option of being dead,
cremated and buried, this is impossible to predict.
Society has a long list of guidelines you can follow, education,
the dole or work, giving you something to relate to.
It is not difficult to imagine the possible outcomes of all the plans
you may have, but you can't count on these to hold up.
So we choose to believe that we will succeed, but you'll be forced to look
at things from another perspective when the World gets real and in your
face, a rear tire blows or something unexpected happens.
Less of a fairy tale, but still an adventure.

Time always runs in top gear.
Suddenly the planned future becomes the past.
You cannot afford to make this mistake more than a few times.
Lost time doesn't come back.

I don't know what the future will bring for me. Of course I hope to be a
wealthy writer. I do what I can to make this a part of my future.
My other goals in life should also be achievable.
The future belongs to no one but yourself.

Walking in Memphis

Crossing the Mississippi for the second time since the Twin Cities, I rode into Memphis and the state of Tennessee. While Nashville is the state capitol, Memphis is Tennessee's largest city. The central city has a population of around 650,000, but when including West Memphis and the greater metropolitan area 1.35 million people lives here, making Memphis the 25th largest city in the USA. Loving useless trivia, the largest employer in Memphis is the multinational courier corporation FedEx, whose global air hub is Memphis International Airport, making it the second-busiest cargo airport in the world.

Dropping in on Beale Street, this was cordoned off for traffic. After parking the bike, I took a quick stroll and found most places being closed for business as I arrived early on a Sunday. I gave some small change to a beggar who in return provided me with directions to the Lorraine Motel on Mulberry Street. On foot I passed what must have been a gated community, an entire block encircled by a ten foot brick wall. Not very charming, but the United States is a land of contrast. Just a few blocks from the White House in Washington D.C. you can find yourself in what is basically a slum. Giving up figuring out the directions given, I end up taking the bike there.

In its earlier days Memphis was prospering from agricultural goods, natural resources like lumber and, with the Mississippi River location, the American slave trade. Memphis has the largest African-American population in Tennessee, and a prominent role in the history of the American civil rights movement.

Starting my journey visiting historical sites in Washington D.C., I am close to coming full circle. Looking down the Mall on July 18th from the Lincoln Monument where Dr. Martin Luther King Jr. made his famous "I have a dream"-speech, to the Lorraine Motel in Memphis where he was assassinated on the second floor balcony by James Earl Ray on March 29th, 1968. My guidebook refers to the Lorraine Motel having been closed for a long time and that a National Civil Rights Center was planned to open in 1990. Well, my old book was a bit outdated as it took me 15 years before I got to use it. A Smithsonian affiliate institution, The National Civil Rights Museum opened in 1991 and is a complex of museums and historic buildings centered around the Lorraine Motel. Its exhibits traces the history of the Civil Rights Movement from the 17th century to the present. Unfortunately, I arrived there on a Sunday where it opened at 1 pm.

An American Baptist minister, Martin Luther King Jr. led the Montgomery bus boycott in Alabama, against the policy of racial segregation on the public transit system. This was a seminal event for the Civil Rights Movement. The campaign started in late 1955 and lasted almost a year, after Rosa Parks, an African-American woman, was arrested for refusing to surrender her seat to a white person. The boycott only ended when a United States Supreme Court decision declared the Alabama and Montgomery segregation laws unconstitutional.

Martin Luther King Jr. is best known for advancing civil rights through non-violence and civil disobedience, inspired by his Christian beliefs and inspired by the nonviolent activism of Mahatma Gandhi. In my view, a true American hero. Like Nelson Mandela in South Africa, he sure made a big difference for a lot of people. I remember when Nelson Mandela was released in 1990 after 27 years of incarceration, becoming president just four years later, forgiving past injustice and working for national reconciliation. Had I received the treatment given to King or Mandela, I would forgive nothing and be out to get even.

Not waiting 2 hours for the National Civil Rights Museum to open, I decided to go see the other sights that Memphis had to offer instead. During a short stop along the shoreline of the Mississippi, I thought this area would be super nice for a picnic. It is getting warmer as noon approaches, so I got on the Monster and went to Sun Studios. This is where Elvis Presley recorded some of his first songs before he became the King of Rock'n roll. Not a big place, the tour starts every thirty minutes and cost $9.99. Not really worth it, this place first and foremost came off as a merchandise shop to me. The most notable thing was actually a couple of other visitors outside, dressed in an impeccable 1950s rockabilly style. The girl with full sleeve tattoos, sharp make-up, polka dot dress and Dorothy hairdo with bangs. The guy looked a bit more like a biker without a bike, sporting tattoos too, a big wallet chain, suspenders, bowling shirt and a low mohawk. Sun Studios wasn't impressive, so been there, seen it.

I am an Elvis man, so there was no way I would miss the biggest attraction in town, Graceland, the mansion once owned by Elvis Aaron Presley. Since the passing of her father in 1977, Graceland has been owned by Lisa Marie Presley. Like Prince and Bruce Springsteen, Elvis has recorded some songs which are absolutely amazing. (Being a horrible singer, the only song I can get away with on karaoke night is "Can't Help Falling In Love.") Located on 3764 Elvis Presley Boulevard, it is a twenty minute ride 7.6 miles down hwy 51 from Sun Studios.

As I was on a motorcycle, I got to park for free at the souvenir shop next door. The normal charge for a car was $2. Here I bought a keyring, some postcards and a t-shirt. Wanting to buy a single-use camera, I somehow ended up in the line for tickets to Graceland Mansion, so I didn't get to take any pictures from inside. Not the worst thing that could happen, as it took twenty minutes to buy the $27 ticket which includes the memorabilia museum, car and motorcycle museum and Graceland itself. There was another wait to get into Graceland, visitors are brought in by minivans in small groups. Waiting for this there is an option to see the inside of the two private jets owned by Elvis, "Lisa Marie" and "Hound Dog 1". Like everyone else, I got some pictures taken in front of the entrance gates too. Here I talked to a Danish couple from Copenhagen. As they were an older folk, they were crossing the USA in a car. Traveling in a car or RV is a very different experience than on a bike, but if you wait too you may not have the health to do this on two wheels. And I must add that novice riders should get some experience with long distance riding before taking on a coast to coast ride.

Graceland Mansion sits at the top of a hill in an oak grove with surrounding pastures and is a two-story residence in the Colonial Revival style with two chimneys and four Corinthian columns. The mansion measures 17,552 square feet (1,630.6 m2) and has 23 rooms, including eight bedrooms and bathrooms.

After purchasing Graceland, the King spent more than half a million on modifications including a wrought-iron front gate shaped like a book of sheet music, with green colored musical notes and a silhouette of himself. He also installed a kidney shaped swimming pool and a racquetball court.

Besides showing the piano and furniture, plenty of memorabilia is on display inside Graceland. Personally I was most interested in seeing the extension called the Jungle Room which features an indoor waterfall of cut field stone on the north wall. Along with the TV room, this was basically the King's man-cave. Elvis often watched three television sets at once, and the TV room's west wall displays Elvis' 1970s logo of a lightning bolt and cloud with the initials TCB, for 'taking care of business in a flash'. TCB is also outlaw biker slang for beating somebody up or killing them, so I found this quite intriguing. The tour ends in the meditation garden, which is the site of Elvis's grave. Some visitors were in tears which I did find a little over the top as he has been dead since the first Star Wars movie premiered in theaters.

Back on the other side of Elvis Presley Boulevard, I got around to buy that camera I needed. I do think the souvenir shop employees have a hard job, having to listen to Elvis songs playing on repeat in the background the entire workday, each and every one of them, must be exhausting.

Elvis was into motorcycles too and he had Harley Davidson Sportsters and Electra Glides. Standing next to his pink Cadillac in the Car museum, this looked just massive.
Elvis Presley's story and legacy is still impressive today and he remains the best-selling solo artist with sales estimates ranging from 600 million to 1 billion albums and singles. Graceland is a must when in Memphis, but I don't really need to go back to see it again.

Elvis Presley's Graceland has expanded since I went, so today there is even more to see than described above. If you are not into Elvis I do suggest you listen to a compilation album of his greatest hits.

He sure was one of a kind.

Like Elvis had a singing talent above average, I truly believe that everyone is good at something. Some motorcycle riders has the ability to ride fast on any road, it just comes naturally to them. Others are great salespeople, have great social skills, are great dancers, highly skilled within a craft or have deep knowledge within a scientific field. A segment has talent within non-legal professions, where they excel at crime, spraying graffiti art or evading the law.

Leaving Graceland, I tried to find Route 78 heading north in Memphis. Asking a white woman for directions, she wouldn't talk to me. This is the first time I had encountered what could be interpreted as racism or bigoted behavior on my trip around the USA.

Well, being open and extrovert is a big advantage when you're traveling. My general impression of southern folk is that they are very friendly.

With plenty of daylight to burn, I decided to go as far as I felt I had the energy for. Riding in the dark is not much fun. I couldn't see too much through the visor as the weather conditions became a bit moist and foggy. American highways have no reflective markers on the sides so I can't recommend going at high speed after dark. Being tailgated by a car for a while, I wave for them to overtake. In the dark, it is difficult to estimate how far off cars behind you actually are. Also, in case you crash it could take a while for someone to discover that you have come off, so riding alone isn't always the best idea either.

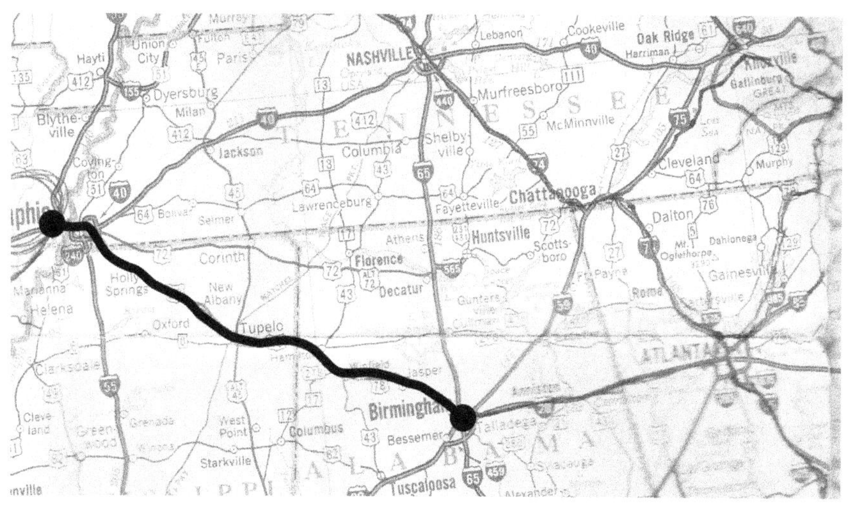

I ended up riding 250 miles through Mississippi and reached Birming-ham, Alabama around 10:30 pm, so dinner at McDonald's was unusually late.

On the parking lot an African American babe next to an SUV smiles at me, I reckon she figured the motorcycle in the parking lot belonged to the geezer with the helmet. Her companion looked like he had been friend-zoned and didn't appear too happy about that. As I rode out she waved to me, the SUV wasn't his! I did find it understandable why this guy would hang around, everybody likes a hot chick in a cool car.
But it did make him look like a beta male.

Days Inn got a room for $58. I discovered the bathtub wasn't watertight, and the floor got flooded. It was close to midnight, so I didn't care to report it. Days Inn's problem, not mine.

Monday, September 6th 2004

The first Monday in September is known as Labor Day in the USA.
A federal public holiday, this honors the American labor movement and the contributions that workers have made to the strength, prosperity, laws, and well-being of the nation. As it falls on a Monday, the long weekend is known as Labor Day Weekend.

As I rode until the late evening yesterday, I checked out of the Birmingham Days Inn at 11 am. Being updated on the serious weather situation in Florida, I decided to give Miami a pass, as "Frances" had made huge damage already. Just three weeks prior the hurricane "Charlie" caused massive destruction there too. To top this off, a third hurricane named "Ivan" was brewing off the Florida coast, and none of the experts had any prediction how this would play out.

This did chafe a bit, but I wasn't going to play tourist in a disaster area.

Eastbound, and alternating between Highway 78 East and Interstate 20 for 160 miles, the landscape became greener and lusher again.

After around three hours I reach Atlanta, the home of Coca Cola, in the state of Georgia. The greater Atlanta area is home to 5.8 million people, but without any research I didn't ride into downtown, and it was still Labor Day. On Interstate 85, the car in the right lane made an emergency stop in front of a rolled up carpet that had come off another vehicle. He narrowly avoids taking me out swerving around it. I was going 65 mph, so that could quickly have gotten nasty.

Out of greater metropolitan Atlanta area I cruised through some soothing green landscape to North Carolina on Highway 23 north.

On July 21st, the very first day after riding out of Moto Europa heading west, I did take a wrong turn trying to get to the Blue Ridge Parkway. After ninety miles I was back in the Smokey Mountains. This time in the south end, so I was close to having travelled full circle for the third time like with LAX airport and the two Martin Luther King Jr. sites.

While the weather conditions in Florida may have been horrible, it also made this part of the days ride awful too. Only encountering serious rainfall riding through South Dakota with Wayne, Al, Ron and Joe, the rain and cloudy conditions made it almost impossible to see through the visor and the traffic being fairly dense, this was no joy.

Fortunately, my jacket was waterproof, so it kept me dry and the rain out.

Even with the shitty weather, the Smokey Mountains are simply beautiful just before sunset. After sixty miles in the Smokies, I turned off Highway 23 onto my "old friend", Interstate 40 to Asheville. At an Asheville gas station, yet another guy called me out with a "Nice bike" compliment.

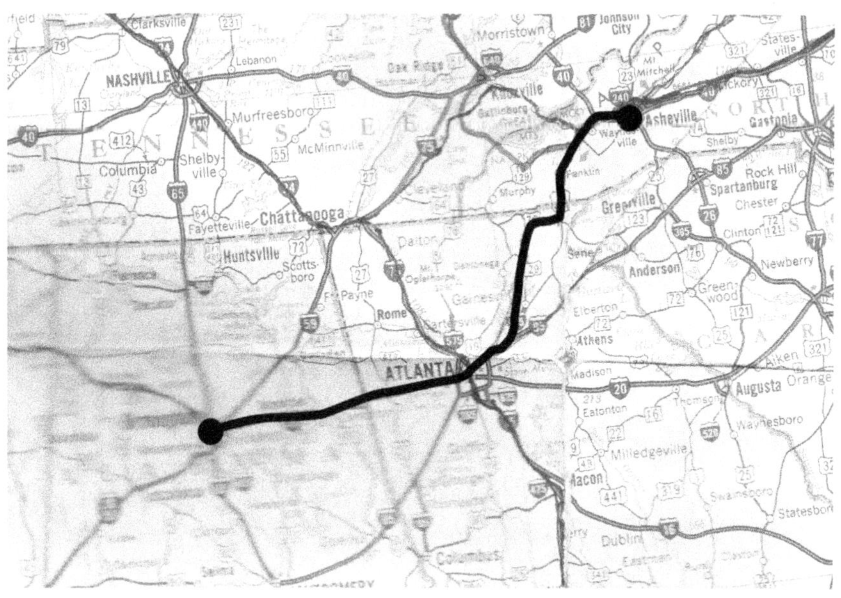

I think I have started to build a preference for staying at Motel 6, so I got a room in Asheville for $46. Had I known about the legendary road called Tail of the Dragon at the time, I would have stayed there an extra day for sure, as it is just 100 miles away.

Designated highway 129, the Tail of the Dragon is also known as Deals Gap, an old Native American trail on the border of Tennessee and North Carolina. This has been paved and has become another must ride destination for bikers from all over the World. What makes this unique is that it has 318 curves in 11 miles with no intersecting roads or driveways. I have had the chance to ride on this twice, in 2009 and 2011, and along with New Zealand it is heaven for motorcycle enthusiasts. The road is bordered by the Great Smoky Mountains and the Cherokee National Forest. That means steep drops in case you come off the road, and usually a few people die there every year. The speed limit is 30 mph but some go at very high speeds and others cross the double center line that runs the entire length of the 11 mile trail. The cops are very aware of this and they do make a lot of speed controls. Personally, I crossed the double center line twice on each run, it really demands absolute focus and concentration. The Dragon is so demanding that I barely averaged the legal speed limit.

This day I rode 310 miles I am now on Eastern time. Checking my map, the plan tomorrow was to get on the Blue Ridge Parkway via exit 53A.

Tuesday, September 7th 2004

Leaving Motel 6 at 11 am, I finally found myself on the Blue Ridge Parkway, albeit much later than hoped. Here I met seven other motorcycles. Unfortunately, the rain and foggy conditions continued the entire day. The rainfall was remnants of Hurricane Frances and turned the mountain sides into small waterfalls. With a measured thirteen inches of rain, this was the largest amount of downpour in North Carolina since the 1960s, leaving three million people without electrical power. The cost of Hurricane Frances was expected to end up between two and four billion dollars.

It wasn't cold, but so incredibly wet that my riding gear couldn't keep me dry. It isn't unusual that Gore-tex can't keep you completely isolated in extreme conditions, as rainwater running from the tank and from the back of the seat will seep down to the lowest point where the rider sits.
Water also has a habit to find its way down your collar.

Not having a car permit, but just a motorcycle license, I am used to riding in rain as a motorcycle has been my only personal transportation option for several years. The twisty mountain roads would normally be super fun but now I had to turn in at a covered terrace rest stop as the rain penetrated my boots and the cooling effect of the Smokey Mountains was pretty harsh. The weather was so bad another guy in a car had stopped to take a break too, he didn't feel safe driving in such piss poor conditions either. A Park Ranger had followed us for at bit beforehand and stopped to check if everything was ok.

While waiting for the water to run off my riding gear, I checked my Road Atlas. This lifesaver had been indispensable without a GPS, and I used it so much that it became so worn and tender that it had started to come apart. With a speed limit of 35 mph, being cold and wet, unable to see the mountains through the fog, I decided to give up as this was not working at all. Getting back on the Monster, the remote to my immobilizer temporarily stopped working. After a few attempts, the fuel pump fortunately primed, and the Monster started breathing fire again.

Sticking my feet in the water ten days ago at Santa Monica Pier in California, I actually had not physically touched the water on the East coast. The plan was to do so in Miami Beach, but that wasn't going to happen as the hurricane season had shortened my journey by a week. Touching the water of the Atlantic Ocean would have to be elsewhere and my alternate choice to do this was Virginia Beach. Taking Highway 421 south, and with a bit of hassle finding my way out of the Smokies, I was back on I-40 again toward Durham 230 miles east. After 300 miles I ended the days ride in Butner on Interstate 85 North. Here Econolodge has a room for $47. The warm shower was worth every penny.

Out of the mountains, North Carolina was super humid. Back in 2004 comfort amenities such as heated hand grips weren't widely available for motorcycles, but today these are becoming a highly requested option. I have had aftermarket heated grips on my last two motorcycles and today I wouldn't buy one without fitting such. I sure as hell could have used them on this day.

The smart phone revolution has snuck in motorcycles, as has bluetooth connectivity, helmet speaker headsets and LCD screens replacing analog dials and gauges. The next big thing is cruise control becoming standard on motorcycles. Not kidding, I'll want that too. More electronics does mean more shit that can potentially break and fail...

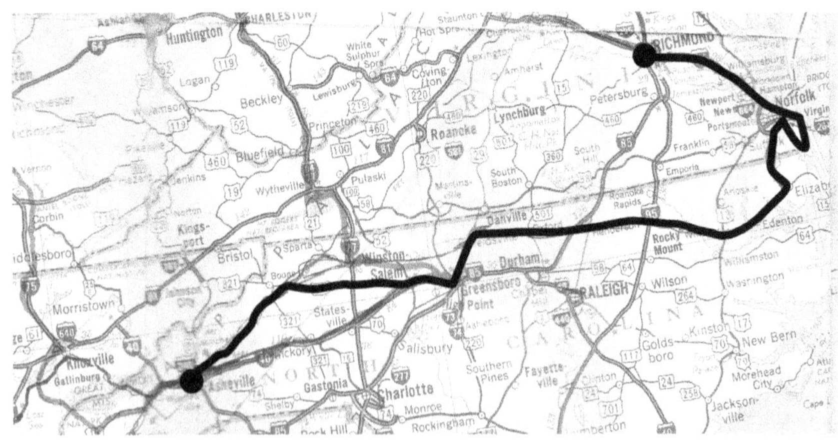

Wet feet in Virginia

Out of Butner I continued up Interstate 85 and my oil warning light came on, forcing me to stop immediately. 25% of motorcycle repairs are electrical problems. This could be a serious issue, but as this was my third Ducati Monster, I knew exactly where to troubleshoot this. The oil pressure contact is located in front of the clutch cover and above the oil inspection window on the left side of the engine. With all the rainfall in the last two days, I expected moisture or water to have gotten past the plug seals. Pulling out the wire plug going into the oil pressure switch proved me right. So the super easy solution was to wipe the water off and blow a couple of times on the plug. This fix sorted the problem immediately.

Part of owning a motorcycle is accumulating some basic knowledge of motorcycles in general and learning specifics about your own specific model. Having a motorcycle garage workshop is a big advantage when it comes to maintenance, especially if you have the space to install a motorcycle lift. It can be a lot of fun tinkering and servicing your motorcycle yourself and this part of the hobby can also save you a good chunk of cash too. Some motorcycle owners are pretty anal when it comes to keeping a motorcycle in mint and almost pristine condition. A fair amount of motorcyclists actually spend more time polishing chrome than actually riding. I am not in that camp. A quick wash and some fresh oil is enough for me to be ready to ride. A motorcycle is meant to be used, the manufacturers always come out with a new and improved model next year.

With a motorcycle as a primary mode of transport for quite a few years, I have also been riding during several winter seasons. I cannot recommend this as road salt really takes its toll on engine cases and especially oil- and water cooling radiators. The fork tubes and triple trees are also vulnerable to harsh weather.

From I-85 I went onto Route 158 East 135 miles to Elizabeth. These were the worst road surfaces I had been on since leaving LA. My wrong turn of the day sent me towards Kitty Hawk, so I turned around as soon as possible. I could have gone to Kitty Hawk Beach but stuck to my decision going to Virginia Beach 60 miles north. My Road Atlas being from 2003, the year prior, the road to Virginia Beach was indicated as under construction. Going through a tunnel underpass I guess they didn't manage to finish this yet.

Finally reaching the beach, it was windy, but sunny. Only a few people were present, but I got a guy to take a couple of pictures of me. My story seemed to impress him a bit, this being the exact point in my life where I had touched water on each side of the United States of America. Having been at both ends of the continent is not the same as having travelled across and making the West and East coasts the end destinations.

Dipping my feet, I made a quick taste test too.

Time to get to Richmond. My Ducati at home was the entry level model, so I wanted to sell this and ship my two-wheeled travel companion back to Denmark. This being the top model, it would be a sweet upgrade. Going on Highway 164 to I-60 to the Virginia state capitol, more monstrous rain came down as I came back into Richmond, so I slid out into the intersection at the I-64 interchange. I fortunately didn't lay down the red beast. It would have been super crap to wipeout on the last day of riding.

Arriving after dark, I checked into the same Comfort Inn near Moto Europa I stayed at once before for $82. To celebrate the end of my grand motorcycle tour I went down to the bar and ordered a Samuel Adams Boston Lager. The bartender asked for ID, which hadn't really happened a lot on this trip. Well, until I started to get some grey hair on my head I have always looked like a kid. Being a short guy didn't help either, my mother didn't bring a lot of money with her on the day she went out to buy legs for me. The United States legal drinking age is 21.
This is in my opinion a bit odd, young people go drinking anyway.

Thursday, September 9th 2004

Order of the day was to get the Ducati serviced at Moto Europa and cart my ass to New York City. Missing out on Florida, I wanted to spend some days in the Big Apple. Calling Holiday Inn in Manhattan I booked a room there for $200. Expensive like Chicago, but right in the middle of everything. Since I had travelled by motorcycle, Greyhound Bus and airplane, a train ride would be interesting to try when I had the chance. An economy Amtrak ticket from Richmond to New York was $99 and departure time was 3:05 pm.

The folks at Ducati Richmond were a bit surprised to see me, expecting my return a couple of weeks later. My trip, shortened by Hurricane Frances, was just two months into my allowed three month visa, and I had planned to stay a five to seven days in New York City, leaving a buffer of two weeks in my initial plan. But with a week cut out in Florida, it did chafe me that I wouldn't get to ride down to Key West.

Moto Europa had seen some changes in the last month. Matt had quit to become a car salesman. I was curious to know what happened to their office assistant Joyce. She had disappeared without notice on August 3rd. This was very mystical as she could have had in a traffic accident or even been murdered. The general manager Stubbs had gotten in contact with her, and physically she was fine, so she had just quit without any warning.

If you have a fair sense of how it is acceptable to behave towards others,
you will want to shift up a gear or two. Show a kind side,
be of use to others and thus yourself. Grow as a person.
Help out, make an extra effort and do your best.
A "thank you" has greater value than what we usually care to remember.
Some people just seem to have forgotten this.

I do know the real world is not that rosy.

The American job market is brutal and you really can end up with the duff end of a wishbone. Fast-food jobs are low-paying work, and some sales jobs are fully commission based, so without performing you're not getting paid. Some employers don't give a rats ass about their employees. But unhappy employees do what they're told and no more than that. A lot of productivity and good ideas stays off the table on that account. Unhappy employees will leave at the first instant a better option comes along, and their productivity often reflects their relation to the workplace. Wrong does not become right with an apology. So something wasn't adding up and I felt I didn't get the full story of what had gone down at Moto Europa.

With my intention to import the Ducati S4 to Denmark, I could make a better deal having some modifications done before shipping it. I wanted to black out the frame, add tapered handlebars including an aftermarket triple three. Waiting for Stubbs to calculate a price, I talked to another customer on a Suzuki DL 650 V-Strom. With everything I had seen, the topic of helmet usage came up. Motorcyclists all have some fantastic stories, and this guy had come off his bike on the Interstate from Newport News.
Not wearing a helmet every time he was riding; he had used a full face helmet on the day of this accident. Facing down and seeing the asphalt sliding by three inches away from his eyes, changed his mind about helmet usage.

My customization idea was a $1300 piece of motorcycle surgery.
With 12,100 miles on the odometer, it was time for another big service and a fresh set of tires too. Besides that, I needed to have the problem with the alarm fixed, as blowing fuses wasn't going to fly. This was sorted as a warranty issue, so it didn't add any further costs. Wrench monkey Curtis said it looked like a serious grounding problem. The broken clutch lever cost $60, I should have had this sorted sooner, as the end bit gnawed a hole in the left ring finger on one of my summer gloves, destroying it. I have ridden with a snapped lever before, and it is a super bad idea. Besides vehicle regulations often states it is illegal to ride with a snapped lever, it can wreck a pair of gloves in a couple of days. So a grand total of just under $1700. Getting this done would be even more expensive in Denmark so I chose to go for it. Luis would then pick up the bike when everything was done.

Having provided some good business for Moto Europa, "T" gave me a lift to the train station. The Amtrak sign pointing to the station was ten times smaller than the one they had at McDonalds, so if you didn't know your way it was easy to miss. Here there is a 40 minute departure delay.

I am not sure why, but there seemed to be a problem as the cops entered the train and took up a report from another passenger. Apparently, someone had stolen some items from another passenger while she had been sleeping. That is the one sure thing in life, leave your stuff unsupervised, and it will disappear. The only place I think this doesn't happen is Japan, but theft in America is incredibly common. While the people on the train were 95% non-caucasian and a lot of them were seniors and children, I don't think theft has anything particular to do with, race, gender or age in the USA.

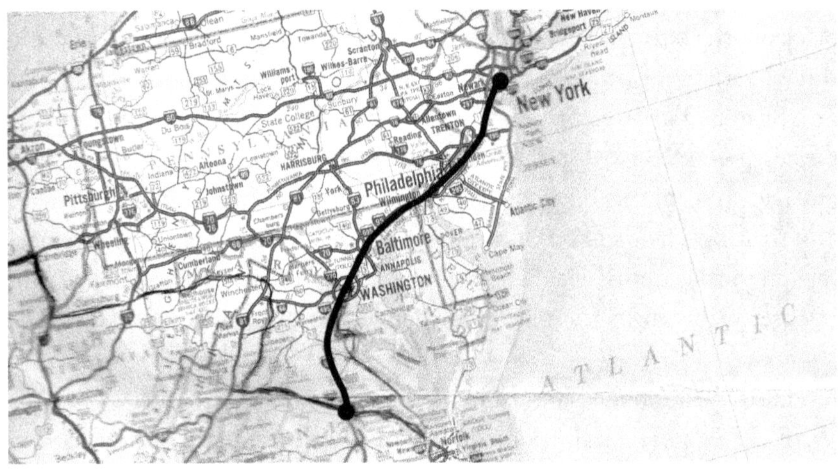

Arriving in New York Penn Station after an uneventful six hour trip, I got on the subway and checked into Holiday Inn Broadway. It dawned on me that this was my first time on the city streets. Going to Richmond I had used the subway and had not been above ground.

I soak washed some t-shirts and socks, these were still wet from the last few days of riding in the rain.

New York City (NYC) is the biggest city in the USA. With a land area covering about 302.6 square miles (784 km2) and a population of 8.4 million inhabitants, New York is also the most densely populated major city in the country. New York City consists of five boroughs, each of which is a separate county of the State of New York. The five boroughs, Brooklyn, Queens, Manhattan, The Bronx, and Staten Island were consolidated into a single city in 1898.

Just to get a quick first impression I take a walk in the Broadway area. The receptionist did warn me that walking around alone after dark could be risky, so I stayed on the larger streets and where there were a lot of people. At a plaza some young African American guys are hanging out. My red and black motorcycle jacket looks a bit out of place and they find it funny, one of them calling me out as "Yo, Johnny Quest". Not knowing who the fuck Johnny Quest is, I thought to myself: "If you only knew what I have experienced while wearing this jacket, you wouldn't believe it".
Well, instead of trying to tell my story then and there, I wrote about it. Johnny Quest did sound familiar and I since found out that the name is without an "h" and Jonny is the main character in an animated TV-show which began in the mid-1960s. Looking like a kid hybrid version of Donald Trump and Steve Jobs, I have a hard time seeing the connection to my jacket. I guess he wasn't a successful popular culture export abroad compared to other cartoon heroes like Superman or Spider man.

While in New York, I had to eat a hot dog. Hot dog stands became a staple fast food in Denmark during the seventies but has been squeezed by competition from other fast food joints such as McDonalds and countless pizza outlets. The garbage I got here gave me some serious bowel issue later that evening. Once again I felt coming full circle, as I got some stomach problems eating from a street stall in China at the beginning of my globe-trotting trip. New York hot dogs sure was a letdown, the Danish interpretation is so much better. After high school I actually had a summer job making burgers, hot dogs and fried chicken. If you ever go to Denmark, I recommend you try a fully loaded roasted hot dog if you get the chance.

Friday, September 10th 2004

My trip was cut short by inadequate planning. Waking up to the phone ringing, the Holiday Inn reception told me that my credit card was not working, so they couldn't charge for the next night. I was traveling with just my Visa card, and this proved to be a very bad idea. I knew there was plenty of funds in my account, so using it on August 13th to pay for servicing the Ducati in Boise, Idaho, I must have maxed the card to the security limit set within a month.

I had left two grand with Luis as a contingency. So I got on the phone calling up Luis' home number. Luis and his wife must have been at work, as nobody was there to pick up on the other end. As I had used all my travelers cheques, my day started with me stuck in New York without access to money. With only around 120 dollars in my wallet I made a quick decision and had the reception concierge re-book my flight to the late Newark departure to Copenhagen at 11:20 pm. This would leave me with just one day in New York City, instead of the five I had intended.

While annoying, this was acceptable. Tickets to New York has become very affordable, so leaving this for another visit wasn't a huge problem. Checking out, I left my luggage by the valet concierge. Tipping the guy an extra buck was much appreciated. It is a bit strange that American dollar notes are the same size, so you need to pay attention to which denomination bill you hand over. A pretty good advantage at the strip clubs, as you can make it rain like Mayweather for a hundred times less than what Floyd spends.

This sudden change of plans gave me around six hours in Manhattan. So I started with taking a walk through Central Park just a few blocks away.

The weather was sunny but not really hot. Continuing south I passed Madison Square Garden, the Ed Sullivan Theatre on Broadway and ended up on Times Square. On this trip this was the second time in this location, albeit I was above ground this time, and not just changing subway trains.

Just as in Chicago and San Francisco, I went for a harbor cruise in order to see as much as possible, especially with the extremely limited time constraint. In Battery Park, located on the south tip of Manhattan, I got on a one hour tour with Statue Cruises, the quick round trip. New York is the premier gateway for legal immigration to the United States, but I simply didn't have time to see Ellis Island and the Statue of Liberty close up and had to settle with the waterfront view. On the cruise I got to see the church at Wall St., the Statue of Liberty, Brooklyn and Manhattan bridges, so I managed to get the most out of it. 2004 was just three years after the 9-11 attacks and three marine helicopters made a low altitude formation fly-by over the cruise boat. Pretty cool, I do like them choppers. Back on terra firma, I headed towards Wall St. to see the NYSE, the New York Stock Exchange building. I have no great history with stocks, I only bought $1500 worth of stock once, and the last time I checked, these were worth 26 bucks.

Looking up I suddenly found myself in front of the Empire State Building. Standing here, I thought to myself that I needed to come back to New York for sure. Architecture and skyscrapers are a manifesto of human engineering and achievement, and it is be a soft spot for me.

Talking skyscrapers, I had to make a stop at Ground Zero. In 2004 this was still a hole in the ground, and a big gaping wound causing a huge shift in politics and American engagement abroad. The 9-11 attacks in 2001 was the second time the Twin Towers was targeted by radical islamic terrorists, the first attempt to bring down the towers took place in February of 1993, around the time I had started this book project.
A bomb was detonated on the second subterranean level of Vista Hotel's public parking garage, below the World Trade Center building. Six people were killed, and more than a thousand people sustained injuries. Having visited historical monuments all over the country, 9-11 is special as events unfolded on TV in front of the entire World, most people know where they were at during these attacks. Hitting the economical hub by destroying the World Trade Center Towers, the military powers in the Pentagon and the political epicenter in the White House or Congress would on a strategical level be a strike of genius. Fortunately, the latter didn't succeed.

Looking at the building site, I talked to some of the other people there, and the common sentiment was a lack of understanding why Osama Bin Laden had not been caught yet. Talking with Aloun in 2009, my thought on this was that the invasion of Iraq and engagement in Afghanistan shouldn't have happened, instead the U.S. military should have black-ops'ed everything until they captured Osama Bin Laden. He was eventually killed on May 2nd 2011, but I think he got off easy with the executive termination order to kill on sight. If it was up to me, that motherfucker should have been lit on fire and kicked out of a tall building.

As said, I am not too forgiving, and believe in getting even. 9-11 might have been an excuse for George W. Bush to initiate the second invasion of Iraq. The claim of Saddam Hussein having weapons of mass destruction was in my opinion a weak spin to gain control of the Iraqi oil supply. Well, Saddam is dead now too and nobody is going to miss his ass.

The destruction of the World Trade Center Twin Towers has had a huge impact on the political landscape in Europe too. Entering Afghanistan and Iraq as a part of the international coalition, Denmark lost a huge amount of military personnel during the engagement against the Taliban and Al-Qaeda. Especially when casualties are compared to the size of the Danish population.
Going to take out Al-Qaeda was justified, but also created a ripple effect against oppressive religious regimes in the Middle East and North Africa. Ghadaffi got himself some street justice in Libya, but ISIS ("Islamic State of Iraq and Syria") grew from the ashes of Saddam Hussein's fallen regime. ISIS has since caused a lot of suffering and refugee streams. It is usually young men who take the long journey to and through Europe as they are least vulnerable to assault and abuse. Groups like ISIS are known to buy and sell refugees as sex slaves. Like Osama, ISIS should be wiped from the face of the Earth. No "if"s, "but"s or "maybe", every single one of them just need to check into hell.

The political right has reaped great benefits from the many people flee-ing for their lives, using refugees as leverage to make cuts for all the weak groups of European societies. This has been the plan from day one, they

WNBA
SPALDING
MADISON SQUARE GA
E GARDEN
COST
OF IRAQ
WAR:
$136,042,976,637
EMPIRE STATE
LATE SHOW
with David Letterman

just didn't tell their voters about this in the election campaign. Those who talk about refugees as being a bunch of moochers conveniently "overlook" that they have lost everything they previously owned in order to be able to reach safety. Anti-refugee sentiment can only be expected to continue as there are votes in it, alienation is the basis for their electoral support. It is obvious that there is no money tree, but most problems in connection with immigration are the result of the discrimination that the majority do not experience themselves. It is ok to make demands, but these will be meaningless if there are not real opportunities for earning a living on your own. It should be clear that I have absolutely no sympathy for immigrants who commit crimes. As is, I have nothing against being patriotic or nationalist, wanting to make your country do better is a fair cause. Nationalism becomes a problem when it is used as a platform for exclusion and discrimination or incites violence.

Children often reproduce their parents' attitudes. If the parents are burning right wingers, the children's pronounced opinions will often be characterized by this, even though they do not actually understand what they themselves say. The counter-reaction often appears when the children reach the teenage years where the young people begin their search for an identity. Division into "them" and "us" forms the basis of parallel communities. The argument "if you are dissatisfied, you can just move" is the classic punchline underlining this. Searching to fill out an inner void, weak and young people who find themselves indifferent and in doubt, ends up as easy prey for extremist or gang recruitment. Alienating a generation already, the politicians created the foundation for new gangs actually competing for dominance against some of the outlaw biker clubs.

The Danish government has become one of the most hostile toward people fleeing for their lives and threw away every ounce of decency when they started to decline receiving UN quota refugees. I believe Denmark has lost a great deal of the identity and self-understanding that I was brought up with. By saying no to UN-recognized refugees, Denmark should at the same time not expect help or support if we one day find ourselves in need.

European civilization reaps what it sows and two world wars were started here. It is naive to believe that a place like Australia will change its refugee policy just because there would be war in Europe. If another grand scale conflict starts in Europe I hope China will be smart and tactical enough to not take sides.

With an American president who talks about building walls against migrants, much of the European perspective can be applied to the USA. While the United States isn't landlocked with most refugee producing countries, the migration towards the West is based on the desire for a better life, and dreams of a safer life with opportunities. The harsh reality is that many end up living in tents under bridges. This is in my opinion, the division of rich and poor, which will become clearer in the future.

Because of deterioration in the social safety net, a lot of people considered middle class are in danger of ending up in the same situation without even being aware of it. This is the real collapse of society making the right wing rhetoric about the "surrender of civilization" a fine but utterly useless academic discussion.

Terrorism by right wing extremists has been far more prevalent than most people remember, and the perpetrators has done much more damage with a kill-death ratio exceeding most Islamist sleeper cells.

Timothy McVeigh murdered 168 people in 1995, including children at the kindergarten, by bombing the Alfred P. Murrah Federal Building in Oklahoma City, Oklahoma. McVeigh was convicted on federal murder charges in 1997 and executed in 2001, so at least the US justice system does something right about terrorists. The Norwegian and Australian white supremacists mass murdering innocent people in Norway and New Zealand will likely get to die of old age.

The 9-11 terrorist attacks may have changed the world a lot, but the balance of power is shifting. China's position is yet to be determined, but from a European perspective I find the biggest threat to western society being a Russian leadership whose wet dream is to resurrect the Soviet Union.

The right wing all over the World seem to be sock puppets playing into the hands of people who are smarter than themselves. This may sound paranoid, but always stay critical of your leadership.

My acute money problems this day in New York is just one of the areas that would be targeted in a larger scale conflict. Water and electrical supplies, communications and financial markets are the most obvious areas that has been digitized to an extent that makes the West vulnerable for tech warfare beyond imagination.

After a day of sightseeing in Manhattan, my journey around the USA and the World was coming to an end. Fortunately I had enough cash to pay for a chauffeur serviced ride from Holiday Inn to Newark International Airport. Truly awe-inspiring to me, Chicago and New York really stood out. I didn't get around to see my favorite piece of architecture in the world. the Chrysler Building, so *I'll be back* in NYC at a later point in life. (The Burj Khalifa in Dubai is still on my bucket list.)

On the plane to Copenhagen I have a small routine I always do before takeoff. Besides the mandatory safety briefing I always double-check the location of the emergency exits from my seat. I like to know how many people I may need to deal with if shit happens and not having to look for the exit in a panic. Have you noticed in case of an emergency landing you're instructed to bend your head down? I think this is because the airlines want to offer you one last chance to kiss your ass goodbye...
Seated next to an American married dane, she wasn't too talkative, Danes aren't that friendly without alcohol. My impression of Americans is that they are generally quite friendly and polite. Courtesy is a two-way street., you get what you give. If you want a better world, you start with yourself. You take a chance and risk a little by trying. Leaving this approach to others, you cannot expect courtesy from other people. To be inconsiderate probably hurts yourself more in the long run. Keeping it real and honest, the most important person in the world is of course still myself. Even including all I've experienced, I believe my value can only be set at zero in comparison with the rest of the World, my time on Earth merely a blip in time.

Arriving at home, it was time to adjust back to normal life. It is all about your everyday life and your attitude towards it, as everyday life delivers the most accurate punches.

Having had about ten really close calls on this trip, I am happy to say that no big accident happened. The Monster was down twice, first when the side stand poked through the hot asphalt near Osseo in Wisconsin and when I stupidly tried to make a u-turn on an incline at the Rush No More Campground in Sturgis.

Moto Europa later wanted to charge me for storing the bike more than five days after the modifications were done. Luis thought they were a "bunch of pricks, after I all the money I spent there". Treat your customers like crap, and the Internet will give you a bad reputation. Ducati Richmond went out of business a couple of years later. I wanted to bring the Ducati to Denmark, but in order to comply with the Euro2 restrictive emission and noise regulation, the registration was made two weeks too late. I could import the Ducati, but unsure it would be approved for road use. This bullshit situation arose just because of bureaucracy, so I wouldn't risk ending up with a bike I couldn't get a license plate for. So I stored it with Luis until 2009. Here I did a partial trade-in for the new factory murdered out Harley Davidson XL 883 Iron. Motorcycles are a money pit; the trade-in value of the Ducati was $4000. I am content that I didn't do this ride on an 883 Sportster in 2004. Torque on an 883 is in my opinion a bit too low in order to keep up with fast moving semi haulers on the Interstates. The stock rear suspension is awful on some models, but a cross country ride could easily be done on a 1200 model with a larger gasoline tank. With a pretty good knowledge of Harley Davidson today, the best for short riders are mid controls in combination with separate highway pegs. With the right setup you can use the rear brake and gear down using your heels on the shifter and brake arm. This is a much better option than forward foot controls.

I did look into a used Ducati Monster S4 at a good price later. The one that had my interest unfortunately had the rear frame shortened. If you want to sell a motorcycle, don't cut the frame and make sure it can be restored to original specs. This will have potential buyers turn away or go hard on the trade value.

Harley Davidson manufactures model FXFB, also known as the Fat Bob. The name has been used since the 1970s and comes from the fat rear wheel with a "bobbed" rear fender. After my tour in the USA, I had gained about 8 pounds, this really shows when you normally weigh around 132 pounds (60 kilos). Maybe I should test ride a Fat "Bob" when I get the chance. Having munched on burgers all over the world, the best bacon cheeseburger I know is actually made in the town I grew up in, Rita's Burgerbar in Esbjerg. I have since learned that I missed out on trying In-N-Out Burger and Five Guys while in California, they should have some great burgers.

There was plenty of other things I missed out on. Being unable to do and see everything was a something to be expected, as I was riding with a bunch of ideas in my head but without a specific plan. So I decided to give the St. Louis Gateway Arch, Monument Valley and Colorado a miss. If I get the chance to go to Sturgis again, I can do with a few days there, and not the entire official event. The Buffalo Chip Campground and the Sturgis Motorcycle Museum & Hall of Fame would be on the to do list as well. Missing out is a good excuse to come back. And yeah, Florida is still where I left it.

After finishing the rough draft for this book mid 2019, I went to Chiang Mai in Thailand to examine the information gathered about my biological parents. Finding out that they died a long time ago wasn't a big surprise but provided the missing pieces of my identity and giving me ease of mind. Expecting to have older siblings I was surprised to find out I have a twin brother and an extra niece, whom I met the next day! This story went viral on social media and I found myself on Thai national TV within 12 hours. Thinking this book was the only one I would be able to write, the framework for a second book is being thought out with a co-writer, the work title being "Bob and Boonshu".

Still thinking about life, my perspective have changed a lot lately. It feels like it was just a few years ago I was 27 -but that was 19 years ago. Time sure flies when you're having fun. At 46 years old I find myself closer to the ripe old age of fifty. This has me thinking about the fact that there is an end of the road. We're all living and loving on borrowed time, so take every option in life and work to make the most of it.

Having some set goals gives you something tangible to relate to. Dreams are best when they become reality. In order to reach your goals it demands initiative, patience and most of all confidence.
It is up to you and nobody else..

The first and most important thing to do is check if the goal is reachable. When I write each word gets me closer to my goal, to write a book.
If I don't write I won't reach my goal. So I take care of business and write.

To win the lottery you need to buy a ticket and participate.
Take action and wait for no-one.
Work hard and focused to get there because
no dream comes true by itself.

If you lack confidence and drive you will only see other people pass you. Start small and learn shifting into high gear. That could be saving up and purchase one of the things you always wanted but never got around to buy. This will feel as a small victory. And victory is as sweet as revenge.
You get appetite for more. You start to think proactively.
And when your confidence grows, you grow.

When things seem to be rolling by themselves it is not unusual that some gunk gets in the gears. Here you find the third parameter to make your dreams come true, patience. It's an opposite to aggressiveness and creates balance. Patience makes it easier to keep your head cool.
Patience is not a brake, it's just a lower gear.

Confidence is also a vital part of my idea of a greater consciousness. But confidence can also be turned upside down. The dream goal shouldn't overshadow your everyday life. Accumulated, the small golden moments has as much value as life's greatest highs. So writing this book has been a great experience, looking up the pictures and reading my old diary, vividly refreshing all the memories.

We are not born equal but one thing we all have in common, no matter if your name is Bill Gates or Joe Average:
No money in the world can buy back time wasted.

Illustrating this try to make a table of the twelve months of the year noted on a vertical line and each year of your life expectancy (say, 79 years) on a horizontal axis. Each field representing a month of your life, cross out each field lived until now. Mark up every month after the age of 68, at this age you might not have the health to travel.

Looking at the result, how much time do you have left?

It always ends with a Harley...

Experiences create memories.
Memories which will last longer if you get them when you are young.

It takes time to get old,
so no need to sit on your ass waiting for that to happen.

If tomorrow never comes,
make sure to live today

Appendix A: I want a motorcycle

After reading my story you might want to get into motorcycles.
It doesn't have to be expensive to get started, but the cost can vary a lot.

Bike

The cheapest option is of course to borrow your friends motorcycle, it could only cost a lifelong friendship. Getting a good starter bike isn't expensive, but I think a 125 cc motorcycle is too small to start on. Being underpowered, you really have to rev the engine to stupid getting up an incline. More important, the brakes on smaller displacement motorcycles are usually not as effective compared to bigger bikes where more mass needs to be stopped.

A used 300-600 ccm bike is in my opinion better to start a motorcycling career on. More wants more, and your starter bike will often feel too underpowered after you gain some confidence and riding routine. But getting a bike that is too big or too powerful can be hazardous to your health. So if you are totally new to motorcycles, I would stick to a used motorcycle as my first bike.

Finally, I recommend buying a first bike without a windshield or fairing. This gives new riders a much better feel for the accelleration and speed motorcycles have.

Safety Gear

Helmet, gloves, boots, back protector, padded pants and jacket. You don't want to skimp on this, it is made to save your ass. I think accidents are almost inevitable for new riders, and trust me, rubbing your body and head on asphalt at 10 mph or faster is awful. Don't take your safety lessons the hard way.

Maintenance and Repairs

The older the bike, the more repairs and maintenance are needed. This does provide new riders with an option to learn about their motorcycle. Motorcycles are not created equal and some are too difficult for amateurs to tinker with. But being able to do an oil change and other small tasks can provide you with some basic hands-on experience.

Insurance

I have touched on this when I bought the Ducati, your age, type of motorcycle and driving experience and history affects this a lot. You do want to shop around as prices can vary immensely.

License/Permit

You can't ride legally without a license, and without one you might not be able to get insurance for a motorcycle. Riding without insurance can really screw up your life financially, so you want to have both a license and insurance sorted before clicking the transmission into first gear on a public road.

Gas

Motorcycles usually offer longer mileage per gallon, fuel consumption does depend on your riding style and engine size.

A way to think about the cost of a motorcycle is to tally your cost of the above up as price per mile. If you only ride 800 miles per year on a $20,000 Harley Davidson, it is an expensive hobby. But if you ride 15,000 miles per year the cost per mile is much lower, and I bet these are more fun as you will see and experience much more.

Appendix B: Travel tips

I might have spent too little time at some of the places I visited, but my aim was to go coast to coast and see as much as possible, including the most prominent sites and significant places. With Internet and smartphones with GPS, it has become easier to get the most out of road trips. You will need a charger for your phone, but a lot of modern motorcycles can easily be fitted with an adapter.

Buying a National Parks Pass is a good idea if you intend to visit more than three National Parks. This has been replaced with (or renamed) "America the Beautiful Pass".

Food
Junk food can be bought for $10 a day, but to be sure you might want to round this up as you'll want to buy water, snacks and other drinks too. Multiplying the cost with the number of travel days should give you a good indicator, unless you absolutely have to dine at the Crystal Palace every night.

Accommodation
Super 8 and Motel 6 chains are the best choice if you want a fair deal and a room quality you can rely on. Both motel chains are economy class, but with my experience I generally think they offer good value for money. As noted riding through South Dakota, hotel and motel costs can be a fraction when you travel as a couple on a bike or as a group, instead of traveling alone. You do have to be able to live with the risk of other people snoring and gassy flatulence.

Fuel
On this trip, fuel for the bike was $3-6 per fill up (2004 prices), So this came to an average costs of $12, refueling around 3 gallons (12 liters) two times a day.

Motorcycle rental or purchase
If you only have 2-3 weeks to travel, and not wanting to buy a motorcycle, Harley Davidson now offer the Eagle Rider rental program. Here you can rent a bike on one end of the country and drop it off at the other. An example is a Harley Davidson Street Glide touring bike. Renting this costs $180 per day for 15 days and coast to coast will run up a cost of around USD 4,000 including insurance. (2019 price example) You can learn more about this on Harley Davidsons official US website.

Crossing the USA in a fortnight is not hard to do, but you need to plan your two week route well to ensure you see and experience the things and sites that interests you, or the most possible.

If you want to buy a motorcycle in the USA, I hope this book has provided some useful information on how to do this, and how not to as well. Besides my story, I recommend that you find the motorcycle you like and let the dealer know about your ideas and wishes.

An option I considered was to buy a motorcycle in Denmark and ship it to the USA. But as this was the final leg of a longer journey, this solution wasn't practical. Riding a motorcycle around the world is a different adventure which would require a better suited motorcycle than a Harley. I think I would have wanted to travel with a buddy too.

As I didn't choose this option, I do not have any pricing as an example. However, having worked in international trade, I can confirm container shipping has become very cheap. My plan for the motorcycle bought in the USA was to ship it back home to Denmark. This didn't happen, but I did do some research around shipping a motorcycle.

Shipping a single motorcycle usually require a pallet or crate to which the bike must be strapped securely.

A lot of airlines and shipping companies will only deal with you through an agent so that they know they get all the correct paperwork.

Using airfreight is faster and can be very expensive. Sea freight takes longer and weather conditions can disrupt transit times, affecting your travel schedule. Traveling in a group, container shipping is a good option. A 20-foot container usually can take up to six motorcycles. Do expect seaports to be very bureaucratic, airline shipping is much more streamlined.

For riding your own motorcycle, most countries will give you a temporary import permit, providing you can prove it's your personal property. For that you need the registration document in your name, your passport and driving license (plus an international driving permit too).

Some countries also require a "carnet de passage" which is an internationally recognized customs document entitling the holder to temporarily import a vehicle duty-free.

The classic traveler way to ship a motorcycle is to hire a cabin on a freighter cruise ship and take your bike as accompanied luggage. With shipping options available, I think that it is only true globetrotters going "the long way around" who does this today.

Here is some shipping tips to keep in mind:

1. Some airlines insist the tank must be drained of all fuel. Otherwise a half-gallon (2 liters) maximum apply. Make sure the motorcycle is clean and free from leaks. Countries like Australia and New Zealand are very strict about protecting their environment from plant and insect contamination.

2. The battery must be disconnected and the connections should be covered with insulation tape to avoid sparks posing a fire hazard.

3. In order to securely strap down the motorcycle to a crate or pallet, let a little air out of the tires to around 27 psi (1.8 BAR) and change the suspension setting to allow for a little softer travel.

4. Remove the screen and mirrors. Using bubble wrap and zip ties will ensure these items don't get lost or damaged.

5. Panniers can normally be left attached. If you have a top box there is an increased risk that this will get scratches.
The people who take your most precious in and out of a shipping vessel may not be used to handle a top heavy motorcycle. So using bubble wrap around a top box may be a good idea.

6. Removing the front wheel can cut air freight charges a lot, as these are calculated by volume.

7. Remove any pressurized containers or liquids, ie. filled jerry cans, chain cleaner spray, chain lube, etc.

Appendix D: The Numbers

Spending 61 days traveling across the USA, here is a rough tally of my spending:

Food expenses
Unsure of the exact number including snacks and drinks, I just set an average at $ 20 a day, so this comes to $ 1220.

Accommodation
This varied a lot, ranging from $ 0 to $ 250 per night. The account of every place I stayed is found in Appendix E. This came to a total of $ 4538 including tax in 2004 prices, so you have to adjust for inflation.

Fuel
Gas prices in the USA are not plagued by taxes, so using six gallons a day for $ 12 (2004 prices), so this expense came to $ 600 with fifty days on the Monster.

Total
Excluding the cost of buying or renting a motorcycle, tires and maintenance, plane tickets and health insurance, the grand total was:

Food	$ 1220
Accommodation	$ 4538
Fuel	$ 600
Total for 2 months	$ 6358

Dividing this with the number of days travelled, the daily average cost was $ 104.22. Adjusted for 2019 inflation this is roughly $ 140 per day

Imagining you have two weeks to cross the USA, the rough 2019 calculation is as follows:

Rental Harley Davidson Street Glide FLHX	$ 4000
Food, Accommodation, Fuel	$ 1960
Total for 2 weeks	$ 5960

To this cost you need to add the price of a plane ticket, which of course is variable and depending from where you live. You do want to make sure you got travel health insurance that covers riding a motorcycle.

Other information

Before buying a Ducati I knew maintenance on an "exotic" would be pricier, but the eight-valve engined Ducati models are among the most expensive to get serviced. The 6000 mile service was $ 980 and to this I need to replace the rear tire for $ 170.

The National Parks Pass (Renamed "America The Beautiful Pass") is super value for money if more than three National Parks, National Monuments and National Forests are part of your itinerary.

Appendix E: Accommodation Account

Prices stated are from 2004 including tax, not adjusted for inflation.

Accommodation

$	Location	Days	Name
150	NY JFK	1	Ramada Plaza
670	Richmond, VA	6	Crowne Plaza
480	Washington DC	3	Holiday Inn
100	Richmond, VA	1	Comfort Inn
23	Virginia, VA	1	Misty Mountain Camping
65	Clarksburg, WV	1	Motel Sleep Inn
45	Indianapolis, IN	1	Motel Indiana
59	Chicago, IL	1	Esquire Motel
510	Chicago, IL	2	Holiday Inn Express MM
63	Manistee, MI	1	Super 8 Motel
12	Escabana, WI	1	Pioneer Trail Campground
70	Milwaukee, WI	1	Baymont Motel
100	Minneapolis, MN	1	Comfort Inn
200	Minneapolis, MN	4	Super 8 Motel
0	St. Paul, MN	1	Alouns house
71	Brookings, SD	1	Motel Brookings
232	Rapid City, SD	2	Foothills Inn
110	Sturgis, SD	7	Rush No More Campground
115	Cody, WY	1	Econolodge
145	Boise, ID	2	Motel 6
9	Diamond Lake, OR	1	Broken Arrow Campground
87	Eureka, CA	1	Econolodge
150	San Francisco, CA	2	Geary Parkway Motel
18	Kings Canyon, CA	1	Sunset Campground
5	Yosemite NP, CA	1	Yosemite Campground 4
175	Los Angeles, CA	3	Hollywood Inn Express
195	Las Vegas, NV	2	MGM Grand
47	Wliiams, AZ	1	Motel 6
46	Gallup, NM	1	Motel 6
48	Lubbock, TX	1	Super 8 Motel
42	Greenville, TX	1	Motel 6
46	West Memphis, AK	1	Motel 6
58	Birmingham, AL	1	Days Inn
46	Asheville, NC	1	Motel 6
47	Butner, NC	1	Econolodge
82	Richmond, VA	1	Comfort Inn
217	New York, NY	1	Holiday Inn Broadway.
4538	Total accommodation cost		

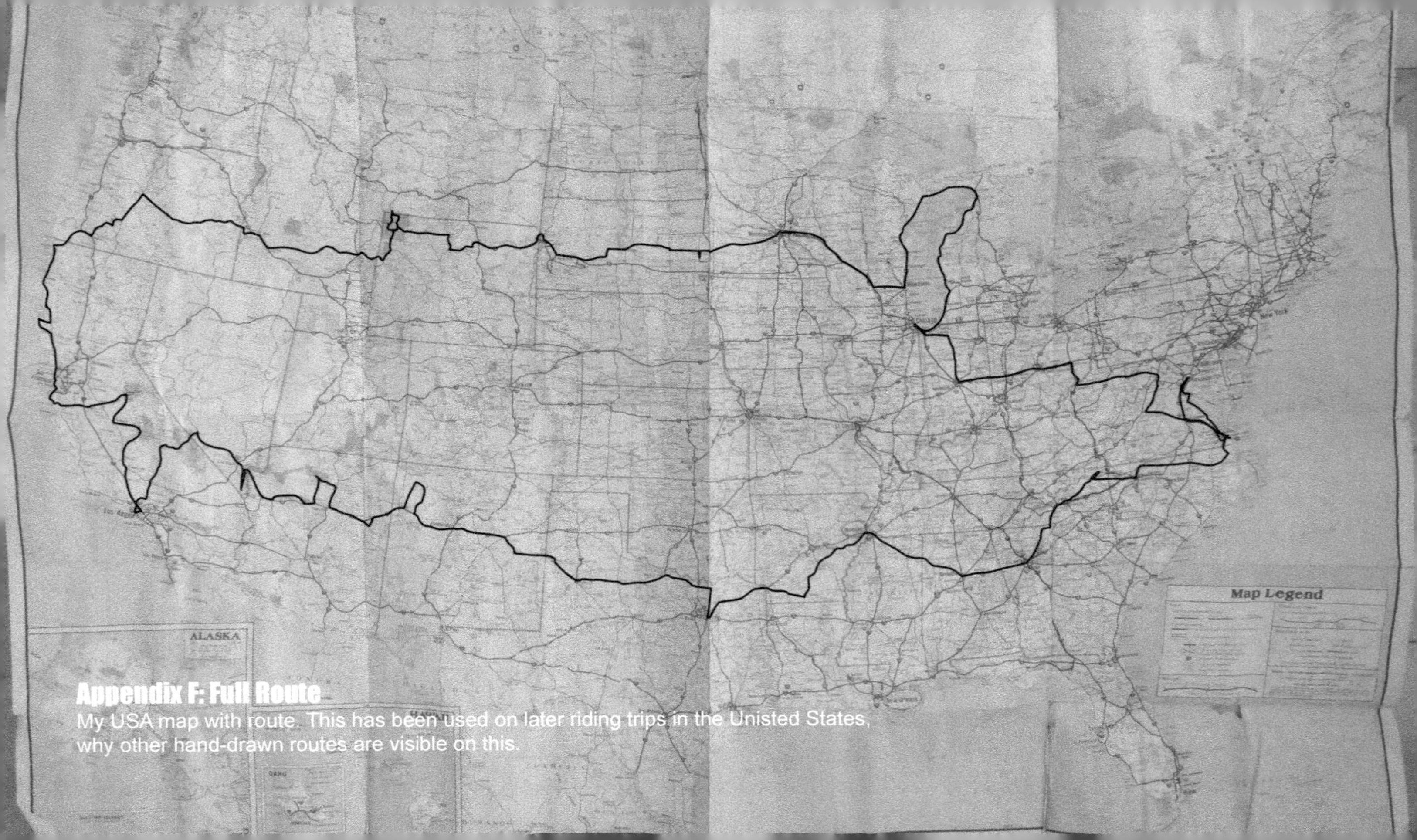

Appendix F: Full Route

My USA map with route. This has been used on later riding trips in the Unisted States, why other hand-drawn routes are visible on this.

Notes: